Cybercareers

Mary E.S. Morris

www.cybercareers.com

Paul Massie

Sun Microsystems Press
A Prentice Hall Title

© 1998 Sun Microsystems, Inc.—
Printed in the United States of America.
2550 Garcia Avenue, Mountain View, California
94043-1100 U.S.A.

The publisher offers discounts on this book when ordered in bulk quantities.
For more information, contact Corporate Sales Department, Prentice Hall PTR ,
One Lake Street, Upper Saddle River, NJ 07458. Phone: 800-382-3419; FAX: 201- 236-7141.
E-mail: corpsales@prenhall.com.

Editorial/production supervision: *Beth Sturla*
Cover design director: *Jerry Votta*
Cover designer: *Anthony Gemmellaro*
Manufacturing manager: *Alexis R. Heydt*
Marketing manager: *Stephen Solomon*
Acquisitions editor: *Gregory G. Doench*
Sun Microsystems Press publisher: *Rachel Borden*

10 9 8 7 6 5 4 3 2 1

ISBN 0-13-748872-6

Sun Microsystems Press
A Prentice Hall Title

Contents

Chapter 2
Trends Shaping Cyberspace, 13

Chapter 7
Business Skills in Cybercareers,   125

Chapter 10
Technical Development Skills,   233

About this Book

The Mission of this Book

If you're interested in work related to the Internet, web, intranets, new media, or information technology, you've come to the right place. This book has one mission: to help you succeed in the 21st century cyberspace workplace.

In *Cybercareers*, you'll learn all this, and more:

- New strategies for developing yourself—and staying current in the face of unprecedented change

- The specific technical areas you need to be familiar with—and more important, the high-level transferable skills you need

- The cyberspace work roles available right now—and how they're likely to change

- How to prove you have the skills an employer needs

- The hot new strategies that can keep your career moving forward no matter how technology changes

Cybercareers briefs you on the buzzwords you'll need to know. It will help you understand what life is really like in the cyberspace workplace. (Frankly, few career books address the "little things!") And perhaps best of all, it shares the personal experiences of more than a dozen men and women who have built highly successful cyberspace careers for themselves—often in surprising ways.

Your *Cybercareers* Journey

Maybe you've heard this saying: your career is a *journey*, not a *destination*. Here's how *our* journey is organized:

In *Part I, Overview*, you'll take a look at cyberspace as it is now, and the powerful trends shaping its future. You'll begin learning about the qualities and skills you'll need to succeed in the workforce—whether you plan to work for a large company or go out on your own.

In Part II, *Cybercareer Roles*, you'll take a look at the specific roles available to cyberspace professionals, how to choose the one that's right for you, and how to prepare for it.

In Part III, *Cyberspace Business Skills*, you'll take a look at the profoundly important *business* skills every cyberspace professional needs, no matter how technical or creative their position may be.

In Part IV, *Cyberspace Technical Skills*, you'll take a look at the technologies driving cyberspace now, and the ones you're most likely to encounter in the next few years.

In Part V, *Cyberspace Arts and Media Skills*, you'll take a look at the creative content and production skills you'll need to publish in cyberspace—and the increasingly important "meta-content" skills you'll need to help people *make sense* of the barrage of information they're facing.

Finally, in Part VI, *Jobs of the Future*, you'll take a sneak preview of some of the jobs that *just might* be in your future.

Ways to Get There

Each person must walk their own unique path through life and through this book. However, here are a few suggestions on how *you* might proceed through this book.

A Student's Path

Read the Overview chapters carefully, understanding the trends that are changing the workplace and the qualities and skills you'll need to develop. Spend some time with the Developing Yourself chapter. Try to set your own personal vision, goals, and milestones. Remember, you can change your life and your vision any time you want: the crucial point is to *get started.* If you find an area where you're especially strong, look for the skills and roles that grow out of it.

A Transitional Worker's Path

Chances are you're here because you want to make a change. All the more reason to read the Overview section carefully: it'll give you insight into the industry trends and personal changes that can have the most impact on your life.

Items of Note

Along the way, we've added icons to help you identify information that might be of special interest to you:

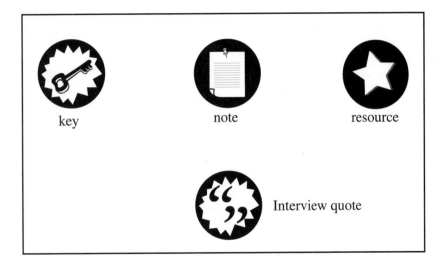

- **Key Icon:**   These are especially important concepts: the ones you should read even if you're skimming everything else.
- **Note Icon:**   These notes give you a little more insight on topics, without interrupting the main flow of the book.
- **Resources Icon:**   These are references to additional resources listed in the back of the book or on the web.
- **Interview Quotes:**   These are quotes from real, successful people. You can learn a lot from their experiences.

About the Author

In many respects, this is a very personal book. It reflects the experiences I've had in building my own cyberspace career: the lessons I've learned, the mistakes I've made. I'll tell you a little about myself, so you'll know where my advice is coming from.

In 18 years in the workforce, I held 17 jobs before I went out on my own. Why so many? For one thing, I value my happiness. If a job doesn't make me happy, and I can't change it, I'll leave. I know a lot of people in my parents' generation who worked at jobs they hated, because they had to. I won't accept that limitation. It may take more work, but my happiness is worth it.

Also, I worked in the oil industry in the 1980s, when that industry was in a deep depression. For years, I went from job to job, just ahead of the latest round of layoffs. Once I was caught in a layoff because I was arrogant enough to believe I was too good to be laid off. I finally realized that *no matter how good you are, if there isn't any work, they don't need you.*

I've been a computer operator, an electronics bench technician, and a system administrator. I've been technical webmaster for the world's leading network computer company, Sun Microsystems. I've worked with PCs and LANs, UNIX and the Internet. Virtually from its birth, I've worked with the World Wide Web.

I've learned in all these jobs. I've learned about teamwork, project management, and quality assurance. I've learned about the importance of mentoring and networking with my colleagues—and how to stand up for what I believe in. I've learned one other very important lesson: "*There are no such things as dumb questions, only the dummies who don't ask.*"

I've worked with all kinds of people—and realized that no matter who you are, a calligrapher, an anthropologist, an Eslan-trained masseuse or anyone else—you have plenty of opportunities in cyberspace, and plenty to offer.

I've learned that I can't afford to stop learning for a moment. I skim about 18 inches of books and magazines per month on everything from business, to evolution, to nutrition, to cognitive psychology, to chaos and non-linear math, to social welfare, with a little sci-fi thrown in on the side. *Everything I read makes me better qualified.*

In high school, I was fortunate enough to take a class called Futuristics, with Alvin Toffler's *Future Shock* as the textbook. It taught me to think for myself. There was only one way to fail: to not have original thoughts. I came to realize: that's the way all education should be.

Once, I planned to be a psychologist, a counselor for the terminally ill. Unfortunately I looked far younger than my age and no one took me seriously, so I set that aside as a potential second career. I figured nobody could spend a lifetime in just one career. (Now I realize that most of us will have *several* careers, if not more!)

I discovered almost by chance that I liked computers, and started learning programming—but the challenge of being syntactically perfect with all those little colons and semi-colons and such was just too tedious. I moved to Silicon Valley, found my way into system administration, and since then, *my income has doubled every other year.*

Here's why I believe I've been successful:

- I deliberately chose jobs for what I could *learn* at them: new technologies, new business skills.

- I've never limited my work life to 40 hours a week—nor do I invest so much time in a job that I burn out.

- I developed skills I could *transfer,* not just specific technical skills that quickly become obsolete. I don't just know one operating system, I know a dozen of them—and the underlying patterns and concepts that apply to all of them.

- I realized how important it is to blend formal education with practical experience. If you don't, you might find you've wasted years learning something you don't actually like to do. You might find you're overqualified even if you don't have any experience. Conversely, you might find yourself spending too much time learning on-the-job when you could have learned the same thing quickly in a classroom.

- Finally, *I* chose to invest in my own development.

Are my successes a fluke? No. But success comes with a price. You have to ride the waves of change, not follow docilely. You have to keep learning, not just hang your sheepskin on the wall and consider your education complete. You need to think, and act for yourself—not wait for your company to promote or develop you.

But enough about me. Now it's time to find *your* Cybercareer. All the best of luck on your journey!

Acknowledgments

No man is an island, and no book is ever written alone. The following people have contributed to the development of this book, and for that we are eternally grateful.

This book contains the wisdom and insight of many people including:

Sandy Ressler - author of The Art of Electronic Publishing.

Debra Winters - Manager of Intranet Operations for SunIR

Mike Troiano - CEO/President of Ogilvy & Mather Interactive

Rosemary MacCallum - Copywriter

Glenn Fleishman - Principal of Point of Presence Company, when interviewed, now he's Catalog Manager of Amazon.com

Kathy Slattery - Technical Writer, Sun Microsystems

Ken Erickson - Developer, SunSoft

Bill Prouty - Chief Webmaster of SunIR

Tim Brady - Director of Production at Yahoo!

Jakob Nielsen - Distinguished Engineer for Sun Microsystems Inc, and author of many books including, Usability Engineering and Multimedia and Hypertext: The Internet and Beyond

Lynne T. Keener - Director, Internet Services at Keener Information Design Group

Rachel Border - Publisher of Sun Press

Karin Ellison - Webmaster of SunSoft

P. Michael McCulley - Webmaster of Knight-Ridder Information

Don "DocDon" Taylor - Internetist

Our reviewers who kept us on track include Sandy Ressler, Wayne Spivak, Raewyn Whyte, Randy Hinrichs, Chris Haynes and Terrell Hayes.

The people that operate behind the scenes to make this book special deserve an extra thanks, including Rachel Borden, John Bortner, Greg Doench, Stephen Solomon, Ray Pajek, Jerry Votta, and Jill Dupont.

Thanks to all!

Cybercareers

PART

An Overview

- Critical Factors for Success

- Trends Shaping Cyberspace

- The World of Work

- Developing Yourself: A Roadmap

Often the best way to begin anything new is to view the big picture.

If you're interested in a career related to cyberspace, don't start your quest by looking at specific jobs or skills. Start by figuring out where cyberspace is headed—and where *you* can intersect with it in the future. Start identifying the subtle success factors that are rarely measured or discussed, but are nonetheless critical.

That's our goal for the first section of Cybercareers.

In Chapter 1, you'll learn the most important success factors for cyberspace careers. They're not what they used to be!

In Chapter 2, you'll be introduced to the powerful trends now shaping cyberspace.

In Chapter 3, you'll enter the world of cyberspace work to see what companies are looking for.

In Chapter 4, you'll discover a set of strategies for developing yourself and the qualities you'll need to succeed in cyberspace.

Three themes run through this section and this book.

First, no matter what career you choose, you'll need to adapt yourself to a rate of change unprecedented in human history.

Second, the social work contract is broken. Your survival and success are now your responsibility, nobody else's.

The third theme is the most important. You *can* adapt to this new environment. You *can* plot your own course. And if you do, you'll have the opportunity to do work that is more important, more challenging, and more satisfying than you may have ever imagined.

Let's get started!

CHAPTER

1

Introduction

Cyberspace, that unlimited landscape between your keyboard and mine, is the new land of opportunity. As you read this, cyberspace is creating millionaires, improving millions of lives, and eliminating national and political barriers that have divided people for centuries. Cyberspace is the key element in an entirely new stage of human development: *the knowledge age.*

But the dangers of cyberspace and the knowledge age are equally profound. Cyberspace is unleashing an unchecked, unmanageable stampede of change—and disenfranchising millions of people who cannot cope with that change. Moreover, radical change is nearly always accompanied by social and political upheaval.

In the new knowledge age, agricultural, industrial and even service sectors of the economy are rapidly fading in importance. In the U.S., for example, the knowledge sector comprises about 19 million people. That's less than 20 percent of the workforce. *But these knowledge age employees account for more than 50 percent of U.S. earned income.*

The change isn't as visible in other countries yet, largely due to politically-mandated workplace regulations. But even there, it's gathering steam.

In the knowledge age, change occurs as quickly as knowledge itself changes: *at the speed of thought.* Change is no longer transient: it's a permanent fact of life. This is the single most important point to understand as you prepare yourself for the knowledge age.

What Does this Mean to You?

No matter where you live, or what you do, if you're planning to work in the 21st century, you will constantly encounter these four issues:

* Rapid obsolescence

* New ways of working

* New jobs

* New skill requirements

Rapid Obsolescence: The social contract for lifetime work has been broken, because jobs no longer exist for a lifetime. In the knowledge age, many jobs only last a few years. All too often, as jobs become obsolete, so do the people holding them. It's time to *stop* thinking of obsolescence as bad luck, and *start* planning for it.

New Ways of Working: Every aspect of the workplace is changing dramatically. Businesses are reengineering, forming partnerships, "spinning off" business units, and competing in new global markets. In enlightened companies, workers are being empowered as never before. Even in *those* companies, however, there are few guarantees for employees. Accordingly, each individual must start to think of himself or herself as a "company of one," and become loyal to *themselves* first and foremost.

The "company of one," a.k.a, the entrepreneur within the organization, thinks as if he or she is running a business. Such an entrepreneur recognizes that his or her success is closely tied to the success of his or her primary customer, the employer. Thus, loyalty to oneself is often synonymous with loyalty to one's employer. However, some employers treat employees as disposable resources, instead of recognizing this mutually beneficial relationship. This leads to burnout, obsolescence, and even more job insecurity than necessary. In such cases, the relationship is no longer mutually beneficial, and as a "company of one," you should be loyal to your own interests first. It's important to remember that loyalty to yourself can express itself differently in different situations; sometimes as cooperation and sometimes as competition.

New Jobs: The nature of work itself is changing. Eventually *all* rote jobs will be eliminated: automation can do that work more effectively. In some economies, as many as 70 percent of today's jobs will disappear by 2050. New knowledge jobs are already taking their place.

New Skills: New jobs require new skills. The ability to turn a screwdriver or punch a button will no longer be sufficient. Instead, workers will need skills that enable them to add value by creating, refining, interpreting, managing, and especially *communicating* knowledge.

Approaching the Knowledge Age

As we've seen, knowledge is no longer a peripheral item that we can shoehorn into whatever process that's currently on hand. *Knowledge is the core component.* So we must optimize how we handle knowledge, relate to it, and grow it:

- We can no longer afford a *parts is parts* world view. A *systems* view, an understanding of the "big picture" or "gestalt", will help us far more than the sum of the parts.

- Everything must build on everything else. We can no longer afford to continually reinvent the wheel.

- Given that our resources are limited, we must focus our efforts more clearly on our most critical goals. As individuals, we can't afford to work towards dozens of conflicting goals, each pulling us in a different direction.

Instead of becoming pure specialists who understand specific, narrow fields increasingly well, we need to build on what we know to learn real, transferable skills. Only by doing so can we achieve survival and happiness in the knowledge age, *with a real career*—not a fragmented series of unrelated jobs and hobbies.

Skills and Domains of Knowledge

Today, employers are looking for two very different things at the same time.

First, employers want people familiar with the specific tools, processes and procedures now in use. We'll call these areas *domains of knowledge*. *Domains of knowledge* may consist of sets of facts and concepts, along with an understanding of how to perform actions within a certain domain, such as an accounting system or a marketing department. Domains of knowledge often go well beyond pure "technical" skills such as knowing how to generate an accounts payable report or run a system backup under SCO UNIX.

Second, employers want people who can use their existing knowledge to move to new tools, processes and procedures as the organization changes. Career development professionals sometimes use the term *transfer skills* to reflect an ability to transfer and adapt knowledge to new environments. A report from the U.S. Department of Labor refers to *cross-functional skills*, defining them as "procedures that extend across general domains of work activities." To keep things simple, we'll simply call these *skills*.

For example, planning a marketing campaign is a *domain of knowledge* action. Project planning is a cross-functional *skill* that can be applied within the marketing realm or in a wide variety of other roles.

Unfortunately, skills in this sense are rarely and inconsistently taught, primarily because skill definitions don't exist for most occupations, especially emerging occupations.

More ways to understand the difference between domains of knowledge and skills

   The most recent Virtual Conference on Lifelong Learning used different terminology to make the same point. It drew a distinction between content (domains of knowledge) and method (skills). Thus, algebraic proficiency is considered content (i.e., procedural techniques within a domain of knowledge).

The importance of *domains of knowledge*

Domains of knowledge are vitally important for three reasons:

- It's expensive to educate an employee and give them enough time to become experienced in a technical field. Employers are concerned that once they train a person, another organization will offer that person more money and their training investment will be lost. Therefore, employers increasingly seek out job candidates who already possess the domains of knowledge they require.

- Organizations want to be productive *now*, not sometime in the future.

- Though skills are critical, people rarely learn them directly. Rather, they learn by assimilating several domains of knowledge and then building a conceptual framework based on what those areas have in common.

   Programming offers a good example. The most common way to begin training new programmers is with a mythical programming language called *pseudo-code*. Pseudo-code often resembles spoken language more than a classical programming language does, but it has more structured syntax than spoken language. Only after students have adapted to this syntax are they introduced to a real programming language.

The importance of *skills*

As important as domains of knowledge are, *skills* are far more important:

- The useful life of domains of knowledge is decreasing rapidly. In the most quickly changing areas of technology and media, most technical domains of knowledge are useful for only two to five years.

- Most organizations are diverse: they don't use a single set of tools, processes and procedures. Thus job candidates who only know one domain of knowledge may have only a small fraction of the technical knowledge the organization requires.

- In emerging technologies, training programs focused solely on domains of knowledge have repeatedly proven to be *long-term* failures.

Critical Success Factors

To be successful, we must identify the factors that are critical to success, assimilate them, practice them, refine them and become successful at them. Specifically, we must

- Adapt to change.

- Continually learn, grow, experience and evolve.

- Start thinking and planning in the long term—not just a few years down the road

- Recognize that success depends upon gaining the domain-specific knowledge needed for today and tomorrow, *and the real skills* needed for long-term success in an environment where domains of knowledge become obsolete rapidly.

Adapt

Adaptation is difficult, and scary. It means accepting that all you know is written in shifting sand—not stone. It means seeking a dynamic balance, not a static one. Nonetheless, for those who take the time to look ahead, failure to adapt is much more horrifying.

Evolve

The day you stop growing is the day you start to die. On the other hand, in the knowledge age, you have the opportunity to transform yourself from a caterpillar to a butterfly—over and over again.

Act Long Term

The bane of modern business—and modern life—is the short-sighted, "fire-fighting" perspective. The key to your future is rising above this perspective, to see the big picture and plan a course towards it.

This Book is a Map

This book is a map, but not to jobs as we've known them, as the Bureau of Labor Statistics reports them, or as our parents lived them. Rather, it's a map you can use to discover *tomorrow*'s work: the jobs and career paths that are emerging today, and the ones that nobody has even imagined yet. Use it to map the most important unexplored territory in the universe: *your future.*

2

Trends Shaping Cyberspace

When you live in a time of change, you must understand how change will affect you—and then prepare for it. Some changes are short-term, and insignificant. Others are long-term, and profound; these changes are called *trends*. In this chapter, you'll take a closer look at six categories of trends that will dramatically impact your career for decades to come.

- Universal Trends
- Geographical Trends
- Educational Trends
- Employment Trends
- Telecommuting Trends
- Business Trends

Make no mistake: these trends will affect *everyone*, in virtually every field. In an era of global markets and instantaneous communication, *everything's connected*. Changes in one company, industry or process can often lead to unanticipated changes in areas that seemed completely unrelated --just as scientists believe that a butterfly flapping its wings in South America can change the weather in Asia.

Many people only see the way trends can *hurt* them. Perhaps that is understandable: our generation has seen thousands of jobs evaporate every year from industries that are automating, business processes that are reengineered to eliminate middle management, and companies that went bankrupt instead of adapting to new conditions.

However, trends can work powerfully to your advantage. You can profit from a trend by positioning yourself "in the thick of it," where the most innovation and change is taking place. You can also profit by staying "on the fringe" and seizing opportunities caused by dislocations the trend causes.

Staying on the fringe might mean staying in a geographical location far from the centers of technology, thereby limiting your competition. Over the past few years, many system administrators stayed 'on the fringe' by becoming experts in UNIX and TCP/IP rather than Novell NetWare. This is now paying off for them, as TCP/IP is growing rapidly and Novell's growth won't continue much longer. Yet another example: those who positioned themselves in online marketing at ad agencies before it became popular are now reaping the benefits. It is the fringes where innovation occurs, not at the center of the fad. Of course, over time the fringe may become the new center.

As you read this chapter, remember: trends can only hurt you if you do not recognize and adapt to them.

Universal Trends

Four overarching trends are dramatically changing the way people perceive the world and respond to it. These are:

- Increased Quantity

- Increased Complexity

- Increased Churn

- Increased Globalism

Increased Quantity

Almost everything is now increasing at an explosive rate, especially data. As a society, we are developing new knowledge faster than even the brightest minds can assimilate it. We are generating new content at a rate of tens of millions of electronic pages per year.

As a result, we're suffering from *data inflation:* the value of each unit of data is plummeting. To compensate, we create more data, like governments that print more money in response to economic inflation.

This trend creates a market that's ripe for the picking by anyone who can transform near-worthless data into useful information, or better yet, into *knowledge*. It sparks the need for substantially more efficient ways of wading through data, organizing it, and managing it.

Computers are the ideal "stoop laborers" of the knowledge age. But computers aren't self-evolving *yet*. They require people to direct them. While less people are needed to manage people, there is steep growth in the number of people required to manage *computers*.

What does this mean to me?

If you can learn how to understand and manage large bodies of data, and *mine that data* to generate new insights and uncover new trends, you will have a major competitive advantage. In many industries, knowledge workers with these skills are already commanding exorbitant wages.

Jakob Nielsen on the Impact of Increased Quantity

One thing that's clearly needed is navigation, especially on the Web, because there's just so much information. It's true even for intranets. Most sites end up being humongous, even when people start out intending only to put a few things up. Visitors can very easily get lost. Nourishing a design information structure and providing navigation through an information space are key design issues.

The role of editors and moderators will expand significantly, and they will begin to see increased financial rewards for their labors. A *perspective* on a large body of data will become more important than the data itself.

For example, some high-volume netnews groups have good quality discussions, but much junk as well. In response, some people have created paid subscription services that edit out the junk and deliver only the information they believe is valuable.

Increased Complexity

The exponential increase in raw data has created a level of complexity that is *qualitatively* new, not simply "more of the same."

The only way to manage this new complexity is through structure. When we increased the complexity of our industries, we added middle management and paid the associated overhead. When we increased the complexity of computer systems, we added more sophisticated operating systems and paid for *that* overhead as well. In fact, the transition from mainframe to client/server created considerable overhead in both the complexity of the operating systems and the number (and skill level) of people needed to manage those systems.

Now we are faced with the increased complexity of computer networks and the data that resides on them. Again, we must add new structure to the content and communications interfaces and pay the overhead needed to keep things manageable.

What does this mean to me?

Whatever you are doing today, look for the structure in it. Look beyond procedures, to identify *principles* that can standardize those procedures, produce repeatable results and automate them.

This applies not only to technical work, but to all work. For example:

1.　**Writing**—All of us, not just professional wordsmiths, must add higher levels of structure to our communications. This can be as simple as adding bullets and tables to make it easier for readers and viewers to understand the points being made. It can mean adding visual cues with fonts and white space. On an even higher level, it means adding "meta-information"—information *about* information—to make the documents standard enough to be manipulated and refined by computers, not people.

2.　**Tools**—We can no longer expect to learn one tool and its descendants and be considered competent. We must learn *many* tools—and extrapolate their similarities and differences, to better assimilate even more new tools. Some examples are in order. To the computer support person, a tool may be an operating system. Thus you can no longer expect to survive only with, say, HP-UX or Windows 95 skills. You must learn UNIX variants, network computers, perhaps altogether new operating systems. An artist's electronic tools are typically media generation programs. You can no longer expect to survive only with Photoshop and its descendents skills. You must grow to encompass other graphics programs until the skill of rendering Gaussian Blur to a bitmap image is second-nature no matter what tool you're using.

3. **Education**—Look at your education the same way you look at your work. You cannot afford to be educated only in procedures. You must be educated in the structure and principles behind those procedures.

Schools must respond

Often, schools fail to teach the ability to synthesize procedure into principle. Make sure the school and curriculum you choose will do so: don't take the school's word for it. Ask why courses were chosen for the curriculum, and what goals they meet.

You pay good money for an education. You have the right to make sure the curriculum is quality-checked for usefulness and appropriateness.

Principles are rarely learned without experience. Thus the most successful educational programs will start by teaching procedures, then let the person experience how those procedures are used and adapted in the "real world," and finally "circle back" to school to deepen one's understanding and synthesize procedures into principles.

This strategy goes against social conventions that call for a clear demarcation between education and work. It will not be easy to change. However, this circular technique is already the hallmark of many successful people and will become the general track for success.

Increased Churn

In the golden, olden days, there were only a few transitions in life. You graduated, you went to work, you married and had children, and you retired—often from the same company you started with. Now change happens constantly; your work life will continually be churning.

And when it comes to technology, there is no "state-of-the-art" any longer: there is a "*state-of-the-moment* ."

Few people can expect to work for the same company for twenty or thirty years. This has significant repercussions. You must be knowledgeable about state-of-the-moment technology and techniques when you're seeking your next position, because you'll be competing with others who are.

What does this mean to me?

Since you won't always know in advance when you will be in the job market, you'll *always* need to stay current. Never let your educational growth stagnate for even a few years.

Study your company's retirement or 401K plans well. Many plans still assume you'll be at the same company for most of your life. Find out how long you'll have to stay in order to become "vested" (eligible for benefits). It may take five years or more.

Study your company's salary review, promotion and career development processes. What levels of reviews will it take for you to get the raises and promotions you need to progress in your financial goals, or even to stay ahead of inflation? More and more often, people change jobs to get raises their companies cannot give them due to restrictive HR policies. Even if raises are attainable, does your company have ways to give you the breadth of experience you'll need? If you don't like the answers to these questions, don't anticipate building a long-term career at your current company.

Increased Globalism

No country is an island. Today, every country is heavily dependent on exports, and consumers in different countries can have dramatically different tastes and preferences. Products must become localized to where they will be sold, and that requires much more than rote language translation. It involves exceptional sensitivity to language, culture and law.

Chevrolet learned the pitfalls of global marketing the hard way when it attempted to market the Nova in Mexico. In Spanish *No va* means roughly "It doesn't go." Why would someone buy a car that doesn't go?

In one country an autumn scene is considered colorful and beautiful—an ideal background for a Web site. Elsewhere, however, autumn is a time of death; a very poor omen indeed.

To sell products around the world, hundreds of government requirements must be met. Failure to account for these can cause significant financial and time loss—and can even bankrupt an enterprise.

Of course, many companies have gone far beyond simply selling overseas: they have themselves become global, doing business in ten, or even 50 countries. You may well find yourself transferred to another country during the course of your career.

What does this mean to me?

Over half of the successful people interviewed for this book had significant life or work experiences in foreign countries, experiences that went far beyond taking a simple language class, or even taking a vacation. For some, the experiences were as short as five weeks; for others, as long as five years.

Many colleges and universities offer exchange programs and overseas study. These are very valuable programs that, unfortunately, few students take advantage of. Nothing can replace the experience of living in a foreign country and learning to work with people of other cultures and mindsets. This is especially important in the U.S. where most people have been very sheltered most of their lives—leading to an arrogance that ruins promising business ventures, and even careers.

Geographical Trends

As much as some would like to believe that cyberspace will make location irrelevant, this is clearly *not* the case today. *Even cyberspace jobs cluster in specific locations.*

Internet and intranet job markets have different geographical profiles; each will be discussed next.

Internet

To discover where the Internet jobs are, *follow the domains*. A quick look at the statistics shows:

- California, U.S., leads the world in the number of Internet domains registered. Almost 15 percent of all Internet domains are headquartered in northern California alone.

- Los Angeles, California, U.S. and New York City, New York, U.S. are neck-and-neck for second and third place.

- Within the U.S., the next biggest Internet domain clusters are in Boston, Denver, Seattle, the Washington, D.C./Northern Virginia area, Dallas, Atlanta, and Houston.

- Outside the U.S., Canada is the largest Internet domain home. The three hot spots there are: Vancouver, Toronto and Montreal.

- Looking beyond the U.S. and Canada...

  —The United Kingdom, Germany, Australia and Japan rank next in
  registered Internet domains.

  —The highest *per-capita* domain and Internet-connected computer
  usage can be found in Sweden, Finland and Australia. In fact,
  Finland beats out the U.S. for the lowest "User to Internet-connected
  Computer ratio" in the world—an obvious sign of a highly
  computer-literate market.

Consider these trends carefully. There are usually many job opportunities in the main Internet clustering areas. However, you may be able to
find a sizable niche in other areas, with fewer Internet-literate competitors.
The trade-offs are companionship and assistance from other Internet
"sophisticates" in the Internet cluster areas, versus little competition but
equally little local help for people remote from the Internet centers.

California highlights

California has two main Internet hubs, San Francisco and Los Angeles.
The San Francisco metropolitan area (a.k.a. Bay Area) hosts two widely
known clusters of high technology, Silicon Valley and Multimedia Gulch.
While there are many exceptions, Silicon Valley tends to focus more on
Internet infrastructure, while Multimedia Gulch tends to focus on content
development.

Silicon Valley: Silicon Valley can't be found on any maps. Its borders
vary depending on who you talk to, though by one common definition, Silicon Valley is the strip of cities from San Jose to Palo Alto.

Silicon Valley was originally known for the silicon-based businesses
that chip makers like Intel and Motorola established. Over the years, the
downstream businesses of computer manufacturing and software development have also grown rapidly there.

With the University of California at Berkeley (the birthplace of the
widely-used BSD version of the UNIX operating system), Stanford (alma
mater of most of the founders of Sun Microsystems), and a dozen or so
other colleges and universities in the area generating raw recruits for
emerging industries, growth has been explosive.

Tim Brady on Choosing Engineering

I went to school around here, around the mid-80s when Silicon Valley was really hot, the legend of Steve Jobs was everywhere. And it was really hard not being attracted to that. That's probably the biggest force in making me become an engineer.

Netcom, now a national Internet Service Provider, helped pioneer Internet access for the general public in the Bay Area—at a time when Internet access was largely restricted to universities and major corporations. Netcom's pioneer spirit was replicated by dozens of other providers, giving the Bay area a highly 'Net-savvy' population. It's no wonder that the Bay Area has the highest per-capita Internet domain usage rate on Earth.

Not surprisingly, Silicon Valley boasts one of the highest high-tech startup rates in the country. But it's also home to many Fortune 1000 and other large companies. On a typical day, available jobs at just eight companies—Sun, Apple, SGI, Intel, AMD, Oracle, Sybase, and Netscape—number in the thousands. Similarly, `ba.jobs.offered`, the main local job advertising newsgroup, also receives thousands of Bay Area postings each month.

More than one Bay Area person interviewed said their location helped make them successful. Speaking for myself, moving to the Bay Area certainly increased *my* ability to land a good high-tech job.

Debra Winters on Silicon Valley

I grew up in Silicon Valley. My dad was working at Memorex and I started going to college, not knowing what I was going to do. I was majoring in English and Art. But I got a great computer job, and it was just computers from that point forward. It just had to do with where I lived. I have no idea what I would have done if I was living in Texas.

On the other hand, the Bay Area is expensive: in the U.S., only New York City, Washington, D.C. and Chicago come close. Don't expect to come here if you don't have at least a small grubstake to live on until you find a job.

To get a rough idea of housing costs, visit the Bay Net World Homes website:

- Go to `http://www.baynet.com/`
- Enter the site
- Choose a county
- Select the demographics information link
- Choose a city

You can find general U.S. cost of living differences at:

`http://www.homefair.com/homefair/cmr/salcalc.html`

Multimedia Gulch: Just as Silicon Valley has blossomed as the Bay Area's hardware and software mecca, San Francisco's Multimedia Gulch, or SOMA (**S**outh **O**f **M**arket St. Area), is the multimedia designer hangout. (Many design firms here have recreated themselves "virtually" as well, in a VRML Web site rendition of SOMA.)

San Francisco is home to many advertising and media firms, as well as *WIRED* magazine and its sister HotWired Web site; the niche market media giant Ziff-Davis; MSNBC, Microsoft's joint venture with NBC; and C|Net, a leading producer of cyberspace-related programming.

Los Angeles: Los Angeles (LA) was once home to many U.S. government contractors and businesses that supported them. While LA does not offer the Bay Area's extraordinary density of technology companies and Internet usage, it still harbors a substantial computing and Internet business community. Moreover, the marriage of high-tech and Hollywood has increasingly made this an area of focus for new media professionals.

New York Highlights

New York City is home to many advertising firms, media houses, print publishers, and a variety of businesses moving into the content realm. New York City has been a recognized home for artists of all genres for generations. It's not surprising that New York is adding the Internet arts to its repertoire. Like the Bay area, New York City is expensive to live in. Nonetheless, technical people are in high demand and many companies are willing to pay relocation fees to get people to work in the Big Apple. New York's increasingly publicized Silicon Alley is the East Coast version of SOMA.

Intranet

Intranets are hot. What's an intranet? Intranets are internal corporate networks that use Internet technologies to achieve some business goal. First-generation intranets tend to provide E-mail and messaging, and make available documents that would otherwise have been printed, such as benefits information and employee manuals. Second-generation intranets are often used to reengineer internal business processes. Third-generation intranets, sometimes called *extranets*, typically encompass customers and/or suppliers as well.

There are indications that intranets are growing even faster than the Internet. For example, a study co-sponsored by Cognitive Communications and Xerox Corp. indicated that 85 percent of Fortune 500 U.S. corporations are implementing an intranet, or will implement one soon.

Not surprisingly, high-technology companies are more likely to have intranets, but companies of nearly all sizes and types can benefit from them. Typically, if a company has more than 100 employees, and more than half of them have computers, the company is a likely candidate for an intranet.

You find intranets where you find corporate headquarters and significant research branches. As with Internet domains, more Fortune 500 headquarters are located in California or New York than anywhere else. One way to find out who is in your area is to look up companies in the Big Book (`http://www.bigbook.com/`).

What does this mean to me?

Consider this parable:

Once there was a man searching for something under a street light on a dark night. Another man approached him, full of concern.

"What are you looking for?" asked the concerned man.

"My keys."

"Where did you lose them?"

"Somewhere in that field." replied the first man, pointing to a field in the distance.

"If you lost them there, why are you looking for them here?" asked the concerned man.

"The light is so much better here." replied the first man.

Jobs won't come to you. You're far more likely to find the job you want if you go where the job already exists. I spoke at a high school in Richmond, California, a community with a large minority population. These students were very concerned about discrimination and job opportunities. At the same time, less than a two hour drive south of them, companies were so desperate to have minority workers that they were holding positions open even after candidates were identified, hoping to get minorities to apply.

Here are some more points to consider about geography:

- Those with entrepreneurial self-reliance, business skills and technical or media expertise can benefit from being in low-technology areas, because they will face less competition and greater need for improved technology.

- Communities of people with shared technical or media expertise often can provide more opportunities for education and mentoring.

- College towns are often good places to get initial experience, but knowledgeable competition and limited business opportunities can make them poor places to work long term.

Educational Trends

It's not easy to be a traditional educator these days. Schools receive flak for not teaching practical skills; on the other hand, businesses complain that new employees only learned specific procedures, not *how to learn*.

Education Has a Place, but Still has Problems says Debra Winters

I think there's always a role in formal education for everyone, in any job. But for Internet careers, there just isn't a lot of formal education available—and much of it is obsolete before you finish the class.

Teaching cyberspace skills is even more challenging. The Internet's rate of growth and change almost guarantees that a Bachelor's degree candidate in Internet technology will have obsolete technical skills by the time he or she receives the diploma.

Classical education programs can't meet the needs of today's exponential growth industries. As a result:

Ken Ericskon's Educational Experience Was Less than Ideal

Unfortunately, I was in college when the PC revolution was just beginning, and the paradigm shift from batch to interactive computing was starting. I say "unfortunately" because the curriculum had not caught up with technology, so we were training to become obsolete as soon as we graduated. This is the primary reason I abandoned school, and took a job in industry.

Colleges and universities now provide only about 50 percent of adult education. Corporate in-house training, product-specific vendor training, and training companies are increasingly filling the gaps left by colleges and universities.

- Employers are turning to vendor-specific and non-accredited education more often than ever before to meet their new skills requirements.

- Hiring managers are beginning to place less emphasis on degree requirements, especially on the west coast of the U.S.

- Certification programs and competence tests are available for over seventy different areas of study—up from just a couple of certification programs eight years ago. Some are offered for vendor-specific knowledge. Others are organized by industry associations as a way to prove the competence of their membership.

- College graduates, even those with Masters degrees, are finding it increasingly difficult to land jobs without previous relevant work experience. At Iowa State University, for example, only 65 percent of all graduating seniors had job offers upon graduation. *However, every student that had performed an internship or taken a cooperative education program had a job offer upon graduation.*

- Institutions like Pomona College in Claremont, California are developing degree programs focused on critical thinking, formal reasoning, data analysis, and exploration of human behavior—in short, *how to think.*

What does this mean to me?

Education is essential for survival in the knowledge industries, *but education without experience is less important every year.* Increasingly, internships, cooperative education, local and international work/study programs, and work on campus are core components of the educational experience.

The Education that an International Experience Offers Develops Self-Reliance According to Tim Brady

For me, living overseas was an important educational experience. It goes back to self-reliance. In an industry like the Internet, you're on the leading edge, helping to forge the industry, and you need self-reliance and confidence to do that. Living in Japan helped give me that self-reliance.

Students will be most successful if their education addresses *all*, not just some, of the following:

• Industry-specific training
• General business knowledge
• General liberal arts education such as formal reasoning, critical thinking, cultural awareness and other human behavior skills

---

Understanding human behavior is the sleeper liberal arts skill of the 21st century.

Many of my interviewees never completed a degree program related to their current careers. For example, I found Webmasters with English and Library Science degrees, and system support people with biochemistry degrees or M.B.A.s. About 20 percent never completed *any* Bachelor's degree program, yet they are still highly-trained people with above average incomes! They've learned what they need to know through vendor-provided training, corporate training or on the job experience.

Your college major doesn't limit what you can do after college.

Alternative Educational Experiences Can Teach You a Lot according to Mike Troiano

I knew a professor at Cornell named Don Schwartz. I learned more about advertising over coffee with him than I did in my Advertising classes. Classes are important, but at the end of the day, it's about people, less about course material.

Employment Status Trends

When you think of earning a living, what do you think of? If you are like most people, you think of getting hired at a company, receiving money and benefits, going to work each day for the same company. At one point, many people expected to go to work each day for the *same* company—for twenty or thirty years.

Conventional employment as a full-time, "regular" employee *is* still a valid way to earn a living. However, it is no longer the *only* way, nor for many people the *best* way. The following table compares four major approaches to earning a living:

Table 2-1 Earning a Living

Type of Work	Pros	Cons
Regular Employee	• Job is somewhat more secure • Benefits are more common	• Pay is usually lower than contract • Power struggles and politics are hallmarks of standard work life
Contract Employee	• Pay is usually higher • Wider range of working experiences • Less political "garbage" to deal with	• Often must provide own benefits • Less job stability
Consultant	• Flat rate contracts can make more money	• Flat rate contracts mean there's a possibility of actually *losing* money
Royalty Work	• Authors can market themselves, improve the sales of their work, and increasing the money they earn	• Incoming money isn't fixed. It is dependent on sales of work. • Contracts are strict and need to be reviewed to make sure both parties benefit.

• **Regular Employment**:   This is often referred to now as regular or full-time employment rather than permanent employment, because the phrase "permanent" employment can be construed to mean guaranteed employment for life.

Jobs are not "for life" anymore.

Regular employment can be either hourly or salary-based. Hourly employees usually receive overtime pay. Salaried employees receive a fixed salary. If additional hours are required beyond the agreed-upon work week, there is no guarantee that additional money will be forth-coming. A salaried employee may be offered *comp time*—time off to replace the extra time that they worked. Even this isn't guaranteed, though. Traditionally, salaried positions are more prestigious than hourly positions, but often hourly pay can be lower, once all the extra hours are taken into account.

Regular employees commonly receive benefits such as health insur-ance, life insurance, profit sharing or stock purchase programs, 401K or pension programs, vacation, discretionary leave or other time off, and possibly tuition reimbursement. Of course, benefits vary from com-pany to company. A start-up is less likely to give good benefits, but may compensate with large stock options.

- **Contract Employment**: Instead of working directly for a company, receiving a paycheck and benefits from them, you can work for a con-tract agency that supplies people as companies need them. Sometimes the contract agency provides benefits; other times you must provide them for yourself. Contract employment is almost exclusively hourly work; thus you do get paid for all the hours you work.

  Contract agencies come in two flavors: employer fee paid and employee fee paid. Employee fee paid means that the job seeker pays to get the job referral. In the U.S., avoid agencies that make you, the potential employee, pay a fee.

- **Consulting**: Some consultants work by the hour. In the U.S., this practice is increasingly limited by IRS regulations and restrictions. To be paid hourly as a consultant, you must play "20 Questions" -- i.e., you must meet twenty standards concerning work environment and autonomy. The IRS wants to make sure you are not a "regular employee in disguise," working for an employer that wishes to evade its share of withholding taxes.

  Most consultants bid by the project. If you underbid, you may be stuck with losses trying to complete the project. If you overbid, you may lose the bid, or your client may be disappointed in the value they receive. However, if you can deliver what the customer expects in less time than your bid anticipates, you stand to make an attractive profit. This is small business at its best.

- **Royalties**: One final option that is seeing a resurgence is earning a living by producing some marketable intellectual property and then earning a portion of the revenue the property generates. Book authors often work this way; so do shareware authors and an increasing number of trainers and lecturers.

A royalty structure can be very beneficial to the creator of intellectual property, but it may also be used to take advantage of you. Review your contracts very carefully, and remember that royalty arrangements mean your pay will vary dramatically based on the sales of your work. This means you can increase your royalties through effective marketing and public relations. On the other hand, if you simply complete the project and depend on someone else to handle marketing and sales, you're at their mercy. If your publisher or partner has other priorities, you can find that you've invested a great deal of time for very little money.

Lynne T. Keener on Various Types of Employment

As an employee I had the advantage of being a team member. This is very helpful when preparing visual/promotional material: the more viewpoints the better. When working for a large firm, the budgets for graphical design and promotional projects are usually higher than those for a sole proprietor. And having "in-house" resources such as printers and scanners can make creating promo pieces a snap.

As an hourly contractor ("temp worker") I had greater flexibility in my schedule, and I could choose only projects that interested me. It was nice to work with many different clients, learning about them and their firms. The pay was usually a bit higher than for regular employees, but I did have to forego benefits such as insurance and 401K plans. I usually enjoyed the same resources (budget/equipment/team input) as a regular employee.

I get many of the same advantages now, as a Project Consultant. But I can work out of my own office, in my jammies, and I can usually command a higher price. Firms which hire a consultant expect more they do from an hourly contractor. You're not just filling in for someone that's out ill or on maternity leave. You're bringing an entirely new source of value to the firm.

These different types of jobs are springing up because the nature of work is changing. Many jobs are becoming more project oriented, and companies are *outsourcing* the jobs that they don't do really well.

A good parallel here is the entertainment industry. Many people come together to produce a movie. They work until the movie is done, and then go to a new job. Except for administrative "back office" employees, creative staff at a few virtually indestructible shows such as the *Tonight Show*, and a few stars with unusual leverage, nearly all work is project-based.

In the knowledge industries, many experienced people find it more lucrative to consult or work through a contract agency. However, companies have tended to either hire low-paid interns or very expensive, experienced people this way.

For those starting out, it's been traditional to work full-time for a couple of years to establish yourself. It's different, however, in the Web and Internet industries. Few people have even a few years experience in these technologies, since they're so new. Moreover, demand for Web expertise is so high, people with only months of experience can land contract positions. This will continue to be the case for the next few years, until Web and Internet roles become well-established, and the supply and demand of Web professionals come into balance.

What does this mean to me?

You're likely to have multiple working arrangements in your lifetime: regular employment for a few years, contract or consulting employement at other times, perhaps royalty work as well. It's important to understand the personal and monetary trade-offs of each role, so you can choose the role that suits you best at the moment.

For example, it can be tricky to accurately compare the value of benefits in regular employment and non-traditional roles.

Many HR departments try to convince employees that benefits add 50 percent to the value of a salary, i.e., a US$ 50,000 annual salary is really equivalent to roughly US$75,000 when benefits are considered. Is this really the case? Perhaps, but you should evaluate your benefits package yourself, rather than making assumptions. For many people, the value of benefits can be far less. While the following comparision doesn't take into account stock options, profit sharing or bonuses, it is still instructive:

Table 2-2 Evaluating a Benefits Package

Benefit	Salary Cost	Contract Wage Cost
Wages	$50,000 per year	$79,040 per year (2080 hrs)
2-weeks Vacation	$0	– $3,040
1-week Personal Time /Sick Leave	$0	– $1,520
14 Paid holidays	$0	– $4,256
Health/Dental Insurance —Individual	$0	– $2,520
Life Insurance	$0	– $120
Matching 401K	$2000	$0
Total	$52,000	$67,700 as W-2 $62,300 as 1099 [*]

* As a U.S. contractor who receives an IRS 1099 form, you must pay additional Social Security tax equivalent to the 50 percent of the tax an employer would pay if you had been a regular employee receiving a W-2 form.

Telecommuting Trends

Telecommuting means using telecommunications technology to work "as if" you were in your company's offices, instead of physically being there. Telecommuters are sometimes said to have "virtual offices." Telecommuting should not be confused with a home-office business, where you work independently, running a business out of your home.

Telecommuting is becoming widespread in many metropolitan areas. Some U.S. states have required telecommuting as part of their compliance with clean air legislation. Whether it's the law or not, telecommuting has many advantages—and some significant disadvantages.

The Pros

Reduced commute problems: Telecommuting places less stress on people and the environment by eliminating the arduous *commute* through traffic. Less stressed employees often have more energy, more time for themselves and a better attitude.

Lower business costs: Telecommuting can save the company money by not forcing a company to heat its building for one or two workers that work late into the night. A few telecommuting plans have reduced real estate costs, by allowing telecommuters to share offices.

More results-oriented evaluations: In traditional work arrangements, people often feel that they are being graded on elements other than their objectives: for example, on the sheer number of hours they are present. Quality telecommuting plans are often accompanied by a new focus on judging performance based on bottom line results, not simply "being there." This leads to better results and better motivated employees. In addition, if performance-based evaluations are used as the basis for terminating poor performers, they're easier to defend in court.

Telecommuters Must be Judged on Deliverables Says Debra Winters

Managers have to know how to manage telecommuters. And telecommuters have to be measured by deliverables. When a schedule isn't met, that's an immediate warning sign.

Telecommuters need to be available throughout *all* of the working period—to *all* co-workers. They should always show up for meetings, whether that's telecommute day or not.

Management needs to be committed. That means, for example, giving telecommuters the right equipment. They need an ISDN line if they're working on the Web, for sure. If they're *not* working on the Web, they need the fastest modem available, and the ability to log in to the company network.

Management commitment and a professional employee who is measured by deliverables: *that's* the recipe for success.

Fewer interruptions: Time management experts will tell you how important it is to prioritize your time. Some people find that they simply can't do so at work, due to constant interruptions from unscheduled meetings, phone calls and visitors. Moving home does *not* automatically solve this problem. People must be consciously, carefully trained to stop operating in reactive, *"firefighting"* mode. Brusquely making yourself unavailable is not the solution. Nonetheless, telecommuting can reinforce a thoughtfully-implemented time management training program.

The Cons

On the other side of the coin, there are several problems with telecommuting:

Employees don't build a workspace: Working at home is just that—work. Most workers aren't paid to be interrupted by their children or the neighbor. Neither are most people paid to be on-call 24 hours a day. Many employees (and employers alike!) fail to separate home life from business life. They find themselves either allowing their home life to interrupt their work, or allowing their work life to intrude on every minute of their day. It takes a disciplined person—and a specific workspace, such as a room with a closed door—to make the separation.

Employees lack autonomy: Telecommuting requires autonomy. Workers can't call their boss ten times a day and ask what to do next. They must be able to schedule their own time, prioritize their work and make decisions for themselves, without constant oversight or nagging. Telecommuting employees must willingly take on these responsibilities—and managers must willingly relinquish them.

Insufficient communication: Most businesses today rely heavily on informal communication to keep processes flowing; the more non-standard the processes are, the more communication is required. When you're not physically present, it's easy to lose the unspoken nuances and subtle communications that are so important. Telecommuters must have well-developed communication skills, especially the ability to perform *active listening* (listening that confirms and responds to what's been said, and to the "between the lines" non-verbal messages as well.)

Insufficient technical self-reliance: Today's office is high-tech. To be effective, telecommuters must be technically self-reliant—which includes both cyberspace literacy *and* the ability to perform low-level comupter support for yourself.

What does this mean to me?

In the real world, telecommuting isn't a panacea. It is:

* **A part time endeavor**—Most telecommuters work at home only one or two days per week.

- **Only for the disciplined**—Those that can create a separate workspace and establish appropriate boundaries between work and home life are more likely to be successful. Those that cannot will either resent their managers and co-workers, or be resented by them.

- **Only for the objective based**—Telecommuting only works when manager and employee agree upon goals, and specific ways to measure them. Without this, employees may seem "invisible" to their colleagues, and find their careers stalled—while managers find that an employee's poor performance is reflecting badly upon *them*.

Having said all this, telecommuting is growing quickly: at the rate of a million telecommuters per year since the late 1980s. At this rate, 10 percent of U.S. workers will be telecommuting by the year 2000. They're likely to be disproportionately knowledge workers, whose jobs are often easier to adapt for telecommuting.

Increased telecommuting has also increased the demand for support personnel who can provide assistance "at a distance," and for a more robust technical infrastructure with better remote access for telecommuters.

Business Trends

Businesses are under unprecedented pressure to deliver results. But results can be hard to measure. After adding millions of computers, many companies haven't been able to point to definitive productivity increases. After spending billions on mass-market advertising, the advertising industry hasn't delivered definitive statistics on its success rate of mass market advertising.

As a result, there's a significant cry for better measurement techniques, often called *metrics*—and for more results-based business practices. Hundreds of business books tout dozens of different buzzwords to meet these needs: reengineering, downsizing, rightsizing, upsizing, outsourcing, management by objectives, -by walking around, -by empowerment, niche marketing, direct marketing, database marketing, network marketing, relationship marketing, one-on-one marketing, TQM (Total Quality Management), Quality Circles, Continuous Process Improvement, Capability Maturity Model, client-server technology, open systems technology, rapid application development, and intranets to name a few.

Amidst this blizzard of buzzwords, business is attempting to restructure its processes, change its relationships with customers and employees, revamp the way it distributes data, and constantly re-evaluate the value of its products.

In the next several pages, you'll take a closer look at these changes—and the buzzwords that accompany them. This discussion will help you decide what kind of knowledge-age working environment you want to be part of, and to help you ask the right questions, so you're more likely to find the environment you want.

Business Practices

- **Reengineering**:   In reengineering, a company attempts to thoroughly recreate one or more business processes, in order to reflect the current and future needs of customers or the business itself. It is often a gut wrenching process.

  Reengineering Successes: Reengineering works best when it optimizes business processes, e.g., reducing the number of people or departments involved between the time a customer signs a purchase order and when the customer actually receives the product. Every time an activity is handed from one silo[1] or department to another, it's possible to lose important information or create confusion, and the handoffs nearly always delay delivery of products to customers. Reengineering seeks to eliminate these handoffs wherever possible.

  Business Units: One common approach to reengineering is to create business units that behave like self-contained companies. A business unit may provide its own research and development, marketing, sales and distribution channels. In theory, an organization focused on a narrower business can become more proficient at serving its customers, and therefore be more competitive.

  The risk of business unit-based reorganization is that the goals of the business unit may take priority over the goals of the company as a whole. This can exacerbate infighting for funding and awareness within the company. It can eliminate economies of scale. It can also confuse customers who don't understand why they must go to separate business units to solve different parts of the same problem. Sometimes, business units may actually have *competing* products, causing even more customer confusion.

---

1.   A silo is a structure on an organizational chart that clearly demarcates the people and the extent of the responsibilities. Moving something from one silo to another is sometimes referred to as *throwing it over the wall.*

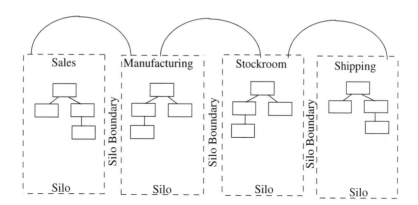

Figure 2-1 Organizational Chart

- **Continuous Process Improvement**:   In Continuous Process Improvement, instead of making radical changes, processes are continually tweaked, tuned, automated or refined to improve quality or take less time. This is sometimes known by its Japanese name, *Kaizen*.

- **Downsizing, Rightsizing, Upsizing**:   Downsizing has two meanings: first, it refers to reducing personnel. Second, it means moving from traditional, large mainframe-style computing to personal computers or client-server architectures. Upsizing refers to the transition from personal computer-based computing infrastructures to client-server infrastructures. Rightsizing refers to doing either upsizing or downsizing as needed.

- **Outsourcing**:   Outsourcing is the use of a third-party to fulfill a particular role. Presumably, every company will have a set of *core competencies*, tasks it is exceptionally competent at. In areas where the company chooses *not* to focus, it may make sense to outsource: hire another firm that *is* focused on delivering excellence in that task.

  Imagine that Acme Toys Inc. specializes in the development, marketing and sales of toys. Handling payroll for Acme employees is a small, "non-strategic" task; Acme may not wish to invest its limited resources to hire, train and maintain a high-quality staff to manage payroll. Moreover, companies that specialize in payroll services have economies of scale that Acme cannot match. So Acme outsources its payroll management responsibilities to a company that specializes in this.

Computing services are often identified as prime candidates for outsourcing. The most common services to be outsourced include: help desk and end-user computer support; lifecycle management/inventory; network and system integration; and disaster recovery. Even application development is increasingly outsourced to lower-cost programmers in India, Russia and elsewhere.

The real goal

In the twilight of the industrial age, it's become apparent that corporate dinosaurs who rely on sheer bulk and power for superiority and being supplanted by more adaptable, more efficient businesses.

Everyone has an idea on how to evolve from a dinosaur into a mammal. At least everyone who isn't too threatened by their own extinction. And *that's* the conundrum. How do you evolve a business composed primarily of neophobic (change-fearing) elements to a change loving organism oriented towards continuous evolution?

At least mammals were able to keep the basic structure of their predecessors: our bone structure and general organ placement hasn't changed much in 30 or 40 million years. But with businesses, even underlying structure must change radically. Gone are the days of "functional" organization and responsibility, when a single heart provided blood for an entire body. Companies are flattening their top-to-bottom decision making structures so decisions happen faster. They're losing task specialties such as payroll, and developing new niche product development and marketing specialties.

Success Rate: Some companies succeed at reengineering; others succeed in part; still others go through the motions without succeeding—or even measuring if they're succeeding. Others reengineer in a way that eliminates or alienates the individuals who generate ideas and vision—thereby showing short-term profits while crippling the company's ability to evolve long-term.

Why the failures? There are many reasons why reengineering fails. The key reasons include:

- **Failure to reengineer processes: a**ttempting to reengineer within the existing functional business structure. Says reengineering guru Michael Hammer, *If it doesn't make three people angry it isn't a process.*

Neither does reorganizing organization charts constitute reengineering. Here's a joke going around a company that suffers from chronic reorganizations:

Welcome to reorgtool. The computer will randomly place names in each slot on the org tree. If this arrangement doesn't work, try again in six months.

Of course, management is trying to do something better than that, but if the employees can't see the rationale or the goals, what's the use?

- **Failure to deal appropriately with the neophobic**: Most people are afraid of change. Change isn't always negative, but *is always* stressful. In an organization that's reengineering, security is constantly at risk. People can fight change through everything from passive resistance to outright Luddism—destruction of technology.

- **Failure to value long-term goals**: It's easy for companies to cut so many employees that they make a short-term profit, which keeps the stockholders happy. But cuts like these often make it impossible for companies to innovate and evolve, especially now that expected product lifespans can be measured in tens of *months*—not tens of years.

What does this mean to me?

As a manager, prepare yourself for the environment you will be working in. Know the goals of your company's reengineering or continuous process improvement efforts. Keep an eye out for risks—and for opportunities to make a positive difference. If you can successfully navigate constant "whitewater" change, you'll increase your visibility with upper management—so after the reorganization is complete, you're more likely to be where you want to be.

As an individual, study up on change management (see Chapter 8). No company will successfully stand still for very long in today's business climate. Whatever approach to change your company chooses, understand it—and be ready. If your company tries to avoid change altogether, it may not be the best place for you long-term. Don't expect to stay forever, and be on the lookout for warning signs of poor business performance.

If you're considering working for a company that is reengineering, be aware that you'll be on a roller coaster there. You won't know whether the ride will be exhilarating or terrifying until you get on board—or speak with friends and colleagues who already work there.

On the other hand, a company that has successfully reengineered itself can be a very good place to work. Chances are high that you can work your way into a challenging position where you can develop yourself. Don't expect to stay in the same position for years on end.

Employee Management

- **Behavioral Interviewing:**   Interviewers are using a new technique called *behavioral interviewing*. For many years, interviewers asked job candidates what they *would* do when confronted with a specific situation. But studies show that people faced with a hypothetical situation *say* they'll perform much better than they actually *do* when the time comes. So expect to hear a different question: *"Tell me about a time when you experienced ..."*

- **Management by Objectives:**   Traditionally, job evaluations have been extremely subjective, and haven't always reflected the goals of the organization as a whole. In Management by Objectives, each manager and employee agree on a set of objectives, and the employee is judged on how completely and well he or she accomplished the objectives.

- **Management by walking around:**   Managers who isolate themselves behind a desk in a closed office can fail to see the little things that make or break a department. Thus, simply "walking around," or better yet participating, is presumed to give a manager much better insight.

- **Management by empowerment:**   In the industrial age, management performed all the "brain work" of the corporate organism—all the decision making. But in today's rapidly-changing marketplace, centralized decision making simply takes too long. So companies are asking managers not simply to make decisions but to *empower* their subordinates to do so as well. Instead of creating bureaucratic friction that slows down the decision making process, management is now expected to alleviate it.

The real goal

The real goal of all these management changes is to give employees and employers a common game plan to operate from. That way, people will know what their goals are, what their roles are, and how much authority they have. They will also know how the corporation wishes them to develop their skills to progress successfully through their careers.

Success Rate: As with reengineering, success rates vary wildly. Most companies more than ten years old have middle and upper managers who are locked into the old industrial mindset. Their learned habits sabotage their own best efforts. After all, it takes a really humble, self-confident manager to change their management style as much as is called for. Additionally, while business school graduates trained in archaic management techniques are being phased out, not all schools agree on what to teach now.

The problem isn't only management. Workers who were originally trained to accept management decisions passively may have no idea how to make the business decisions they're now called upon to make. They may also have little idea as to how to develop themselves in this new workplace.

What does this mean to me?

Your evaluations, pay raises, promotions, awards, bonuses and advancement potential depend on the management style currently in vogue in your company. Your evaluations also depend heavily on getting management to agree with you as to *how* you should be evaluated. Don't simply let management choose your objectives: *be aggressive in charting your own development.*

I got an M.B.A. so that I would know how to manage my manager.
– Kathy Slattery

When I started to work at Sun, my supervisor prepared a Development Plan for me. Since I knew myself better than Sun knew me, I rewrote the plan to reflect where I wanted to go and what I wanted to do. I was the first employee of that supervisor to do this. Admittedly, he did change a few things to reflect Sun's needs. But overall, I had a much more customized plan—which enabled me to receive a good raise and exceed Sun's expectations of me.
– Mary E. S. Morris

Marketing

- **Niche marketing:** Niche marketing means appealing to a small but clearly defined market segment. Niches are becoming narrower and narrower. A few years ago, it might be sufficient for a software manufacturer to identify a niche of "Power users of PCs." Now that the Internet provides an easy way of reaching "niches of one," a niche definition like that becomes inadequate. One rule of thumb for Internet marketing: define a sufficiently small niche that you can locate gatherings on the Internet where at least *80 percent* of the audience is interested in your product or service.

- **Direct marketing:** Direct marketing means reaching the customer and selling your product directly to them without the usual intermediaries such as value-added reseller (VAR), distributor, retailer, or mass marketing media. Direct marketing has existed for many years using bulk mail instead of advertising in newspapers and magazines. Because of the high cost of paper mail, direct marketing developed some very effective audience targeting skills. Direct marketers also learned to write advertising copy in a very different style than classical mass marketing advertisements.

    With the advent of a commercial Internet, direct marketing has taken on many new audience generating strategies, and a new name, *disintermediation*. Disintermediation is a form of direct marketing that continues to eliminate the distribution channels while using a variety of new customer awareness generating strategies.

    Both of the key elements of direct marketing have been successful on the Internet. The hallmark style of direct marketing copywriting has remained popular and effective on the Internet. Those who have adapted the direct marketing targeting strategies to the more refined niches found on the Internet have met with significant success. Even with alternative methods of getting a message into a person's sight, these strategies have proven to be critical success factors.

- **Network marketing:** Network marketing involves using customers (often with a financial interest of their own) to advocate a product or service. Network marketing has sometimes been associated with Multi-Level Marketing (MLMs) schemes of questionable value, but MLMs are only one example of network marketing, not the only one.

- **Relationship marketing:** In relationship marketing, an entire company—management, marketers, sales professionals, customer service professionals, *everyone*—works as a single unit to build a relationship with a buyer. While network marketing is a personal relationship between *one* advocate and a buyer, relationship marketing is a team sport.

The real goal

The real goal of *any* marketing program is to impress your product, brand or corporate image upon a customer's mind, and motivate that consumer to purchase. In an industrial, mass-market age, industrial mass marketing was sufficient. In an age of customized products for customers who view themselves as having unique needs, marketing must change dramatically. It must focus on *individual* customers: "niches of one."

The Internet not only *allows for* the delivery of personalized messages, it virtually demands such personalization. Therefore, the Internet is the latest and most telling example of the trend towards customized marketing (or *mass customization*), and away from mass marketing.

The Internet is a culture unto itself, a culture as unique and important as Japan or Germany. Marketing personnel must make radical changes to adjust to this marketplace.

Success Rate: A few companies have been wildly successful at applying new marketing strategies on the Internet. Many companies have been very disappointed.

Why the failures? The failures generally fall into these categories:

- Belief that the Internet culture will evolve back into a classical marketplace with enough influx of new blood.

  Despite the current historical mythology, the Internet culture did not evolve from a bunch of geeks. *It developed because it was the most effective way to deal with the new online environment.* For example, the need for marketers to focus on "niches of one" evolved because the stress of information overload has made people ruthless about disregarding marketing messages not directly relevant to them. Internet novices won't evade this problem; if anything, it will be worse for them.

  The Internet culture will continue to evolve, but it will *never* "de-evolve" to resemble the corporeal cultures that came before it.

- Failure to understand how focused the target market must be.

  To make the point one last time, *mass marketing is really dead on the Internet.* Even targeted marketing must be used with care and precision. The perception that "people who like sports" constitutes a targeted audience on the Internet is definitely invalid.

- Failure to understand how market expectations change with technology.

  The Internet is developing new technologies every day. These technologies invariably affect the customer, and usually *empower* the customer. Augmented by these technologies, customers are evolving into new creatures who do not respond to old philosophies, strategies, and tactics.

For example, the Internet has developed a *pull* mentality instead of the classical *push* mentality of classical broadcast media. Web pages generally don't show up on a user's browser unless the user clicked on something to get them. In a broadcast medium, like TV, ads and shows come whether you want them or not. The only choices are on, off, or change the channel. If you recall the TV show *Outer Limits*, "pull" means that the user finally controls the horizontal, the vertical, and the focus. The user is in command, and expects to *stay* in command.

While push-style technology is being implemented on the Internet, it defies the philosophy that made the Internet popular—and annoys many users in the process. Internet marketers should recall the old salesman's adage: "Buyers don't want to be *sold* a shoe, they want to feel they've just *purchased* a pair."

• Failure to understand that the Internet is truly a global market.

The Internet may have had its birth in the U.S., but it has quickly outgrown the nation-state mentality. Governments may try to control the Internet, but they can only isolate themselves from it. Business and government are truly divorced from one another in this environment. Businesses must deal with the emerging social constructions of the Internet. They cannot turn to their classical supporters in local government for support or protection. For example, Canter & Siegel, two U.S. lawyers, attempted a marketing strategy on the Internet that involved *spamming* newsgroups -- overwhelming them with junk commercial postings. People on the Internet were annoyed with the spam, and developed a program called Cancel Moose which deleted it. In the U.S., this would have been grounds for a "restraint of fair trade" lawsuit. However, since the Cancel Moose author and executor was outside the U.S., Canter & Siegel had no recourse and eventually ceased their efforts to spam.

• Failure to understand the intensely immediate and human aspect of the Internet marketplace.

Relationship marketing isn't a buzz word on the Internet. People expect real responses from the e-mail addresses that they send to. They expect to find a **human@company.com**. Corporations that are used to the anonymous 1-800-numbers or taking 6–8 weeks to respond to an inquiry will alienate their best potential customers.

What does this mean to me?

As a student: Challenge your business school to develop a curriculum that reflects the new marketplace and can teach focused marketing practices that will work in the 21st century. Expect training that has been proven successful in the real world. Don't settle for theory and practices that can't demonstrate a success rate. Marketing can prove itself—and should be expected to do so.

In the business world: Take the new marketing style to heart. Don't waste time trying to figure out how to send large quantities of unsolicited e-mail that isn't "spam." That's just looking for a way to make classical techniques work. Let the old ways go. Take some human behavior classes, and use new techniques that don't create ill will or pollute the information infrastructure.

IT Goals

- *Client-server* is best defined as a strategy of putting the things that are best centralized on a server, and the things that are best distributed (usually for performance reasons) on the client system.

  Unfortunately this is not the client-server that is implemented in many companies. Some see client-server as simply networking a ragtag bunch of personal computers. While this allows resource sharing, it fails to centralize items that are best centralized. For instance, why install a copy of a word processor on every desktop when less than half of a company's employees use one regularly? By centralizing software, companies can save on disk space, excess licenses, upgrades—and especially *support*, which takes the biggest bite out of many IT budgets.

  Others see client-server as an extension of the old-fashioned mainframe mentality, which says *everything* should be centralized on the server. This is equally inept. The UNIX community experimented with the concept of a *diskless workstation* for many years. But in most environments, placing *everything* on a server overloads both the server and the network, and costs far more in hardware than it saves in IT staff costs. Unfortunately, the network appliances appearing on the horizon appear to presage yet another rebirth of this server-centric philosophy.

  True client-server is an intelligent balance of resources on server and client. This balance isn't set in stone. It will vary for every implementation. If you're looking for work in information technology, ask your potential employer for *their* definition of client-server -- and expect to be asked how *you* define it. It's one of the best ways to weed out those who really know from those who don't.

- *Open systems* is an approach that is built around the concept of using common, usually off-the-shelf, commodity products that can be purchased from—and supported by—many suppliers, rather than proprietary components available from one or only a few vendors.

The Internet became what it is today because it strictly adhered to an open systems strategy. TCP/IP, the Internet's protocol, is open. (In contrast, Novell's IPX is not open, because only Novell controls and evolves it.) The standard that defines how Web pages are displayed, HTML, is also open, at least in theory. (In practice, it is becoming oriented towards Netscape's proprietary enhancements, which please the marketplace but often fail to live up to the spirit of openness.)

"Open" is a buzzword: in the early 1990s, it was so widely applied that it has lost meaning. Many people didn't understand that for something to contribute to an open systems strategy, its evolution could not depend on a single company. To identify a truly open product or standard, ask who controls its evolution. To determine whether you'll be working an open systems environment, find out whether the platforms and standards in use there fit this definition of openness.

- *Intranets* are classically defined as using Internet technology to create a document sharing environment on a private or internal network. In reality, intranets are far more than their current external counterparts. A true intranet is not based solely or even primarily upon document sharing. Intranets are based upon database-Web combinations that extend the accessibility of legacy systems and bring coherence to the entire concept of workflow, not just data flow. The best way to identify a sophisticated, next-generation intranet is to ask how much of it is based upon sharing information and how much is oriented towards automating workflow and business procedures.

The real goal

The real goal was and still is to use computers to make businesses more productive. Unfortunately, computers are best used with precision, not brute force. When used as a blanket panacea, they don't recoup their expenses.

Success Rate: Success rates in intelligently using computing power are very low. The potential of computing is usually fulfilled only when the IT department has strategic goals that address the specific needs of the business, and are flexible enough to evolve into the next generation without rebuilding from scratch.

Why the failures? In postmortems for failed technology projects, the same factors recur over and over again:

- Failure to have a good business rationale and strategy for using technology.

  Many IT purchases are made because someone read about a new trend in a magazine and decided it needed to happen at their company. Technology works best if it is used precisely for specific problems. Upgrade to the latest and greatest only if there's a specific reason to do so. Be specific. Say, for example: "The new version of this word processor will create Web pages automatically at the same time we develop print documents, saving 20 of my people 80 hours each per year." It's not enough to say: "It'll make us more productive".

- Failure to architect a realistic design.

  Bill Gates' heady optimism in "The Road Ahead" is very contagious. Unfortunately, it bears little resemblance to historical trends. Many people do not share Gates' enthusiasm for growing bandwidth because historically, programs and multimedia content have increased in size much faster than bandwidth has become available. Companies that design systems assuming they will have virtually free bandwidth to work with will be disappointed when their systems fail to perform.

- Failure to prototype and test an architecture before implementation.

  "Your mileage may vary" is the technical person's way to say that the real world confounds any guarantee. Product A may work very well with Product B in the test lab. However, Product A, Product B, Product C, and Product D, can't all co-exist peacefully in the same computer or on the same network. The real world is far more complex than any vendor can reasonably test for. When designing your own solution, it is vital that you take a customized prototype for a spin before investing heavily to deploy a full-fledged application company-wide.

- Failure to forecast Information Services (IS) costs accurately.

  Most IS budgets fail to factor in "peopleware" costs, such as training, support and employee development. Extended or long-term costs are also rarely spelled out—including rework costs associated with not doing the job right the first time. As IS almost invariably overspends, executive confidence in IS organizations is often very low.

What does this mean to me?

If you're an IT professional and you want to become a star, you face a challenge your predecessors may not have faced. Many corporations are now realizing their addiction to technology, and the cost of that addiction. Funding for new projects must be justified more diligently than ever before. This "due diligence" can involve more work than the project itself.

Understand what management wants to know, and provide it as concisely as possible, complete with facts, figures, and proof of testing. If you're proficient in effectively "reality checking" projects for management, you'll do well.

Quality and Value

Some companies believe quality is merely a fad, not a long-term trend. Others believe that quality, good or bad, just happens. In reality, quality will be the most powerful trend of the next twenty years, because it will affect *all* business processes. Companies will go beyond measuring "objects" for quality. They will apply quality measurements to processes, structures and even ways of thinking.

In a world of exponential change, where new products are rapidly reduced to undifferentiated commodities, quality will be a prime measurement of added value, and a key measure of business success.

The buzzwords

- **Quality Circles**— Quality Circles were the first application of Japanese-style quality control techniques by U.S. business. In Quality Circles, frontline workers spend time in groups developing ways to improve quality. Since they experience the work every day, they presumably are in a good position to notice problems—and to identify root causes and solutions.

- **Continuous Process Improvement a.k.a.** *Kaizen*—As discussed earlier, Continuous Process Improvement is an effort to improve quality incrementally, on an ongoing basis.

- **Reengineering**—As discussed earlier, reengineering assumes that a process needs to be torn down and rebuilt from the ground up in order to improve quality.

- **ISO 9000**—ISO 9000 is a set of international quality business practice standards. Many companies and governments, especially in Europe, require ISO 9000 certification from their business partners and contractors. Companies seeking ISO 9000 certification must demonstrate that they adhere to ISO 9000 practices, and especially that they have quantified and documented detailed quality processes. Presumably, once they have standardized their processes enough to document them, they will be able to identify and prevent problems and ensure a standard, high-level of product quality. Once certified, companies must consent to regular quality audits to maintain certification. ISO 9000 is a pass or fail certification.

- **Capability Maturity Model**—The Capability Maturity Model (CMM) was developed for the U.S. Department of Defense to measure business practices and quality control. CMM was created to measure hardware and software development practices, and has been modified to apply to personnel and document management practices as well. Unlike ISO 9000, CMM is not a pass or fail system: it has five levels of achievement. Some people prefer this approach: companies can achieve certification and then upgrade it as they keep improving their business practices. However, since more businesses in more countries require ISO 9000 certification, there's more pressure to use ISO 9000.

The real goal

Increasingly, the physical value of a product's components has shrunk, and the knowledge value has increased. The goal of the quality revolution is to maximize the knowledge embedded in their products, thereby adding value building a sustainable competitive advantage.

Success Rate: Success rates vary widely, primarily because many companies go through the motions, instead of expecting a specific outcome. Since quality programs invariably must be adjusted to make them compatible with the real world, many fail. Simply throwing "quality" at a problem doesn't work any better than throwing "technology" at it.

However, there are some shining successes as well. Tom Peters is famous for demonstrating the successes in many of his books.

Why the failures? Failures are linked to many causes.

For many, quality and reengineering programs are incredibly stressful. Stressed-out employees display fear, anger, and diminishing self-esteem, becoming the victims of change, not the instigators.

Many programs fail because participants fail to understand their goals. Thus departments are re-organized in the name of quality, without apparent purpose or measurable improvement.

What does this mean to me?

Increasingly, quality will not be a buzzword, but rather a measurable quantity. You need to understand the quality programs and techniques in use at your company, work with those techniques, and deliver results.

Implementing better quality metrics and methods can make you a shining star. Above all, never complain about a problem without having at least a hint of a viable alternative.

Summary

In this chapter, you've reviewed the workplace, technical and societal trends that will make or break careers in the 21st century. In Chapter 3, you'll take a hard look at what it now means to be competent.

CHAPTER

The World of Work

Competence —"You don't have to be competent to work here— but it helps."

The more competent people exist to fill a position, the more competent each applicant must be.

The Competency Problem

Life isn't fair. Neither is work.

Here's one reason: the more competent people exist to fill a position, the more competent each applicant must be. Conversely, with few competent people available, an average applicant doesn't need to be very competent.

Some people believe that if they haven't been fired, they're competent. But getting a job, or even keeping one, is no proof of absolute competence. It just means you're more competent than whoever else is available at the moment. When an organization's needs significantly exceed the number of competent people available, organizations make trade-offs, temporarily accepting lower levels of competence.

When I was in vocational school for digital electronics, there were guys who graduated with straight D averages—and promptly found jobs. Were they competent? Probably not when they were hired. But the industry was so desperate, it took virtually any warm body that could go through the motions. Those "warm bodies" had a chance to *become* competent before the market was saturated with people that were *already* competent.

Eventually, however, overall competence levels rise. Then, people who were previously acceptable aren't any longer, unless they improve to match the competition.

Where few highly competent people exist, the less competent are unlikely to be terminated. This often gives people a false sense of their skills. Years later, they find themselves out of work, with a long and difficult future ahead of them.

Judging Competency

How do you tell if you're really competent? If you're in a new field, few people are truly competent. Keep these rules in mind:

- Stay humble: even the gurus still have a lot to learn.

- Never turn aside opportunities to learn. The best thing to know is how much you still *don't* know.

- Listen to your manager's development suggestions; if you don't get any, *ask*.

- Compare yourself with others in the industry. Your manager may not be the best judge of competency in a new field: he or she may be learning it at the same time you are.

- *Ultimately, real competence can be measured by consistent, successful completion of tasks and projects. Measure your own competence this way before others do.*

Increasing Competency

If you aren't competent when you're hired, ask yourself if you're willing to commit the effort needed to become competent. If not, invest your time preparing for some other job: in new industries, you can't coast for long.

If you *are* willing to commit the effort, stick with it. Most people don't become competent without a lot of practice. If you can come up to speed in a new position in just a few weeks, you're the exception, not the rule.

Competence is Relative

Again: competence is *relative*.

Back at my electronics vocational school, women were few and very far between. Why? It wasn't because the guys scared the women away or harassed them.

I knew a woman who received a B one quarter, and promptly dropped out. I believe the women viewed competence differently when approaching a male dominated field: they judged themselves on an *absolute* scale of perfect competence that no novice, male or female, could possibly meet.

Education

We've all heard that a college degree is the key to a good job; the better the degree, the better the job. Numerous Ph.D.s working for minimum wage will tell you this is a myth. Like all myths, it's rooted in fact, but a traditional degree alone guarantees you *nothing*.

 Theoretical knowledge without practical experience leads to the "book-smart street-stupid" individual many businesses fear to take on. Experience and theory are *equally* essential. As a result, at more and more schools, degrees will not be awarded until students have proven themselves in the workplace.

A combination of education and experience is the only ticket to success.

The Combination of Theory and Practice is Key According to Jakob Nielsen

Theory and practice—you have to have *both* hats. That's one difference between somebody who's been trained and a hacker. The person who's been trained also understands some of the theory.

Experience is even more critical when you're training for a global business environment. Once, two or more years of language education was enough: now, some employers expect you to have spent time overseas as well. Similarly, most technical translators now need experience *in the industry* as well as in the language.

You're more likely to retain knowledge that you gain through internships and similar programs. It's well known that if you don't use what you learn, you risk losing that knowledge—and nobody can afford to lose knowledge anymore.

The field of UNIX system administration clearly shows the importance of *relevant* experience combined with *relevant* coursework. Most college computer science curricula focus on programming. However, system administrators, support staff or technical architects require a more well-rounded mindset than computer science programs traditionally teach.[1]

In the short-term at least, software developers can restrict themselves to a single programming interface, standard, or language. However, administrators in today's multivendor environments must deal with near-infinite complexity. They need a different set of knowledge skills.

Today, non-traditional education is more likely to impart these skills than university education. Remarkably, UNIX system administrators *without* four year degrees were better paid than those with a four year degree or even a Ph.D. according to a SANS salary survey.

---

1. In many companies, management "expects" computer science graduates to be successful as system administrators, support staff and technical architects, and they hire accordingly. However, managers who have evaluated the success of the candidates they've hired often find that having a computer science degree isn't highly correlated with success as a system administrator. Big picture logic is more highly correlated with system administration success. No wonder many successful system administrators have had music degrees, advanced bio-chem degrees, and even MBAs. Second, there is a significant difference between programmers and software developers. It is an unfortunate reality that many computer science degrees focus on programming specifically, *not* on the big-picture thinking, lifecycle issues, in-depth formal design and analysis that are critical to successful software development.

It's not only technical curricula that often suffer from a lack of practical focus. Consider communications. It's a rare employee—management or otherwise—who doesn't attend at least two or more meetings per week. Unfortunately meeting participation skills aren't even offered, let alone a mandatory part of a well-rounded education. Once again, corporations and non-traditional educators are called upon to fill these gaps.

Multi-Disciplinary Jobs

Most college education still assumes a "specialist mentality," but in an era when specializations flit in and out of existence, specialization isn't a good career move anymore. The demand for multi-disciplinary skills is increasing far faster than multi-disciplinary education is being provided to meet that demand.

Human computer interface (HCI) design is a good example. HCI people require some human evaluation skills based in psychology and anthropology, some technical knowledge based in computer science, and some typography, graphics arts and aesthetic expertise typically learned in Graphic Design or Fine Art programs.

Technical marketing is another good example. Technical marketers must not only understand their technical products, but also be skilled in communicating and presenting those products' advantages in public. They must also be skilled marketers who understand business strategy. It's common for technical marketers to start with a technical bachelor's degree and return for an M.B.A.

Cyberspace is rapidly becoming the realm of the generalist, where those with only one skill cannot compete.

Some Employers Still Favors Degrees over Experience

Having said all this, many old-line company recruiters still believe the person with four years of on-the-job experience is somehow less *"professional"* than someone with a bachelor's degree. Some companies even close many positions to those without a degree. Admittedly, a person with both education and experience is likely to be on the fastest track.

Still, progressive managers in these companies are likely to find themselves increasingly at odds with human resources departments that prevent them from promoting highly-experienced non-degreed individuals into professional positions.

It is change, continuing change, inevitable change, that is the dominant factor in society today. No sensible decision can be made any longer without taking into account not only the world as it is, but the world as it will be. . . .

Isaac Asimov

Change

Jakob Nielsen says Keeping Up with Change is Accomplished by Understanding Concepts

Look at the Web as just one of 50 hypertext systems. It happens to be the most important one, but it will change dramatically. You can't necessarily predict that change, but you *can* enhance your ability to keep up with it—if you learn the underlying concepts of *all* hypertext systems.

If you're just graduating high school, consider how change will impact *your* work life:

• By the time you get out of college, you stand a 1 in 3 chance of not having a full-time job. ("Upwards of 35 percent of the U.S. workforce will be contingent workers by the year 2000."—Richard Belous, *The End of Work.*)

• If you choose to go to vocational school *instead* of college (not in addition to college), your skills may be outdated 5 years after graduation. (*The Economist.*) While some colleges may provide longer term educational assets, even they can't provide career-long education in one degree program.

• About 70 percent of current jobs are potentially automatable within the next 50 years, and automation continues to accelerate. ("...more than 90 million [U.S.] jobs in a labor force of 124 million are potentially vulnerable to replacement by machines."—*The End of Work.*)

- If you choose a job in a knowledge industry (i.e., directly or indirectly related to computers, education, management or the sciences) you stand to be in the top wage earning brackets. ("The [U.S.] knowledge class, which represents 20 percent of the workforce, receives US$1,755 billion a year in income, more than the other four-fifths of the population combined."—*The End of Work.*)

What are the knowledge skills you need simply to *get* work in this new environment?

- Knowledge about job openings and how to make hiring people aware of you.

- Excellent interview techniques.

- Current skills.

- Experience before graduation.

You can't predict the precise job you'll wind up with, but you can plan your general direction—and aggressively move in that direction before you graduate.

Once you're on the job, plan to routinely update your education—and above all, take control of your own personal growth, through after-hours course work, networking, or whatever's necessary.

Ken Erickson Says There's No Way to Plan a Lifelong Career Any More.

Because our industry changes so rapidly, it's crucial to remain involved, and expose yourself to as many different technologies as possible.

I don't think many people really envision what they will be doing 15 years after they start out. I didn't: I just had a vague notion that I wanted to work with computers. I'm not sure what I'll be doing 15 years from now, either. I enjoy my work, but the industry changes so rapidly, its hard to predict if there will be any fun jobs left in computers by then.

Having the Right Attitude

Competence is great, but it isn't enough. *Your attitude can make or break you.*

Many managers will hire a person with a good attitude over a person that is highly technically competent every time. Bad attitudes don't just diminish one person's performance, but the performance of everyone who comes in contact with them. When there's a shortage of trained personnel, people with bad attitudes can "get away with it." But shortages don't last forever—and then, those with the bad attitudes are history.

What are the elements of a good attitude?

- Perseverance
- Paying your dues
- Avoiding "victimization"

Have a Fearless Attitude Towards Learning, Says Glenn Fleishman

I hire people who are fearless, who just will go out and learn stuff quickly. If you work with somebody for even a few hours, you can see how fast they can get up to speed, and how timid or outspoken they are about getting ahead.

It's so important to find somebody who learns fast, someone who isn't afraid to learn. Someone who isn't one of those people who says "I don't want to know anything about that." Because every week there's something new, and if they don't want to know about *that* too, we're all sunk!

Perseverance

Once, I wanted a job. Not just *any* job: a special job at a special company. I applied. I was interviewed. I didn't get the job.

End of story? No way. I asked the manager if I could keep in touch and be considered for future positions. He said yes. So I called him, sometimes every week, sometimes every other week. "Hi, how's it going? ... Anything new?... How's the new home?...Talk to you soon..."

I interviewed with him twice more, and didn't get *those* jobs, either. Was I frustrated? Yes, but I didn't let it show.

I finally got the job ten months later, the *fourth* time it came open. I had called thirty times. I was interviewed four times. According to the manager, it was pure persistence that earned me that job.

"You must have *really* wanted it," he said.

Rejection doesn't mean you're a bad person. It can mean that there are things you still need to develop. Or that others are more qualified *at the moment*. It can mean a lot of things. If you choose to retreat when things don't go your way, you won't get nearly as far.

You Have to Pay your Dues

We've all heard the saying: *you have to pay your dues*. For centuries, you've had to do the "grunt work" before you were allowed to do the fun stuff. Consider the tradition of apprenticeship.

As an *apprentice*, the junior person was given the most menial tasks to accomplish. After many years of menial tasks, that individual was promoted to *journeyman*, and allowed to participate in the simplest parts of creative work. Finally after many years of service and proof of accomplishment, a journeyman was promoted to *master* status.

Modern business maintains this tradition as well. There is good reason to start a new person off with simple tasks, and work them up to more complex tasks.

One important thing has changed, however. In a traditional industrial corporation with a large accounting staff, there were always junior people to sort the reports. In a new intranet organization where you're the only Webmaster, who can you delegate grunt work to? *Nobody.*

It's not just large vs. small companies, either: even large organizations have typically been reengineered into multiple business units that are doing their best to resemble entrepreneurial startups.

Don't look forward to the day when all your menial tasks will be magically lifted from your shoulders and passed on to some other poor plebeian soul. If you're arrogant enough to believe that as a system administrator you're too good to do backups, or as a publisher you're too good to address your own FedEx slip, or as a software engineer you're above fixing bugs, you're likely to find an amused management, keeping one eye out for someone more willing.

The only real way to get rid of the grunt work is to give it to a computer. Learn how!

Make Sure They Need You More Than You Need Them

Many people have experienced discrimination or other unfairness. Most either quietly bear the situation, or run crying to mommy ... err, Human Resources or a lawyer.

Unfortunately, this doesn't always help: for one thing, it makes *everyone* resentful.

Unfair situations happen when one party is weaker than the other. Seems obvious, doesn't it? *The solution is to be the stronger party.* You don't become the stronger party by allying yourself with an outside power like HR or a lawyer. You merely emphasize that people must walk on eggshells when your ally is nearby. Once your ally is gone, they can take advantage of you even more.

You won't be the stronger party as long as you're too attached to the security, comfort or ease your current job offers.

If you're afraid to lose your job, you are at a disadvantage.

If you don't want to have to work harder or learn something new somewhere else, you're at a disadvantage. You must be willing to change, and confident enough to make change happen.

Finally, you must become so valuable that if you left, there would be a serious problem—and you must make sure the bully in question *knows* your value.

If you wait until you encounter problems before you develop this strategy, you're too late. But if you make yourself valuable *wherever* you go, and you're competent and confident enough to move on if necessary, the world can be at your feet.

Doing an "adequate" job won't get you this power. You must be exceptional. *Most people can become exceptional if they simply make the commitment.* But they consider a job "*just a job.*" Thus when bad things happen, they don't have the reserve of personal power they need to overcome. They just resign themselves to complaining and remaining a victim.

Motivation

Most people invest too much energy and time in surviving, not enough in self-actualization. They view their jobs and education in terms of survival; their hobbies and limited free time as the only opportunity for personal growth and satisfaction.

No wonder they resent their work, watch the clock, and try to get away with the bare minimum 40 hours a week, or even less.

Unfortunately, 40 hours a week simply aren't enough to succeed: they don't leave enough time to learn what you need to know, or network with the people you need to meet, so you'll have the visibility you need to get ahead.

40 Hours Isn't Enough, According to Bill Prouty

You must do 50 hours or more to stay really current in a high-tech job here in Silicon Valley. Maybe you do 40 hours of work, then another 10 or 20 hours of networking and investigation. And you can't just do it at home—you have to extend your work day to get your work done *while* you're networking and learning about new technology from people that know it here at work.

Never Underestimate the Power of the Network, Says Mike Troiano

It's the power of the network. I got my first job from another Cornell guy. From my perspective, relationships like those justified the degree. Yes, I learned how to think at Cornell, but I probably could have done that for less money at a non-Ivy League school.

Go somewhere you'll develop a solid set of alumni contacts and have some organization you can use to make inroads with people in the business.

And besides, why work just to survive?

When you split your time between survival and the pursuit of happiness, you're not likely to achieve either. As Marsha Sinetar says: "*Do what you love; the money will follow.*" In the Knowledge Age, more and more people can eventually find work they love, and make a living at it.

Your ideal job won't be the first job you ever get. It probably won't be any job that you get, when you first get it.

Until then, try to choose jobs you can "massage" into work you enjoy. Yes, there will be times when you must devote your whole body and soul to survival—but don't do it for too long.

As many Yuppies discovered, pursuing a goal without enjoying the ride isn't what it's cracked up to be. The journey is worth more than the goal.

The key to long-term success is motivation: if you're motivated to do something, you will usually do it well. But motivation to acquire more money or possessions often fades once survival needs are met. *For most people, the only motivation that lasts is the internal motivation that comes from loving what you're doing.*

Debra Winters on Her Motivation

I work because I want to. Once I thought, maybe, gee, I'll have another child and I'll stay home. But the Internet made work so much fun that would be absolutely pointless.

My Webmaster job was a rainbow I pursued because I really thought it was fascinating and fun. When I see something pop up and I'm surprised, like *wow! that looks really cool*—I go after it.

Specialization

In the industrial age the ability to turn *this* screw or weld *that* joint was all you needed to get a good union job for life. That changed somewhat with the advent of the service economy. It changed more when reengineering started making people responsible for a process, not just a task.

The specialist is an "endangered species"

On the Internet, it's changed completely. The most valuable people on the Internet have a wonderful combination of technical expertise (or at least lack of intimidation!), business savvy, and communication skills.

There will still be a place for a savant, but people like that will be the exception. Most truly successful people will understand business well enough to recognize a customer's needs, have enough vision and imagination to discover a solution, and have enough technical or artistic skills to help make that solution a reality.

We have not always been a species of specialists. The farmer could build a house or barn, plow a field, plant crops, tend farm animals, and do whatever else was needed.

We once valued the "well-rounded" individual, the "Jack of all Trades" who could understand and do many things. In the knowledge age, we must return to that mindset.

Be a Generalist First, Says Mike Troiano

I'd much rather have someone who understands the industry in which they're going to work, someone who can relate to my client, than someone who knows the intricacies of C++.

Being an effective generalist is the price of entry. You need to understand the world the clients live in.

Discipline: Practice Makes Perfect

I interviewed dozens of people to write this book. I asked them all: *How did you learn how to think?* I wanted to know how people moved from the *"cookbook," rote approach to work, to understanding why they were doing what they were doing, and when to change their tactics.*

The answer I heard most often was *discipline*. That may conjure up images of monastic retreats or martial arts exercises. But take a closer look. Different disciplines teach their "thinking" skills differently. Business schools use case studies. Engineers learn from problem-sets. Librarians may learn to think using word logic. Regardless of the technique, they all learn by *disciplined hard work.*

Sometimes, this consists of time-consuming repetition. As engineer Tim Brady put it, "problem-set after problem-set after problem-set." You have to keep at it until it becomes second nature. If you have to consciously review what steps to take, you haven't got it yet.

Of course, repetition only helps if you're also being taught the concepts that make everything fit together. *Newsweek* debunked the myth that German and Japanese students spend more time on education than U.S. students. In fact, U.S. students spent slightly more time on studies. But they achieve much lower levels of competence, because they spend only about 22 percent of their time thinking and discussing how to solve a problem, and 78 percent of their time doing repetitious drill work. For the Japanese, the numbers are almost precisely reversed.

Why do you think Leonardo da Vinci produced dozens of drawings of hands and faces? In art, as in science and technology, there's no substitute for knowing something *intimately*.

A Closer Look at How People Learn

When a person initially learns something, they learn it in "declarative memory space." It is rote practice that transfers the skill to "procedural memory space." Once you have learned to ride a bike, that is now a procedural memory. When you still had to think about the balancing act involved, that was declarative memory.

Another example: learning to shift gears in a car with a manual transmission. At one point, you had to think about how far out to let the clutch pedal and how to coordinate that with the accelerator, and then using your hand to change gears. After awhile that becomes "second nature," i.e., it has been transferred to procedural memory. Procedural skills aren't limited to physical skills like riding a bike; they include semantic manipulation, such as applying an algebraic procedure to both sides of an equation.

Domain of knowledge skills (not necessarily facts, though) are best converted to procedural memory. At that point the declarative memory is free to think "about" what you are doing. You need your declarative memory free to conceptualize and apply principles. Until you transfer that knowledge to procedural memory, you don't have any free compute space to think "about" it. You cannot move to the higher level of thinking where improvisations or variations on a theme occur.

Now you understand why discipline is so important; you need to practice things until they're transferred from declarative to procedural memory. In fact, it's the ability to move basic semantic manipulations to procedural memory which allows people to think abstractly about computers and knowledge in the first place. An experienced programmer can think conceptually about a program, and then render it in a programming language using correct syntax and keywords without even thinking about the rendering process — just as some writers write by thinking about concepts, not individual words.

This intimate level of knowledge wasn't needed in day-to-day "industrial-age" repetitive work, but it is a cornerstone of the Knowledge Age, which is characterized by endless variations and change. Since not all variations work, a creator must know the material well enough to identify the ones that are most likely to work.

Summary

In this chapter, we've considered what it takes to be competent in the Knowledge Age. But competence isn't an end in itself. In Chapter 4, we'll take a closer look at what you need to do to become not just competent, but also *happy* about what you're competent in.

4

Developing Yourself: A Roadmap

When it comes to your worklife, don't fall into the mental mindset of previous generations. That mindset is very limiting. It holds that:

• **You should know "what you want to do *when you grow up.*"** People have been asking children what they want to do when they grow up for generations now. Admittedly, having a choice is better than being told you must follow in your father's footsteps no matter what. Nonetheless, children today are rarely exposed to anyone's worklife. They have no experience with which to make that choice.

Programs which allow parents to take their children to work for a day barely scratch the surface. Many of these programs allow only passive observation, with little if any narration about what is actually happening in the workplace. Moreover, they rarely expose the child to a wide variety of jobs, since the child usually stays with their parent and is only exposed to their parent's close colleagues. And even the best "work for a day" program can't change the reality that today's jobs and careers may well be gone by the time a child is ready to enter them.

Today's high school graduate probably will have several careers, not just one. Asking them to choose one thing "to be" is asking them to buy into yesterday's workplace—and setting them up for the same anger people are experiencing today when their life's work is replaced by a computer or robot.

- **To succeed, a person needs "a good education."** This phrase, taken literally, is quite true. *Education* is a key indicator of salary, growth potential, and satisfaction. However, *a good education* is often interpreted to mean a bachelor's degree—usually in a scientific or engineering field for those that want to get into computers.

  In reality,

  —Some of the best paid systems administrators do not have a bachelor's degree, even though they are highly-trained professionals in a highly technical field.

  —Some of the most important growth industries in the knowledge arena require only basic computer skills.

  —The role of the specialist is quickly shrinking.

  —In the information age, a good education *really* involves:

    —Skill in the core competencies: Cyberspace Literacy, Communications, Change Management, and Practical Reasoning.

    —The ability to learn *transferable* skills you can use and adapt as your industry changes.

    —Continuous learning to stay current throughout your life.

- **A "good work ethic" will ensure success**. Again, taken literally, of course this is true. But for many people in previous generations, this simply meant showing up for work on time, waiting for the bosses' instructions, staying loyal to one company, and expecting that company to take care of you for life. Yes, a good work ethic will ensure success—but a good 21st century work ethic is very different:

—**Your employer is your customer**. Think of yourself as a company, and your employer as your #1 customer. Most often, what's best for you is to meet the needs of your customer—your employer. It's a win-win situation. However, if push comes to shove, you must do what's best for *yourself*—your "company of one."

—**Think and do for yourself**. In the industrial age, a management hierarchy was in charge of day-to-day thinking and decision making. That was *then*. Now, front-line workers are increasingly empowered to make day-to-day decisions, set priorities and establish schedules. If you don't learn to work autonomously, you'll be gone—or you just might find yourself with a *computer* for a boss.

—**Do what you love**. Good work comes from employees who are motivated to work hard, surmount obstacles, and go beyond their job descriptions. When survival is your primary long-term goal, you can invest a great deal of yourself in your job, simply in order to survive. But if you've experienced life beyond the bare minimum, survival won't provide the same motivation—and if you don't have a high level of motivation, you're likely to be among the first to be downsized. *You need to be self-motivated, and your strongest motivator is likely to be love for your work.*

Debra Winters' Motivation: Her Son, and the World She's Creating for Him

My son has changed my life altogether.

We've always done computers together. My hand was always on his hand on top of a mouse, even when he was ever-so-little. It's inspiring. And it drives me into the Web even more. We've stopped going to the library and using the encyclopedias: we do all his school research on the Web. I feel like I'm taking bricks and helping build the foundation for his house.

My son keeps me very career-oriented, believe it or not. I look at my job as much more important, because everything I do today will impact what *he* can do tomorrow.

—*Debra Winters, Manager of Intranet Operations, SunIR*

Where to Begin

There are always a lucky few that knew they wanted to be a doctor even at the age of five. But most people don't know what they want to do until they're doing it. A more reasonable goal: know where you want to be *tomorrow*.

- **List what you like and don't like.** You may not know exactly what you want to do, but your basic likes and dislikes can help you decide where to explore next—or what to avoid. There may be quicker ways to reach your career goals than "process of elimination," but it's a start if you don't know where to start.

- **Survey things.** Try "one of everything." That's what students are expected to do in college. Unfortunately, college classes are often the poorest guide to whether you like a field. College classes teach "given" knowledge; they rarely promote exploration. If you're fortunate, you'll have a great teacher who can bring insight and motivation to even the most mundane subject. If you're unlucky, your instructor's dry presentation can sap the life out of even the most thrilling field. Always search out the best teachers: the ones who are genuinely excited about their subjects. And don't rely only on teachers: seek out professionals and associations that can give you an insider's view of a line of work.

Choose a Wide Variety of Classes, Says Tim Brady

Take a class in psychology, one in economics—*take the whole spectrum*. Don't think you're going in at 17 years old already knowing what you want.

— *Tim Brady, Director of Production, Yahoo!*

- **Do *something*.** When confronted by an oncoming car, a deer will often freeze. It's a survival instinct that worked for centuries—but it's not a successful survival technique for deer today, who are more likely to be confronted by a speeding semi-truck on a highway. Faced with a life-or-death decision, people often freeze in indecision, too. Always do *something*.

If you're unsure of your commitment to a course of action, don't make a long term commitment. But failing to do anything is always worse than trying something and discovering that you don't like it. Everything you do gains you experience, knowledge and self-understanding you can apply elsewhere. Do nothing, and you *rot*.

Planning Your 21st Century Education

In *Digital Economy*, Don Tapscott noted that a medical doctor of seventy-five years ago couldn't function in today's hospitals, but a teacher of seventy-five years ago would find themselves quite at home. That's frightening. It's no wonder *less than half* of today's high-technology education takes place in traditional post-secondary institutions.

Take a cue from this, and plan your education for the 21st century—an education that goes far beyond the walls of a classroom. Plan your education to include:

General skills. If you're planning a career in the 21st century, you'll need these general skills:

- **Cyberspace Literacy.** Cyberspace Literacy involves proficiency with the World Wide Web, e-mail, Usenet Newsgroups, word and web processing programs. You need to understand not simply how to use these tools, but how to use them *effectively*, so they magnify your capabilities. For example, you need to understand how to perform a Web search that delivers the right results quickly, and how to use agents to retrieve the information you need autonomously.

- **Communications.** Oral and written communication skills are more important than ever. Moreover, traditional skills aren't enough. Today's skilled communicators must:

  —Structure their messages for fast and effective communication

  —Communicate within new, computer-mediated media

  —Know their audience and tailor their communications appropriately

  —Complete the communication process with active listening and feedback, and

  —Use appropriate "situational communications" skills, such as archiving, moderation, meeting participation and networking.

- **Change Management.** Change is rarely addressed in secondary education: nobody knows what to teach about it. Nonetheless, you need to know how to anticipate, forecast and prepare for change—and how to *initiate* change that doesn't quickly turn into chaos.

- **Practical Reasoning.** Practical reasoning takes practice—lots of it. Few graduates can demonstrate consistently practical reasoning right out of school. But practical reasoning skills are the most important critical success factor for long term employment, and they *must* be developed. Those who succeed in the workplace demonstrate entrepreneurial skills, and change jobs frequently (although they don't necessarily change employers). Those who can't demonstrate these attributes last only as long as the company retains its old attitudes. Practical reasoning, sometimes called "out-of-the-box" thinking, correlates highly with senior-level and consultant positions.

Procedural training for specific jobs. This type of education is widespread in vocational and non-accredited institutions, but colleges and universities do offer some of it, too. It's often essential for those starting out in a specialized job, whether that job be systems administration, accounting, or anything else. But it isn't enough to see you through your entire life. In fact, studies in Germany found that procedural training provided only about *five years* of employability, on average.

Theoretical knowledge in a specific field. Of course, colleges and universities specialize in theoretical knowledge—though you still must determine whether the school teaches the specific theory *you* need. For example, schools that offer only systems programming theory may not be the best place to learn database or applications programming theory.

Specialization is best done *after* you have some experience in a field, if only a summer internship. Theoretical knowledge becomes far more pertinent after you see how it's applied in the real world.

Theoretical education can give you the background you need for an entire career—but since most people will have several careers, even this type of education isn't enough to see you through an entire lifetime.

Learning to evolve. If you learn *how* to learn, and how to adapt and grow continuously, you'll have skills that can last for a lifetime. In large part, "learning how to learn" is the same thing as learning practical reasoning skills. Learning is merely the classification, modeling and application of logic to a new field of endeavor—and these are the core elements of practical reasoning.

The Importance of a Degree

To some people, post-secondary education is impractical, irrelevant, and twenty years out of date. To others, a degree is a rite of passage, the initiation to professionalism. Here are the key factors you should consider in deciding which degree to get, or even *whether* to get one:

1. **Lack of a degree is a barrier to entry**. The lack of a degree is still a barrier to entering many professional positions, even if having a degree isn't necessarily proof of competence—just proof that you have jumped through the appropriate hoops.

2. **Proof of accomplishment**. Having a degree proves you've accomplished at least *one* long term goal. It *does* demonstrate perseverance and tenacity. It *may* also show that you know something about a particular field.

3. **Often, no longer enough by itself.** As we've said, many people now realize that a person with a degree *and nothing else* isn't always the best person for the job. If your education was focused solely on theory, you still must acquire procedural knowledge, either with non-accredited education vendors—or if you're lucky, on the job. Even if you get on-the-job training, you'll need continuing education to acquire your next job, and succeed at it. It is not rare to find two jobs that share many of the same skills. But virtually every new job requires at least one or two new skills.

Experience

Education is like preparing a field for a crop. Education is the *plowing* process that loosens the dirt and makes crops easier to grow. Education is the *fertilization* process that provides the sustenance plants need to grow. However, actually planting and growing the crop: that's *experience*. It doesn't matter how much preparation is done, if you don't actually do something, you'll never get results. In this section, you'll learn how to *plan for experience*.

Planning the Development of Experience

We've said you should think of yourself as a "company of one." Successful businesses, including yours, must define a vision, goals, objectives, milestones and "inch pebbles."

Once you've defined where you're going, you can build a gameplan for getting there. And with goals in place, you can also establish metrics to measure your progress.

If you don't measure your progress, you won't know when you're off course—or when your entire industry has swerved and you're still going full-steam in the wrong direction. And without measuring progress, you're unlikely to realize how much you *really have* accomplished.

* **Vision**. A vision is the dream you want to achieve. It's your highest, most general statement about where you're going and how you'll get there. Some of the best visions talk about where the world is headed and how a company will "meet up" with the world as it *will* be.

  Your vision doesn't have to focus on work. In fact, it is probably better if your vision spans *all* your activities. The vision of many people during and after the Great Depression of the 1930's was simply to live a comfortable life, not want for necessities, and offer their children better opportunities than they themselves had. The vision of many counterculturalists of the 1960's was to change the world and make it a better place. My vision is to pursue the best and never settle for just "adequate".

* **Goals**. Goals are things you want to achieve long term. You might set a goal to earn $100,000 per year, or to be a published author, or to live in a particular place, or to be an executive. Some goals are common to the vast majority of people. These include:

  —**Sufficiency**—A well known psychologist, Abraham Maslow, defined seven levels of achievement: the first, lowest levels involved survival. Everyone needs resources *sufficient* to survive.

  —**Self-sufficiency**—For many people, sufficiency isn't enough. When sufficiency is provided by someone else—parents, spouse, or even government agencies—it may come at the cost of self-esteem. For many, providing the necessities *for oneself* is a critical goal.

  —**Comfortable Reduced Work Periods**—When many people think about reduced workloads, they think about retirement. Retirement is an important goal that requires planning: we don't die on the job as routinely as our ancestors did. But it isn't the only reduced work period the average person will experience in the 21st century. People have children, get ill, are laid off, and go back to school. Each situation reduces the opportunity to work and earn income; each situation requires advance preparation.

- **Objectives.** Objectives are steps towards achieving your goal. To make $100,000 per year, you probably must first make $20,000 per year, then $40,000, and so on. To be a published author, you may need to understand the publishing industry, learn how contracts are handled, dream up an idea for a book, and get a publisher interested in you and your idea. If your goal is to become self-sufficient, your first objective may be a year's training at vocational school to obtain enough knowledge in a domain to start working immediately—above minimum wage. (Remember, vocational schools teach *domains of knowledge*, not skills. They're the first step of the ladder. They can help you earn enough money to be self-sufficient, but you'll still have to develop the transferable skills you will need.)

  Objectives don't have to be oriented towards just *one* goal. For example, if your goals include becoming self-sufficient *and* acquiring a bachelor's degree, you might complete a year's education at a vocational school whose credits can be transferred to a four-year college. Similarly, if you're working towards an art degree, you might start with one or two semesters at a vocational college like *Master's Institute* learning how to create graphics with Photoshop and Illustrator. With this training, you can get a job immediately, if needed—and your courses can be put towards a degree program. This technique of optimizing your efforts to meet multiple goals or objectives is called *leveraging*.

- **Milestones**. Milestones are smaller steps towards an objective, en route to a long-term goal. For example, to get a raise to $40,000 per year, you may need an excellent employment review. To get an excellent review, you might need to perform your core job well, complete at least two special inter-departmental projects successfully, and get some specific education. Thus completing one of those inter-departmental projects or a class is a milestone.

- **Inch Pebbles**. Always have your next stop on the road of life within sight. Break your milestones down one more step, to "inch pebbles"— week-to-week accomplishments. Inch pebbles are your microscopic steps towards your milestones, objectives and goals. If you run into problems, you want to discover them while moving from one inch pebble to the next, not from one milestone to the next, or half-way to the next objective. Spend a few minutes each week reviewing accomplishments, finding ways to resolve problems that will crop up in achieving future inch pebbles, and recording your progress.

Inch pebbles are useful for many reasons. A week is about as long as an average person remembers their small accomplishments—the accomplishments that make good discussion material in interviews and periodic evaluations. Three months from now, when you sit down with your boss and she asks you what you accomplished last quarter, you can impress her with a list achievements that demonstrate real growth.

Inch pebbles are also important because course corrections at this level are easier to accomplish. If you get feedback that your status reports are missing key elements, you can note that information in your weekly self-review, and follow up on your improvement in weeks to come.

Getting Experience

Getting experience—especially initial experience—can be very hard. You know what people say: *it takes experience to get a job, and it takes a job to get experience*. However, there *are* solutions:

- **Paying Your Dues**. To get your first bit of experience, you may find yourself taking a job with a less than spectacular salary, or even doing volunteer work. Everyone must start somewhere.

  —**At school, in labs**. Some schools offer labs, commonly staffed by bright, but cheaply paid students. In these labs, the students may prepare class materials, administer computers, or act as tutors or mentors.

  —**Internships, Cooperative Education**. Internships and cooperative education are among the most productive ways to gain experience. Interns are often low paid workers, and they often bear the bulk of the menial work. Nonetheless, an internship can make the difference between having a job waiting when you graduate from college and spending another six months looking for one.

  —**Volunteer work: CompuMentor, VISTA, others**. Volunteer work is often far more than manning the ladle at a soup kitchen. Like everyone else, non-profit groups want to take advantage of new technology and the new opportunities it offers. However, most don't have the money to hire professionals. Consider investigating

CompuMentor, an organization that matches people with computer skills to organizations that need those skills.

Even more conventional volunteer organizations need skilled professionals. VISTA (Volunteers in Service to America) often requests people with computer and cyberspace skills. VISTA pays a little money and contributes towards your college education, before or after the fact. Beyond these organizations, there are literally hundreds of others. A local volunteer coordination service can assist you in finding positions in your area. Visit the Cybercareers website (`http://www.cybercareers.com/`) for more ideas.

- **Job Search**. Once you have some experience and can be more selective, start looking for jobs that offer the specific experience(s) you want. You might want experience in a specific technology, like UNIX systems, or you might want to develop a specific skill, such as leadership. Don't choose jobs strictly for salary and benefits. You could find yourself making a great deal of money short-term, while you fall far behind in developing the skills that are most critical to your long-term success.

- **Develop broadly**:   Don't repeat the same job. If you were a Xenix system administrator at one job, don't settle for being a Xenix system administrator in your the next job. You might learn a few new operating procedures, but you won't broaden your experience.

- **Develop at your own pace**. If you try to go too far, too fast, you won't get the depth you need—or you'll forget what you learn because you haven't repeated it enough. The world may be moving fast, but it's still not moving at the speed of light. It's more like a caravan, with different companies and people, each moving at different rates. In *Crossing the Chasm*, Geoffrey Moore*,* presents the world's many segments, from *innovators* to *early adopters* to the *early and late majority* and even *laggards*. You don't have to live on the leading (or so-called "bleeding") edge *all* the time.

Tracking Your Experience

Tracking your experience is critical to developing yourself, but most people do it rarely, if at all. They miss many opportunities to collect proof of their skills and experience, and keep their accomplishments alive. There are several useful techniques for tracking experience:

- **Diary of Experiences**. Keep a diary, and update it every week when you evaluate your 'inch pebble' accomplishments. If you don't write your accomplishments down at least once a week, you're likely to forget many of them. Why does it matter? Performance reviews are one reason. They're usually very infrequent, no more than once or twice a year. Both parties enter these reviews with few memories of the small events that prove consistency or improvement. Only the events of the past few weeks stand out—and if some of those events were negative, a performance evaluation is likely to be unfairly colored by them. If you can point to a record of many positive events over a long period of time, you can offset any negative short-term issues.

  Many people are required to create status or progress reports only once a month. If you don't track your accomplishments more regularly, your reports can suffer from "accomplishment shortages."

  Third, people often overcommit to projects, misjudging what they're capable of doing. By reviewing how much time it actually took to complete similar work, you're more likely to accurately estimate your next project. Again, track this information at least once a week, or your memory may start playing tricks on you.

  Fourth, documenting your work history may be useful in earning college credits later, as colleges begin to admit that life experience may be equivalent to certain college courses.

  Finally, as we've mentioned already, many interviewers are now using "behavioral interviewing"—asking how you acted when faced with a specific situation. By keeping a diary of your experiences and reviewing it prior to an interview, you'll have more positive examples to draw upon.

- **Samples of Work**. Most artists come to job interviews with portfolios of their previous work. The arts are volatile: people may come together for a specific project, and then disperse. This makes it difficult to locate people for later references. Your portfolio may be your only reference.

  Portfolios aren't just for artists and models any more. They're used extensively by Web developers and designers to demonstrate accomplishments, personal style, techniques, and levels of expertise. They are also used by many new professional developer associations as a method of certifying Web professionals.

  In fact, portfolios come in handy for a wide range of people that must demonstrate design, communication, software or knowledge creation skills. Even system administrators can benefit from documenting their project plans, automation scripts, bug reports, and status reports, proving their ability to manage projects and communicate appropriately.

Finally, portfolios are important for demonstrating life experience. As we've said, many colleges now give credit for life experiences—but only if you can prove what you've done.

- **Document After Interviews**. Many interview books will give you pointers on preparing for the interview, completing the interview, and following up with the interviewer. But one important task is often forgotten: *debriefing yourself.*

  Write an account of the interview shortly afterwards. Note what went well, and what you can be proud of. Also note what didn't go well, and what questions you had trouble answering, so you can prepare for your next interview more effectively.

  Be explicit, and be detailed. We sometimes believe a few words will be all we need to spark our memories. In reality, six months later, those few words may seem like gibberish. You want to remember the interview well. Then, in your spare time, replay it in your mind, and change things you would have liked to have done differently. Many performance professionals say this technique can refine your skills.

- **Document Job Research**. When you research jobs, write down what you learn. Write down the types of jobs you investigated, what you learned about how your target companies operate, and who the key players are. Even if this information isn't important now, it will be later. You may not get the current job, but if you find out about similar positions, you'll be well positioned to go after those jobs.

  Keep names of people you can network with in the future, and information about those people. Down the road, you might use this information to estimate how likely a company would be to get into a specific new technology you're interested in, or use a specific product you're familiar with. Documenting your job research is also good practice if you find yourself in sales. The more a salesman knows about a company, the more likely he is to find the right product, and make the sale.

- **Achievements and Awards**. Your achievements and awards help differentiate you from other candidates. Extra company courses that you took can prove your interest in staying up with the latest technology. Awards for going beyond the call of duty can demonstrate your dedication. Bonuses that you received for your hard work can help make your case for a future promotion or raise.

- **Aptitude Tests**. Aptitude tests offer insights into the areas that you appear to have strong interest, natural ability and/or significant experience. As you mature and grow, your test results may change. More importantly though, when reflecting on where you've been and where you're going, aptitude tests can remind you of something you've forgotten you're really good at. They can suggest directions for the next career or job change.

  They can also remind you of the places where you *don't* have natural skills and must work harder to develop yourself. For example, one person may be a natural "opener": they start projects really well, but may have trouble finishing them. Of course, projects need to finish just as much as they need to start, and knowing that you have this weakness is the first step towards resolving it.

- **Reviews and Feedback**. It's good to review your past activities, and reflect on both your accomplishments and challenges. These reviews, both formal and informal, can offer insight into areas where you need to develop yourself.

Summary

Developing yourself is your first opportunity to practice the skills that determine long-term success. You can establish a big picture "vision," and build a plan for self-development that includes objectives, milestones, and even the "inch pebble" steps you need to take next. Your weekly diary can be a powerful tool to help you develop yourself.

But the real key to developing yourself is simple: *decide for yourself to do it*.

PART

Cybercareer Staffing

- Where the Opportunities Are

- The Business Impact of Cyberspace

- Business Skills in Cybercareers

- Change Management

Looking for work in cyberspace offers unprecedented challenges.

You can't simply point to a degree and say, "I'm qualified."

You can't always know in advance what your job description will be.

There are few established standards by which employers can judge you.

It can be disconcerting. It can also be liberating. You can progress much more quickly and achieve much more than you could in a traditional position. There's nobody telling you what you *can't* do. It's a once-in-a-lifetime opportunity -- and when it's gone, it'll be gone forever.

Since traditional job titles aren't meaningful in cyberspace, in this section you'll take a close look at the practical roles that cyberspace professionals are filling. You'll learn about Internet and intranet roles; technical infrastructure roles, content deveopment roles -- and the business roles involved in making virtual spaces *real*.

CHAPTER

5

Where the Opportunities Are

Cyberspace is a big place. It includes current belles of the ball, the Internet and intranet—as well as the computers, networks and information services that predate the Web-based intranet. It's big enough to provide a wide range of opportunities for *all* kinds of people.

In this chapter, we'll show you where the opportunities are in:

- Information technology (IT), Information Systems (IS) and Information Resources (IR) organizations

- Internet Services

- Intranets

You'll also learn about opportunities with organizations that provide Internet-related outsourcing services. These include:

- Advertising Agencies
- Web Service Providers
- Internet Service Providers

Roles and Job Titles

We're in the habit of judging jobs based on their titles—and expecting job descriptions to resemble those found in sources like the U.S. Department of Labor's Occupational Outlook Handbook.

But job titles for knowledge workers are rarely found in the Occupational Outlook Handbook; they're too new and varied. Even job titles are of limited value, in an era when both technology and roles are changing at near light-speed.

The Limits of Job Titles

In many cases, there simply are *no* fixed job titles and job descriptions for knowledge age work: the traditional labels have broken down completely, as if Humpty Dumpty were in charge of Human Resources.

In one organization, an Internet Engineer might find herself integrating SSL (Secure Sockets Library) into a new electronic currency program—a development role. In another organization, someone with the same job title might be called upon to set up a firewall between the company's servers and the Internet proper—an administrative role.

The most mangled title of all is "webmaster."

- A webmaster should be an accomplished system or network administrator with in-depth knowledge of web products, including servers, search engines, publishing tools and HTTP security.

- But a webmaster may also be called upon to program to the CGI specification in any of a half-dozen languages, and do some database programming on the side.

- *And* a webmaster is typically a company's web evangelist and greatest advocate, a.k.a. "Web Maven."

- If that's not all, a webmaster is expected to be a gifted writer, content consolidator, graphics production specialist and layout professional.

- Meanwhile, the webmaster must be a savvy marketer and advertising genius—designing a site that coaxes recalcitrant buyers into parting with as much money as possible.

- And finally, the webmaster must be a public relations specialist, expert at getting the site registered with search engines, promoting events and additions to the site, and garnering accolades from the numerous groups now awarding prizes for web sites.

Throughout this book, we've often said that it's important to broaden your skills beyond a narrow discipline; *this* is why. But in reality, a webmaster who can do *all* those things well is about as common as a six-handed person — and people like that are as costly as they are rare. Instead, hiring professionals find themselves seeking *several* people, each skilled in one, or a few, of the areas needed. Once hired, these people may be "allocated" into as many roles as they can reasonably handle.

In this chapter, we'll give you insights into each of these roles — and tell you how IT managers and hiring professionals are thinking about them right now.

Cyberspace: Eight Major Roles

In one way or another, most computing and cyberspace job descriptions fall roughly into one or more of eight general roles. Of course, these are only rough guidelines, but you'll find them very useful in understanding what you may be called upon to do.

These eight roles are:

• Administrator (Support)	• Architect
• Analyst	• Developer (Programmer)
• Tester (Quality Assurance)	• Designer
• Producer (Artist, Illustrator, Writer, Author, Musician)	• Manager

Administrator (a.k.a. Support): An administrator typically installs, configures, troubleshoots, and repairs software. This is a highly challenging support role, given the diversity of software and hardware now available, and the inherent complexity that results whenever they're combined.

Architect: An architect is a planner or high-level system designer. This is often a company's highest level of technical achievement, one that few people reach. Architects research and sometimes prototype systems, in order to develop a long-term technical strategy for an organization. This strategy must dovetail with the *business* goals of the organization, and must be economically feasible. Therefore, successful architects must not only be superior technologists; they must have business savvy as well.

The need for people skilled in research and complex configuration design is growing at a phenomenal pace. Few companies can afford to hire the architects that they will need—assuming that high-level technical people *could* be found to fill these positions.

Sun Microsystems, Inc., has come up with an alternate approach. They hire *principal investigators*, who perform the primary research work in a narrow niche. Above these investigators, an architect consolidates the information learned, and develops strategy. Bill Prouty, Web architect for Sun, indicated that even though he had almost 40 percent of his staff devoted to researching new technology, ideally it wasn't enough. In the fast-changing world of cyberspace, this is not an optional role — and in a leading edge organization, it is certainly not a trivial one.

Commonly, architects sit atop the "administration" career ladder in an IT organization. Analysts, whom we'll consider next, are on the top rung of the development ladder.

Analyst: The term "analyst" has been widely used for decades. *Systems* analysts model processes, so programmers can render them into code. Nowadays, there are also *business* analysts, *market* analysts, and *network* analysts. All these people model processes so they can be reduced to simpler terms, and then delegate responsibility for appropriate action. For example, just as systems analysts pass their results to programmers, business analysts typically pass their results to managers.

As the business importance of software becomes more critical, even systems analysts find that their roles have a significant business component.

Developer (a.k.a. Programmer):   There have been programmers as long as there have been computers. In the mainframe era, there was a clear division of labor: programmers wrote code, and systems analysts developed designs. While "programmer" is still a very common title, most programmers now perform at least some design, and many depend on code-generation tools that automate much of the actual coding. Therefore, they prefer the more descriptive title "developer."

Having said this, for the most part, analysis of the business process and conversion of business terms into programming requirements is still often handled by analysts.

Tester (a.k.a. Quality Assurance):   Testing is a clear, distinct role that is typically considered part of software development rather than administration. Some companies have started using the term Quality Assurance instead of testing. Quality assurance *should* be far more than just testing: it should involve following errors back to their source and remedying the problem there, rather than simply rejecting failed products. However, some companies use the terms QA and testing interchangeably, so if you want to know exactly what's intended, you'll have to ask specific questions.

Designer: The term "designer" is used occasionally in the technical world, but it is primarily a media term. The designer is the visionary, dreamer, and strategist who develops an idea; the *producer* implements what the designer came up with.

Producer (including specialty terms for specific media):   Once, when fewer media existed, unique terms sprang up to describe content producers. They were called writers, authors, artists or musicians. With the proliferation of new media, these people are increasingly called "producers". For example, now that sound has gone beyond just music, there are now *sound producers*. The term Producer or Editor may also identify people who combine various types of media into a complex whole. In this case, "production" is viewed as a stage of the media development process, and the producer works at that stage. The specific job title then refers to the business task associated with the production, e.g., *CD-ROM producer*.

Manager: Ideally in modern business, managers are there to support their staffs, clearing the business obstacles that prevent people from getting the job done. Of course, many managers still hold the traditional view that they are supposed to direct people.

Other more difficult to describe descriptors are...

You'll sometimes hear other terms that, like webmaster, are so overused that they've lost much of their meaning:

Engineer: "Engineer" is a title that has come down from before the dark ages. It means someone who *applies science*. Accordingly, the title of engineer is generally accorded to anyone with at least a four-year degree in applied science. In information technology, the respected term "engineer" has generally been accorded to programmers and developers; administration has not traditionally been given the same value. This is changing quickly, however. A small but growing minority of administrative personnel are achieving the title of engineer—often without the degree requirements.

Specialist: When you've created a job title with plenty of adjectives, but you're not sure what the noun should be, the easiest word to toss in is "specialist." ("Client/server networking... umm, *specialist*.") Obviously, it implies that someone will work primarily with a specific technology or will have specific expertise, but the title "specialist" tells you nothing about the actual work involved.

(In this book, we'll talk at times about *generalists*, not simply to balance the specialist, but to underscore that some jobs simply cannot be done by people with purely specialist knowledge and experience.)

Member of Technical Staff: In government work, some information is classified based on *need to know*. Some job descriptions are a bit like that: if you knew someone was a *satellite astronavigator*, you'd have a pretty good idea how important they were to the government. To hide information useful to competitors, some corporate titles have become *very* general; witness the currently-popular title Member of the Technical Staff (MTS). Many companies have also adopted this title because it gives them more flexibility in assigning work.

Technologist/Technician: "Technologists" are more often encountered in support than programming/development roles, but can be found in either role. Often this title signifies an administrative job with small amounts of programming. Years ago, a technician or technologist was similar to an engineer, but with less status—and often with a two-year or trade school degree instead of a four-year degree.

Organizational Staffing

Often, IS organizations staff their frontline support positions first — the support positions that deal with the customer or user. However, databases, servers, and complex or multi-user software also require support, often from professionals with specialty expertise beyond that required on the "frontline." Most Internet and intranet support falls into this "premium" category.

IS/IR/IT Staffing

There are wide differences in IS staffing, depending on company size and the company's view of the importance of information management. In a company of forty people, the IS department is usually a staff of one, if that. In a company of ten thousand people, the IS department can comprise a few hundred people. The larger the company, the more it can benefit from economies of scale when hiring information technology professionals — especially support specialists.

When planning support, many companies use the rule of thumb that one person will be required for every 40-80 computer systems in use. The more a company has standardized on a single platform, the more computers one person can support. It's reasonable to assume an 80:1 ratio in highly-standardized, "homogeneous" computing environments, and a 40:1 ratio in highly diverse, "heterogeneous" environments. As companies get larger, economies of scale may reduce these differences: one person can be devoted to supporting Macs, another to PCs, another to UNIX workstations.

Large companies can also devote support resources to improve the way they deliver support. With a good support infrastructure, one person may be able to support 100 computers instead of 80, and some exceptional support organizations have reached 130 computers per support person. A few companies are aiming at 500 computers per support person — which will require extensive investments in infrastructure and user training, along with an exceptionally controlled environment.

Small companies (1–150 computerized employees)

Small companies rarely have enough computing support needs to develop specialists: support people become jacks-of-all-trades who are called upon to do just about everything. Companies like these often depend on support contracts to provide specialized support when it's needed. As you can see, IS organizations like these tend to have flat organizational charts:

Mid-sized companies (151–600 computerized employees)

Once you get a few support people together, they can start pooling their resources, and specializing. Tom may find himself specializing in Word-Perfect support — resolving WordPerfect problems faster than other support people, and fixing problems that might stump his colleagues.

When IS departments reach this threshold, they often begin to build a core team of second-level, specialized staff members. These roles are created because the organization needs in-house expertise in more complex areas that require special training or knowledge.

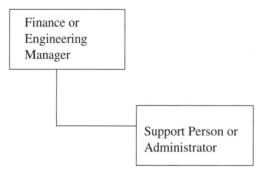

Figure 5–1   Small Companies

In some companies the specialists are clearly defined and removed from day to day work. In other cases, they're asked to devote part of their workday to specialist work and the rest to general tasks. Once a company has a team of specialists, it may be cost-effective to move premium support activities, such as database support, in-house.

Often, the first specialists to emerge are network support people. They may be followed closely by people devoted to infrastructure improvement. Infrastructure support professionals may work to automate tool and resource usage, centralize software servers, implement name services, or automate software installation, configuration and upgrades. Some companies may assign a specialist to e-mail, web and other online work at this point.

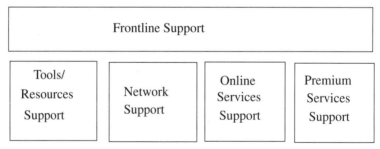

Figure 5–2   Mid-sized and large companies

Large Corporations (600+ computerized employees)

Once a company grows beyond about 600 employees or about 20 IS personnel, these specializations typically evolve into separate departments. Thus, Tools and Resources people may not answer to the same manager as Frontline support people. Planning takes on a significant (and more formal) role, and architects become more prominent. Management is organized into "people" management, project or program management, and strategic futures management. More technical specialists are added, as well.

Internet Services Staff

The size of a company's Internet staff has little to do with the size of the company, and far more to do with the ambition of the company's Internet-related goals. At a company like Amazon.com or Virtual Vineyards, which depends on the Web as its primary way to reach customers, more than half the employees may be involved in Internet development or support. In more traditional companies, a staff of 1,000 might require only one part-time person for web activities.

As we've already discussed, the Internet requires a highly multi-disciplinary team, with extensive business *and* technical skills. This often leads to internal disputes over "who owns the Internet," with both IS and Marketing claiming leadership — and Marketing winning slightly more often. In making these decisions, companies with successful web presences recognize that their sites must constantly change, improving both content and usability.

Internet Network Administration: An Internet Network Administrator is typically responsible for establishing the Internet connection, registering the company's domain name, implementing an effective security firewall, monitoring traffic, and resolving connectivity problems. In some larger organizations, planning or architectural functions are performed by different people than day-to day support. In other organizations, roles are divided into *network* and *security* responsibilities.

It takes more work to set up an Internet connection than to maintain one. Many companies find it cost-effective to hire a consultant to set up the connection and firewall, and then have a Network Administrator support the connection after appropriate training.

Sponsor: In all successful projects, someone's at the helm planning the course — someone with the clout to make it happen. For a web or intranet project, this typically is an executive. Though few companies can spare an executive entirely for Internet projects, executive-level sponsorship is essential.

Web Architect: Web sites grow and change, and much of that change occurs in technical areas. The web architect is typically responsible for ensuring that a site evolves to keep up with technological change.

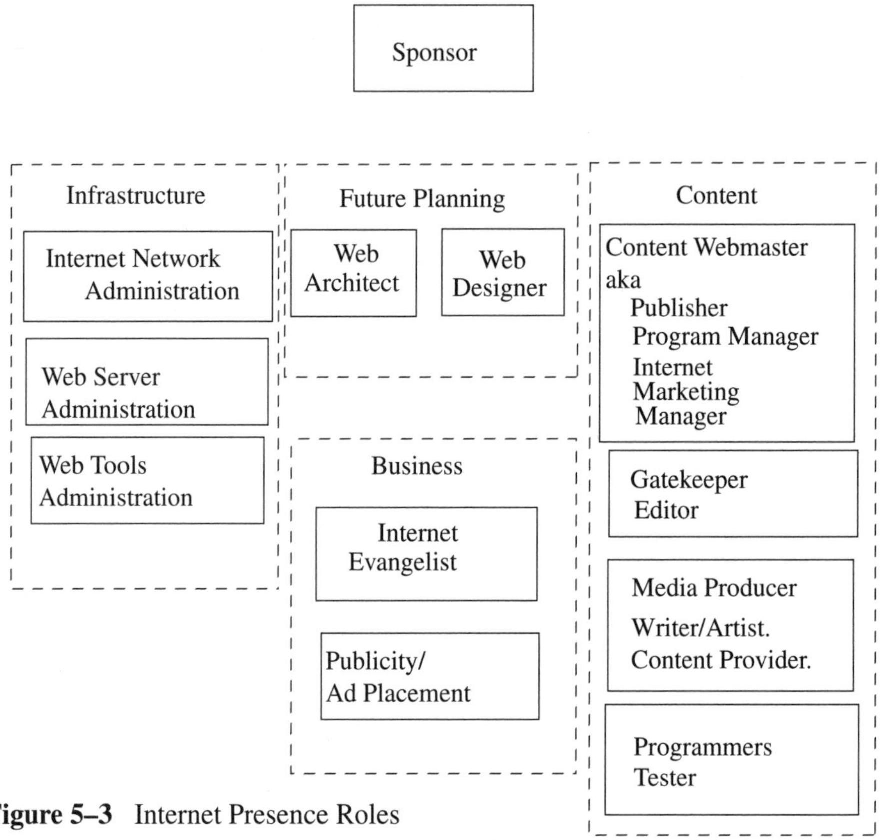

Sponsor

Figure 5–3   Internet Presence Roles

Web Server Administrator: The Web Server Administrator supports the web server. If you're a good LAN server administrator, chances are you can get up to speed with web servers in a few days of intense training — but if you try it unprepared, or you're likely to waste weeks on trial and error.

Large-scale web servers like Sun's site (`http://www.sun.com/`) with tens of thousands of pages and hundreds of people submitting material require extensive support. Once a web server holds 5,000–10,000 pages, or has multiple applications installed, a full-time web server administrator is needed.

Web Tools Administrator: There are always client-side tools to go with the server applications. Some tools are for users, others for contributors. The Web Tools Administrator decides which to use, then installs and supports them. For non-technical resources like media libraries, even an ambitious secretary or administrative assistant can be drafted for initial resource building.

Internet Marketing Manager/Content Webmaster: In many organizations the top of the content chain is the Internet Marketing Manager — the marketing person who oversees the entire web effort. For sites devoted primarily to producing content, this role is roughly equivalent to a magazine's publisher. The Content Webmaster oversees both programmers and editors who are responsible for content creation in specific areas.

Web Designer: *Web design is a business issue*. Enlightened companies recognize that a Web designer isn't a frivolous extra to be added only when there's extra money floating around, but rather one of the most critical parts of the web team. Poor design can cost a company customers, miss opportunities to off-load expensive 1-800 number and fax response systems, and simply make the site a losing proposition.

A Web designer creates initial design specifications, develops a style guide and templates, and verifies usability. Many companies save money by hiring consultants or contractors for web design during the development process, and for annual or semi-annual "checkups." At these companies, day-to-day implementation is overseen by editors or gatekeepers.

Gatekeeper/Editor: Someone must manage the thousands of files that exist on many large web servers. Someone must make sure they're organized properly, that they reflect the "look-and-feel" of the company style guide, and that they're written appropriately. In some places, these people are called editors. Others call them document managers. Sun calls them Gatekeepers. Netscape calls them Traffic Coordinators.

Often, the Gatekeeper is the person with a vested interest in getting the right message out: for example, a product marketing manager.

Many companies haven't defined the role at all, leaving the responsibility with the Web Server Administrator. That's fine for organizational issues, but it doesn't address content quality control or message management — issues a technical professional may not be well-suited to oversee.

The evolving rule of thumb is to plan for one Gatekeeper for each 200–500 new web documents per month, plus one Gatekeeper for each 1,000–5,000 old documents that must be maintained. Thus, smaller sites won't need a full-time Gatekeeper, but large sites may need several full-time Gatekeepers, or even more.

Media artists: Only design firms and large companies can justify keeping online graphics professionals on staff full-time. Most creative work is contracted out.

Content providers: Just about anyone can provide *some* content: business or technical writers, knowledgeable employees ("subject matter experts") or managers. But every document needs an owner, and every document should be reviewed periodically for continued accuracy and relevance.

Programmers: Simple response forms can be created with shareware software or pre-packaged programs, but it isn't long before the need for a "real programmer" becomes obvious. Often, a company's first web programmer is its Web Server Administrator. That's justifiable in smaller sites, but companies with larger sites benefit from separating programming and administration. Programmers and administrators rarely have the same strengths.

Testers: Any web site that lets programmers test their own code is asking for trouble. Often, the programmer is too close to the project to see problems. In complex projects, the programmer may be so technically focused that they fail to consider the interface adequately.

Interface testing can be done by recruiting employees with technical knowledge equivalent to the "average user." Simple testing can be done by systems administrators. But any mission critical application, or application that involves commerce should be *fully* tested by a professional.

Internet Evangelist: Internet marketing goes far beyond simply setting up a web site. E-mail communications with visitors and potential customers must be staffed. A good Internet Evangelist can generate significant traffic and improve a company's reputation by participating in Usenet newsgroups and e-mail discussion lists. An Internet Evangelist can also research customer needs, and set up filtering tools to watch for mentions of a competitor — helping a company keep abreast of competition in real time.

Publicity/Ad Placement: If you build it, they *still* won't come until they know your site is there — especially with half a million other sites to visit. Companies must generate publicity, both offline and online. They must register with search sites, negotiate links, and purchase web advertising.

Web Mentor: If you really *are* one of those multi-talented Renaissance people, with all the skills of the "classic" webmaster we discussed earlier, you don't want to spend your life converting FrameMaker documents to HTML. If you're skilled in administration, design, content creation, marketing and maybe even programming, you'll make a great Web Mentor.

The Web Mentor is a leader and a trainer, responsible for sharing experience, developing solid project plans, but most of all, providing one-on-one guidance to help others come up to speed.

Intranet Staffing

Staffing for intranets generally resembles staffing for Internet services, with a few exceptions. There are typically more technical and infrastructure people involved (both for support and programming). The top of the content hierarchy tends to be the corporate communications or human resources department. The sponsor may be the CIO or another executive level information professional.

Many intranets leverage infrastructure work already done for a company's Internet presence. intranet publishing tends to require less gatekeeper oversight, less control, and less quality assurance. On the other hand, since more "amateur communicators" are involved, more editorial training and guidance are needed.

There's one more big difference between a company's Internet site and its corresponding intranet: the amount of content involved. *Typical intranets have at least ten times more content.* At one point years ago, Sun Microsystems had just under 10,000 documents on its external web server — and over 250,000 pages on its intranet.

Technical Webmaster: A senior technical person is often needed to manage an intranet's growing technical staff, and to provide a single point of contact that can negotiate additional support services with other departments. When the IS organization supplies intranet software developers, the Technical Webmaster may have to negotiate for their services as well.

Web Server Administration: Only large Internet sites can keep a Web Server Administrator busy full-time, but it's different for intranets. There isn't just a production server and a staging server to manage. Most intranets also use "proxy servers" to reduce the network load between sites, or from the Internet connection. Remote workgroups may set up local web servers; large departments want servers, too. Of course, someone has to *maintain* all these servers.

Companies with multiple servers that share a common configuration can automate administration and reduce staff needs — but again, someone has to be there to introduce and manage the automated administration systems. Companies don't hire small armies of Web Server Administrators and let them twiddle their thumbs once the automated systems are in

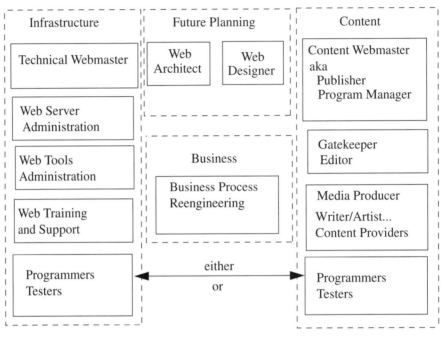

Figure 5–4 Intranet Staffing Roles

place: they typically use contract employees to fill the roles that will only exist during ramp-up.

Web Tools Administration: This role is similar for Internet and intranet work, though some companies expect their intranet Web Tools Administrators to provide more internal training and support.

Web Tools Training: Companies are discovering that their user support and training needs increase significantly with the advent of an intranet. Generally, companies don't have to support their Internet site's users, but they *must* support intranet users. Most people can learn to click on a link or enter a URL in a matter of moments, but teaching them effective search techniques and acquainting them with the structure of the intranet can dramatically improve productivity.

At most companies, intranet authoring isn't limited to documentation professionals, because the intranet isn't limited to professional documents.

Employees benefit from having a wide range of corporate documents available including memos, meeting minutes, and status reports. It isn't cost effective to retain HTML conversion staff to translate these documents: thus the average employee now must learn "web-style" word processing.

Web Architect: An intranet architect may have far more research to do than his or her Internet compatriot. More features can be implemented on an intranet because a company's intranet tools and software can be standardized and controlled. Security also becomes even more important, necessitating a common user and system identification system or naming service.

Lastly, intranets can place significant demand on a company's network infrastructure. The web architect must work with LAN and WAN network architects to monitored traffic, forecast upgrades, and implement them before the network becomes congested.

Web Designer: Some companies see the importance of professional web design on their Internet sites, but believe that a web designer isn't required for their intranet, because it's not a marketing tool. They're wrong. Design has a dramatic effect on productivity. Those organizations which fail to staff for design will find their ROI degrade year after year, as their intranet gardens start to grow more weeds than productive plants. An intranet web designer can add enormous value by focusing on usability and the development of easy-to-use templates for less experienced web publishing employees. Since the enormous amount of information on intranets leads to increased complexity, intranet web designers are increasingly called upon to create customized content solutions that make this information more manageable.

Content Webmaster: Often the Content Webmaster's role is a rather political one. One webmaster jokingly referred to herself as a web-o-cop on days when she found the policing effort not to her liking.

Gatekeepers and Content Producers: Gatekeepers have the same role on intranets as on Internets — but they have more work, since there are more documents. It isn't uncommon to see multiple part-time intranet gatekeepers reporting to other gatekeepers, who in turn report to a Content Webmaster. It's too soon to tell if this will change.

Programmer and Tester: A first-generation intranet devotes itself to simple publishing endeavors. Second-generation intranets orient themselves to workflow issues more than data flow issues, migrating corporate applications to web technology or creating entirely new applications. Netscape's AppFoundry gives a small glimpse of the ways intranets can be used to automate business processes.

Programmers are usually in the thick of things in this stage. Since most business processes are critical to the company, effective quality assurance is equally important.

Business Process Reengineering: Intranets can help automate many labor intensive processes, allowing staff to be redeployed elsewhere. But changing the technology while keeping the same business processes is a recipe for long-term failure. There's increased demand for people who can analyze business processes and work with intranet programmers to redesign both the technology and the processes in parallel.

Specialty Firms

Companies that don't have web content or technical experience in-house — and can't afford to develop it — have the option of outsourcing. There are many different firms outsourcing web work, and therefore many opportunities to *get* web work from these companies.

Don't overestimate the amount of experience you need. The web is a new medium. *There's only one person on Earth with six to eight years of web experience: Tim Berners-Lee, who invented the web.* Most experienced people can demonstrate 18–24 months of time in the Web field. If you learn fast, you can make up ground in a hurry — especially if you're willing to work overtime, as most of today's web professionals do.

Advertising Agencies: Advertising agencies tend to focus on Internet Marketing, and some can offer direct sales assistance as well. *However, it's important to remember that most agencies are just as new at this as anyone else.*

What an Interactive Marketing Agency Offers per Mike Troiano

As a specialized interactive marketing agency, we're not just a "bag carrier." We're trying to get inside the client's business, really understand what they need to achieve, then help them develop a strategy.

—*Mike Troiano, CEO/President, Ogilvy & Mather Interactive*

Web Service Providers: Web Service Providers offer a wide variety of web services, from marketing and advertising to sophisticated web database programming. Web Service Providers aren't all small fry anymore. There are large franchise-like organizations such as USWeb. Many large technology companies, such as Sun Microsystems, offer Web services as well. Of course, there are still thousands of small one- or two-person Web service providers out there, many of whom have as much experience as the large corporate providers.

Internet Service Providers: Many Internet Service Providers (ISPs) have been in the Internet business for a long time, and can offer significant infrastructure support. But they're "hit-and-miss" when it comes to content skills, just like everyone else we've discussed.

Summary

If you're *buying* Web, Internet or intranet skills, the old saying is true: caveat emptor, let the buyer beware. But if you're *selling* them, you've never had a better opportunity to move ahead quickly — and you'll probably never have an opportunity like this again.

PART

Work Skills in Cybercareers

- The Business Impact of Cyberspace

- Business Skills in Cybercareers

- Change Management

Every year, technology and business become increasingly intertwined. The days are long gone when you could survive as an information technology professional without understanding or caring about your company's business goals. If nothing else, downsizing saw to that.

Even if you don't care about your employer, you need strong business skills to survive as your personal "company of one." If you find yourself performing independent work, as a contractor, consultant, or in any other role, you'll need skills like planning, communication, relationship management, leadership, and change management.

In Chapters 6 and 7, you'll take a close look at the business tools and skills you'll need to survive — and thrive — as a cyberspace professional. Some of these skills show up in business school programs. Others never do. Then, in Chapter 8, you'll take a close look at the change management skills that will be critical to both technical and business professionals in the knowledge age.

The Business Impact of Cyberspace

Cyberspace now touches upon virtually all areas of business. Cyberspace leaders must become familiar with how businesses are organized, how they interact internally and with each other — and of course, how information technology can improve the way business is done.

In this chapter, we'll show you specifically where companies are focusing their cyberspace-related business improvement efforts, and what their most serious cyberspace-related concerns are. In other words, we'll show you where *your* cyberspace expertise will be most valuable to them.

Businesses exist to make a profit. That seems obvious, but it's often forgotten, especially by technical experts who are enthralled with a new technology or medium. Such people expect business executives to embrace new technology or media with open arms, and cannot understand their reluctance.

To convince business executives to adopt a technological solution, you need to understand how the business operates, and present your solution in terms they can understand: *profit*.

For example, while a proposal to advertise the corporation on the World-Wide Web (Web) may be accepted, it may get little executive sponsorship, dooming it to likely failure. On the other hand, a proposal to take orders through the Web will be a big hit in the executive suite if it can be shown to reduce costs and increase revenue. To clearly define the competitive advantage that cyberspace can provide, you need a strong understanding of how your business functions.

Overview of Business Functions

Virtually all businesses have several standard components that must exist in one form or another. These include legal, sales and marketing functions, finance, information systems, and business management. Businesses that make something must have a manufacturing department, and businesses that create new products usually need an engineering and/or R&D area.

Small businesses may satisfy some of these needs with part-time consultants, whereas very large corporations may have hundreds of people performing the same functions. For example, the legal department for a small dry cleaning business is probably one attorney who gets consulted a couple of times a year, whereas GM's legal department consists of many full-time attorneys with full staffs. Nonetheless, both fulfill the same function.

Many (though not yet all) of these business functions can be improved via cyberspace technologies. For those functions where cyberspace offers little advantage today, this may change as new ideas and tools become available.

Most of the work of businesses hasn't changed much for hundreds of years. The tools are new — computerized cash registers replace a pencil and paper — but basic processes haven't changed much. The multi-fold advances promised by cyberspace will change all that. It won't be long before many manual functions will be completely automated. Sales will be made, inventory replenished, orders placed, manufacturing done, and products shipped directly to the consumer with no human ever seeing any piece of the transaction. While this may be a bit scary, it also has great promise in terms of reduced cost and delays.

Receiving Orders

All businesses must be able to receive orders. In rare cases, a business may receive only a couple of huge orders in a year. But most companies must handle from a few orders per day to many thousands. Since this area is so busy, improvements can dramatically reduce costs.

All orders must *at least* include accurate, fully-detailed information about the customer and what has been ordered. Failing in either area will mean an unhappy customer, since items will either be incorrect when delivered, or not delivered at all.

Most companies now receive orders directly from their customers via personal contact or telephone. Some companies, typically large and forward thinking, have automated parts of this process via Electronic Data Interchange (EDI), which allows orders to be placed electronically. (EDI will be covered in more detail later in this chapter.)

The most progressive companies are now developing processes to receive orders via the Web. If handled properly, this has great promise. Security is the most critical issue, since such transactions will usually contain financially sensitive information. Once security issues are addressed, the performance and reliability of the systems handling the transactions will be primary considerations.

Consumer Orders: Companies that can accept orders via the Web have immediate, low-cost access to millions of potential customers today, and *billions* of customers in years to come. No matter where those customers are, their orders can be received with similar ease. Since all that's needed is one Web server with the appropriate Web pages, the cost to access these customers is surprisingly low. An early pioneer of Web-based sales is the Amazon.com online bookstore, (`http://www.amazon.com`), which lists more than a million titles, any of which can be ordered via its Web site.

Business to Business Transactions: The Web can also streamline business-to-business orders and reorders. Since most of these orders are based on ongoing business relationships, companies can set up Web pages that are tailored for specific customers, and accessible only to them. Orders placed via those pages go directly to the seller's internal systems, where they can be processed and filled automatically, without human intervention.

Virtual Corporation: "Virtual corporations" are sets of business partners, electronically linked so they appear to customers as a single enterprise. The internal systems at one business may take an order electronically, then electronically pass the order to another business, where internal systems receive it, build the product, order more raw material if needed, ship the product and collect the payment, all automatically. In fact, several companies could be involved. For example, Fedex could act as the "shipping department," or one company's staff could be "leased" from a staff leasing company that handles many human resources functions.

Sending Invoices

All businesses must request payment for their products or services, and nearly all use invoices to do so. Most consumer business is conducted on a cash basis: payment is expected at time of sale. Most business-to-business transactions are handled on a credit basis, where payment is expected some time after delivery.

While it is true that most invoices are now generated by computers, typically a person still prints the invoice and mails it to the recipient. Invoicing can be further automated, significantly reducing the time it takes to be paid, and thereby reducing costs. The best way to implement electronic invoicing is to have the seller's and purchaser's computers communicate. A product's arrival is noted in the purchaser's system, which sends an acknowledgment to the seller's system, triggering an invoice to be electronically dispatched.

Purchase Requisitions

In most larger companies, there's a formal process for requesting the purchase of products and services: employees fill out a Purchase Requisition (PR). These requisitions specify what is needed, what it will cost, who to buy it from, and when it must be delivered. Additional internal tracking information is usually added. The PR is signed by the requester, then passed around for other authorized signatures: typically at least one layer of management, and someone in Finance to verify that money is available.

Many companies now keep PR forms in electronic format: a requester fills it out on the computer, then prints it and circulates a paper copy for signatures. This is little improvement over the previous system.

With intranet technology, companies can make the forms accessible from internal web pages. Now, requesters can fill out PRs on the web page, then route them electronically as needed. Each person receives notification the form has arrived, signs it electronically, then routes it to the next person.

This eliminates most of the time and errors typical of the older, paper-based process. It does require developing a form on a web page, which is not very difficult. More challenging, companies must set up *automatic routing tables*, so requests are routed to the right people. Since the "right people" will vary depending on a PR's dollar value and type, this can be complex. Security is also essential: *only* the right people must see and sign the request, or else there would be no control over what the company purchases.

Stock Option Status

Stock options are a common tool used to retain and motivate key people. They allow employees to purchase company stock at bargain prices: the more the company's stock increases in value, the better the bargain. Managing stock options can be highly labor and paper-intensive, and highly error-prone. It's a challenge for many businesses to track who has how many stock options, and answer frequent employee requests to exercise stock options or get current information.

Now, this entire process can be automated on a company's intranet, dramatically reducing both errors and cost. A password-protected web server can be set up that allows authorized users to view current and historical details on their accounts, and take appropriate actions. The system could even be linked to employee accounts at outside brokerage firms, so stock purchases can be immediately transferred to that brokerage account. Of course those without stock options could not access the server.

Travel/Expense Reports and Requests

Traditionally, travel requests have been handled much like PRs: by printing a paper form and circulating it for signatures. They can be automated the same way, too, except that intranet-based forms may be routed to a Travel department rather than Purchasing after they're approved.

After the trip, most companies expect employees to fill out a Travel/Expense report. In most businesses the same form may be used for non-travel-related expenses. Of course, these forms can also be automated, with appropriate routing and electronic signoffs.

Organizational Charts

It's appalling: few large companies really understand their own structure. You'd think *all* companies would know where their people are, but they don't. Once people have transferred between departments a few times, or been part of a few re-organizations, internal records may well be out of date. It is rare for all such changes to be accurately recorded.

Most Directors or Vice-Presidents have administrative assistants (AA) who are responsible for maintaining an organization chart for that person's group. Since AAs are typically computer-knowledgeable, they usually use some type of graphics package, such as Microsoft PowerPoint, to maintain the organizational chart. A huge amount of time is spent researching, updating, printing and distributing organizational charts that are often obsolete by the time they're delivered.

Enlightened companies are placing their entire organizational charts on an internal web server. Every employee is then responsible for ensuring that their position on the chart is correct. Updates can be submitted by individuals, with electronic signatures by their managers. The approved updates are automatically sent to the AA responsible for maintaining that organization's chart.

In the near future, even the chart entry will be automated, so the chart updates itself. An early attempt at a web-based interactive organizational chart is available from the AppFoundry section of Netscape's home page. Even in its current form, this tool is better than what is available at most companies, and source code is included, so it can be enhanced and tailored to fit specific company requirements.

Suddenly, anyone with authorization can see where everyone else is placed. If all of a company's organization charts are maintained on one central server and properly linked, the company will always have an up-to-the-minute, companywide organization chart.

A tool like this can be integrated with other tools to automate many common "human resource" tasks, such as creating business cards, maintaining personnel directories, employee change notices, expense report authorization lists, and many more.

Several other AppFoundry applications are available, and more are on the way. This is a tremendous resource that can help companies avoid much expensive applications development. Many AppFoundry applications can be used with few if any modifications, particularly in small companies. Even when major modifications are required, much of the initial work has already been done, so the development effort is reduced significantly.

Legal

Companies must understand the laws and regulations that apply wherever they're doing business. While it is certainly possible to operate a business for months or years without ever getting legal advice, this can be very risky. There is a point in the growth of each business where a steady source of legal advice is required. Smaller businesses may keep one or more attorneys on retainer, while larger businesses maintain an in-house staff of attorneys. Very large businesses usually keep an in-house staff of attorneys, with others on retainer as needed.

Unfortunately, cyberspace is opening up a whole new area of legislation and litigation. Legally, it's much like the American Wild West in the 1860's, where the only law was what one could get away with. In many areas, no rules exist; elsewhere, the rules that *are* in place are ineffective. While nearly all laws are national or local, cyberspace knows no boundaries, negating the effectiveness of virtually all attempts to restrict it.

Intellectual Property Rights

For businesses that own intellectual property, enforcement of intellectual property rights becomes an acute challenge as the Internet, Web, and similar communications media expand.

Once, virtually all such issues were covered by patent or copyright law. It was difficult to extend this law to the new world of computers. Some cases have dragged on for many years before being settled (for example, the copyright infringement suit brought by Apple Computer against Microsoft and Hewlett-Packard, which Apple eventually lost). But most are settled by now, and the case law is now reasonably clear.

Unfortunately, cyberspace is changing *all* the rules. The legislation in effect to date is unclear, and the case law is insufficient to cover the issues businesses are running into right now, on a daily basis. For example: how public or private are documents, or parts of documents, that are available on the Web? If they're copyrighted, who may reproduce them, and how? When documents are freely available for anyone to read on the Web, is it legal for someone to copy one of them and sell it to others without paying a royalty to the author?

When is it legal to copy and reproduce on the Web parts of a copyrighted document? For example, newspapers are typically copyrighted documents that cannot legally be reproduced. Yet it is quite common and legal for a person to clip part or all of an article from a newspaper and send it to someone else. This is in effect reproducing the document: is the author entitled to a royalty?

These and many other intellectual property issues remain unresolved, and are hotly debated in Congress. It's likely some legislation will be passed in the next several months — and equally likely that the legislation will face several years of court challenges before the issues are finally resolved.

Of course, the entire issue is complicated by the international nature of cyberspace. Since there is no effective world court, and none on the horizon, laws can rarely be enforced beyond national boundaries, and are likely to be ignored by the majority of cyberspace users beyond those boundaries.

The Berne Convention equalizes global intellectual property laws. It is an agreement made between most industrialized countries, which essentially states that each country will respect the copyrights and trademarks of other countries, and treat them as it treats their own trademarks and copyrights. This is an excellent beginning, but not all countries have agreed. In general, the countries that have signed the Berne Convention are the more industrialized countries — the ones with the most intellectual property.

Even when countries have signed agreements like the Berne Convention, international enforcement is another stumbling block, especially where the offending country has little at stake. The United States and China have recently had several trade confrontations on this issue. Only the threat of major trade sanctions has forced China to act on the United States' intellectual property concerns, and even now there are questions as to the effectiveness of China's enforcement. Moreover, the cost of pursuing legal action internationally is frequently prohibitive, except for giant companies like Microsoft or IBM.

Free Speech Guarantees

Free speech issues are as difficult to deal with legally as intellectual property rights. How far does the right to free speech, guaranteed in the United States Constitution, extend in cyberspace? The U.S. Congress has already passed legislation to address this, but the new law was immediately challenged in court,struck down by the U.S. Supreme Court. It is likely this issue will remain hot for several yearssince the law was declared unconstitutional, the legislators will probably try again with new laws.

Cyberspace is essentially open to everyone. Pornographic materials cannot be hidden by putting them in a back room or covering them with a brown paper cover. Even warning labels require voluntary compliance, which is unlikely to happen. How, then, can free speech rights be maintained while the public is protected from explicit pornography and other things considered wrong by American society?

Free-speech issues are also complicated by the international nature of cyberspace. Many countries do not have a free-speech clause in their Constitution. (Some do not even have a Constitution!). Much of the material banned in some fundamentalist countries is completely legal in the U.S., and there are countries where material banned in the U.S. is perfectly legal.

Such questions pose a grave threat to the future of cyberspace. Some countries require local Internet Service Providers to censor the materials they deliver, under threat of legal penalties. Other countries may very well ban such censorship, again under threat of legal penalties. This could place Internet service providers in an impossible position.

It seems likely that most countries will eventually recognize the futility of trying and will either explicitly legalize cyberspace content, or (more likely) simply ignore the problem. It's unlikely that an equivalent to the Berne Convention will be established for cyberspace. Copyright law is based on commerce, which is amenable to compromise. Free speech cuts to the heart of religion and politics, and these are not issues where compromises are easily found.

Privacy Issues

Privacy issues have been the subject of numerous court cases in the United States. Some areas are relatively clear-cut. Information contained on a person's PC is treated the same as personal documents, and is subject to the same privacy safeguards. Privacy issues become somewhat less clear-cut when personal information is contained on a PC or mail network belonging to a business. Most companies now provide PCs for many of their employees. While those PCs are clearly intended to be used for company business exclusively, most are also used by the employees to maintain private information. Companies rarely acknowledge this officially, but most tend to consider it harmless, and ignore it.

Privacy issues can easily arise, however. In such cases, who owns the information — the individual, or the company? If a company designs and builds cars, and someone discovers a competitor's proprietary design information on one of its PCs, who's liable? If someone is discovered to be maintaining a list of customers for a prostitution business on a company PC, again, who's liable?

Who owns the information transmitted by electronic mail networks? Can the company legally read any message, or does that invade the privacy of the senders or recipients? Courts have generally held that companies *do* have the right to read the information on their networks and computers, as long as that right is clearly stated in company policies that have been distributed to all employees. Companies are well-advised to develop and publish clear rules on this issue.

Required Filings with SEC and Other Agencies

To ensure that publicly-held U.S. companies protect their shareholders' rights, these companies are required by law to file numerous reports with Government agencies. For example, companies must file quarterly reports showing the current financial status of the company, including revenues, profits, expenses, assets and liabilities. Annual reports must include additional information, such as how much stock is outstanding and how the officers of the corporation are compensated.

Most companies now file these reports on paper; more progressive firms may provide a computer tape or disk to the appropriate agency. At some point it may be technically possible to set up a Web page that allows the appropriate agency to access all required information directly from the company as needed. To date, however, the issues of security and Government conservatism have prevented such an approach.

Legal Issues with Information Security

Information is rapidly becoming one of the world's most valuable commodities. Valuable objects are targets for thieves, and must be secured.

Information security issues impact both privacy and usability. Lack of security not only can damage companies, it can also expose people's privacy. But increasing security makes it more difficult for everyone to access and use information, including the people who legitimately need it.

Companies that fail to provide sufficient security may be held liable if their security failures are found to damage others. For example, a company that keeps medical records can be sued for negligence if that private medical information is made available to the wrong person. Companies that allow critical product or financial information to become available may be sued for negligence by shareholders.

Security risks aren't always obvious. If a company transmits sensitive information across the Internet without extensive security precautions, it could be considered negligent, since the Internet is open to many. Leaving critical information on a computer without security controls can also be considered negligence. Even losing data from a disk crash or accident can be construed as negligence if the data was not backed up.

Legal risks also exist if someone is damaged because the security precautions on a piece of information are *too* great. Suppose an employee has a history of violence in one division of a company. The employee's record is sealed to protect his privacy. The employee then transfers to a new division, where one day he kills a fellow employee. The security people in the local division did not know his past record, and consequently paid no special attention to him. The victim's family might sue the company for not providing critical information to the security staff at the new division.

Sales and Marketing

Tremendous hype surrounds the idea of selling and marketing products via cyberspace, and Internet-based sales direct to consumers get most of the media attention. The Internet allows a company to reach millions of potential customers with minimal cost.

However, very little has been achieved to date, whether because of concerns about the security of transferring credit card numbers across the Internet, or more likely because the right products have simply not been presented to the right set of customers. This area clearly has potential, but it may take longer than expected to realize that potential.

An area with more immediate promise is company-to-company selling via cyberspace. This avoids most of the limitations of company-to-consumer selling. Cyberspace won't *replace* traditional selling methods in the near term for company-to-company transactions, but it will facilitate those transactions.

Classical Marketing vs. Cyberspace

Cyberspace presents a unique opportunity for companies to reach potential customers anywhere in the world. Within a matter of minutes, one can make purchases from companies located in Israel, Russia and Japan. Companies with a presence in cyberspace are immediately available to people anywhere in the world. Unfortunately, businesses dazzled by this potential may overlook some basic realities. It's rarely been sufficient for a company to succeed simply by making a useful product and offering it for sale. *Companies need marketing, too.*

If you "build a better mousetrap," it's rarely true that "the world will beat a path to your door."

Marketing is the process of attracting customers and encouraging them to buy. Cyberspace has changed the location and number of potential customers, and the ways they must be attracted. But it has not changed the basic requirement: they still must be attracted, and they still must be encouraged to buy.

For business, the strength of the Web is also its weakness. Each storefront can reach millions of potential customers, but each customer can also choose from thousands of stores. Each business can sell to customers around the globe, but so can other businesses located anywhere on Earth.

Unless a business has a product that is truly unique and valuable, marketing will be the key to success (and if the business *does* have a truly unique and valuable product, advertising it on the Web guarantees clones will immediately appear in a dozen different countries).

The problems of marketing in cyberspace are manifold, and they have not all been solved. These include getting the business noticed by the customer, convincing the customer to buy, and working out the transfer of funds. This is complicated by the fact that the Web does not allow the customer to touch or see the product.

Getting the Business Noticed:　When thousands of businesses are competing for the same customers, the first problem is simply getting noticed. Many businesses now advertise themselves and their products on the Web. Free stock quotes, news pages, and search engines are all widely available on the Web, all paid for by advertising.

Convincing the Customer to Buy:　Once a customer has been attracted to your Web site, how can you convince them to buy when it isn't possible to see or touch your product? Some companies, typically software or information providers, offer free demonstration copies of their products. These may be limited in functionality, time-of-use or content, but allow the potential customer to experience the product. Most successful businesses on the Web today are selling information in some form. Information is uniquely suited to Web marketing, because it does allow customers to sample before buying.

Transferring Funds:　Most people are reluctant to transfer credit card numbers across the Internet, due to very legitimate security concerns. Many encrypting schemes are promised or are now in use, but none have been widely accepted. The most common approach today is to find the product on the Web and then actually order by phone.

It is clear that cyberspace is transforming marketing. The most promising marketing techniques involve giving away something of real value to get a potential customer's attention. Since these techniques work well for only a limited range of products, the short-term sales potential of cyberspace may be limited. Information and software products will be successful, as will extremely familiar products (the Web is a great way to obtain follow-up orders for consumable products). New products, particularly ones more suited to touching and seeing, may not be successful for many years.

Building Relationships with Customers

Cyberspace can be an excellent way to build relationships with customers, but only if used appropriately. Many marketers believe "relationship marketing" works best online for businesses committed to *two-way* communication with the consumer. Intelligent relationship marketing can help a small consumer business compete equally with large businesses online. Web trends like "mass customization" will make relationship marketing even more important.

Relationship marketing is less effective in business-to-business sales to large corporations. There, relationships must be built with executives, who expect to get to know real people, typically in person. Only after a personal relationship has been established can it be enhanced or supplemented by electronic communications. Even then, personal attention remains a requirement.

Cyberspace can accelerate and ease relationship-building, by allowing the easy, quick and frequent transfer of information. This information can be detailed and specific, as will be discussed later. It may include general announcements, invitations to seminars, chatty newsletters, and the like. These have traditionally been done via paper mail or telephone, media that are relatively time-consuming and expensive. E-mail is much faster and cheaper: mass e-mail mailings can be done at nominal cost.

With the right software, these mass mailings can easily be customized to each customer. Such customization can include tailoring content to include only information likely to be of specific interest to the recipient.

Mass e-mailing is the subject of considerable controversy. Done properly, it is a tremendous marketing tool. That means sending e-mail *only* to people likely to have interest in it.

Unfortunately, the minimal cost of e-mail has led to a practice known as "spamming" — sending ads to anyone whose e-mail address can be found. This is the electronic equivalent of junk mail. The practice is not well regarded, and some Internet Service Providers will drop accounts from anyone caught doing this. Spamming must be stopped before it becomes widespread, since it could make the entire e-mail system unusable.

Product/Quote Information

Cyberspace excels at disseminating current product information.

Salespeople have traditionally carried volumes of product information: brochures, technical documents, parts numbers, pricing documents, and more. Salespeople go through extensive training to understand these documents, to configure products for customers, and to provide accurate cost estimates — official "quotes" customers can base their orders on.

This is a woefully inefficient and error-prone process, particularly for businesses with complex product lines. More advanced companies now have computer programs their salespeople can use to generate quotes. These salespeople get the requirements from the customers, input them to the computer, and the computer configures the product and quotes a price. This greatly reduces errors, and helps salespeople provide quotes more quickly.

Some companies have given salespeople laptop computers they can carry to customer sites. With these computers, requirements can be gathered and input; configurations and quotes can be generated on the spot.

Now, on the Web, product information can be made available directly to existing and potential customers. Customers can specify their own requirements, and generate their own quotes immediately, whenever they wish. Given appropriate security, customers with pre-approved credit can even place orders on the Web. No salesperson could be *that* responsive.

It is critical that salespeople still maintain personal contact with the customer, but they no longer need to spend that time doing paperwork.

Order Status

Customers tend to be impatient to receive a product once it's been ordered. Salespeople spend a lot of time responding to order status inquiries. It's a frustrating process, particularly when orders are taking longer than expected. The customer demands to know what's going on, while the salesperson would rather be spending time making new sales.

Again, the Web can help. Authorized customers could be given access to internal order status systems. Federal Express, a leader in this area, now allows customers to track shipments from a Web page (http://www.fedex.com).

Any business that allows a customer to access internal systems this way must provide stringent safeguards to prevent damage. Of course, access to the web page should be limited to authorized persons, via a password controlled by the company. Then, most companies only present a *copy* of the critical data to customers. Even if there's a security breach, and data is changed, only a copy is damaged. In addition, database administrators establish "security profiles" that determine what information and databases customers may access.

Customer Information

Marketing departments are always desperate to obtain accurate and current information on customers. Cyberspace surveys and tracking methods can facilitate this. Few people fill out traditional paper surveys any longer; phone surveys are a bit easier and have a somewhat higher response rate. Web surveys, created as Web pages, are still sufficiently novel that more people are motivated to fill them out. They're also considerably easier to use, since they can employ multiple-choice questions where the preferred answer is selected via a mouse click. At the end the survey is returned by clicking another button.

Surveys are most useful in determining regular customers' satisfaction and tastes. In general, only regular customers are likely to care enough about a company's service and products to take the time to fill out a detailed survey.

Much precise, valuable data can be obtained, however, by tracking the choices people make as they interact with your web pages. This information reflects the actual interests of the customer, and can be used to tailor both products and marketing.

If the systems also keep track of individuals and their preferences, a relatively detailed profile can be developed over time. This allows the presentation of material to be further tailored. It's quite likely that customers can be divided into several groups, with presentations tailored to each person. This way, each person sees first the Web pages of most interest to them.

Bookings Reports

When an order for a product or service is taken, it is "booked" — entered into the company books. The near-term future success of the company can be accurately predicted by the status of "bookings reports," which show how many orders have been taken, and for what.

This is where the well-known semiconductor industry "book-to-bill ratio" comes from. When an order is taken it is "booked", and when a product is shipped it is "billed". The billings show the current amount of products being shipped, and the bookings show orders for future products. When the ratio is greater than one, more orders are being taken than are being currently shipped, which implies industry growth. When the ratio is less than one, fewer orders are being taken than shipped, which implies diminished revenue.

Bookings reports are extremely sensitive, so security is of paramount importance. Once security is in place, however, an internal web server can be set up, with web pages fed information from the company's internal databases. These pages can be updated daily or even hourly, giving executives near-real-time access to this information whenever they need it.

Return On Investment (ROI):
Hot Button for Senior Management

Return On Investment (ROI) is a simple concept. It asks: "If I invest money today, what will be my return at some future point?"

If you invest $1,000 in a savings account paying five percent interest, you can expect an ROI of five percent. Conversely, if you invest the same $1,000 in the stock market, you can't predict your ROI: nobody can accurately guess the value of any stock in the future.

Companies analyze ROI so they can choose the best discretionary investments. (Some investments are essential to stay in business; these shouldn't be evaluated by ROI.)

ROI calculations can become extremely difficult. Consider a company with $10,000 to invest. One manager wants to use this money to repave the parking lot. Another wants to purchase a billboard on the local highway, advertising the company's products.

If they repave the parking lot, the employees will be happier and (presumably) more productive. A billboard won't do much for employee morale, but could bring in substantial new business. On first glance, the billboard appears to offer the best ROI.

But this is a superficial judgment. How bad is the parking lot? Bad enough to keep customers from coming to the company? What's the traffic level on the local highway? Enough to be worth installing a billboard? Are the company's products suitable for advertising on a highway billboard? Each of these questions must be considered — and the answers must be quantified — to make a useful ROI estimate.

Placing a dollar value on competing issues is difficult. Once this is done, however, ROI is an excellent way to remove emotions from the decision and make it on the basis of what's right for the company.

Most cyberspace-related projects are relatively new to senior executives. The best way to obtain such approval is to demonstrate a high ROI. ROI doesn't just motivate upper management to act: it's also the metric they use to evaluate the success of the projects they've approved. If a previous project failed to generate a reasonable ROI, you'll have to show why your new project won't fail in the same way.

Information Systems (IS)

Once, Information Systems (IS) organizations were seen as pure overhead, adding little or no value. This perception is slowly changing. As should be clear to readers of this book by now, sophisticated computing is — or ought to be — integral to the success of almost every aspect of business. Since IS (also known as MIS, IR or IT) is usually responsible for managing computing, IS is pivotal to the success of the company.

Tomorrow's successful companies, large or small, will be linked by a common thread: their networks and computers. IS will install and maintain those systems. But successful IS departments won't just provide a usable infrastructure: they will become business enablers, helping the company achieve and maintain a competitive advantage. Successful IS departments will work closely with all other departments, suggesting better ways of doing business, and innovative ways to leverage cyberspace.

In this section, we'll cover just a few of those opportunities for business advantage: Electronic commerce, EDI, and data warehousing. Many other opportunities exist as well.

Electronic Commerce (EC) and Electronic Data Interchange (EDI)

EDI is a set of standards for exchanging orders, invoices and other transaction data between companies automatically. EDI has been around for years, almost as long as the idea of the "paperless office." And as with the paperless office, there's been more hype than reality. Some companies make limited use of EDI. A few companies, notably in the banking industry, use it heavily. But most companies utilize EDI rarely, if ever.

Electronic Commerce (EC) extends EDI, with the goal of performing most commercial activities electronically. Many progressive firms now have active EC projects. This book has mentioned several roles for EC, including placing of orders, providing shipping information, invoicing, and perhaps even funds transfer.

EC projects challenge IS departments to flawlessly coordinate their computer systems with those of their customers and business partners. While IS departments are accustomed to setting up *internal* systems that operate virtually flawlessly, and they are becoming accustomed to providing at least *some* connectivity with outside systems, they've rarely been asked to provide flawless integration with external systems.

When external systems are tied directly into internal systems, and can even modify information on those systems, potential problems multiply. An IS department has no control over systems owned by another company. And the impact of a mistake is far greater. Accidentally allowing a shipping clerk to see confidential product plans is bad, but allowing another company's manager to see them could be disastrous.

IS departments implementing EC applications must provide an apparently seamless connection between the companies, while ensuring that security is not breached. This is not a trivial task, and until it has generally been solved, progress on EC applications will be limited.

Information/Data Warehouse

One of the major paper-generators in most businesses is the ever-present report. Every department wants a report on something. Some reports are only a page or two; others may require a stack of paper three inches thick. Why are these reports requested? Because someone needs information that's in the computer system *somewhere*, but too difficult for them to find and understand.

A better approach is quickly becoming popular with large businesses, however: the Information or Data Warehouse (IW).

The IW is a separate system devoted to providing current information that would otherwise be obtained via paper reports. IWs are usually based on relational database systems such as those provided by Oracle™ and its competitors.

Establishing a separate IW system has two disadvantages: the additional cost of the separate system, and the challenge of ensuring the data maintained on that system is current with the primary database.

The advantages, however, far outweigh the negatives. Since the IW is separate, people using it aren't bogging down the systems that are actually running the company, nor are they risking the security of those systems. Also, the IW can be designed from the beginning as a *reporting* system, while the company's primary systems are primarily transactional systems.

As its name implies, the IW is a warehouse containing data or information. Since users can access this information themselves, via Graphical User Interfaces (GUIs), they won't need most traditional printed reports. The GUIs don't just make it easier to get pre-formatted online reports, they also make it easier to develop custom reports.

Typical IW users include executives, salespersons, and service organizations. Executives may want to see how sales were yesterday; a sales manager might want to see how much revenue his area has generated this month; and a service organization might want to know which contracts are most profitable.

IW databases can be much larger than traditional transactional databases. A small but growing number of companies now have IW databases in excess of a terabyte in size — a *thousand* gigabytes. Not surprisingly, the greatest challenges facing IW developers are managing this vast quantity of data, ensuring its accuracy, and providing access to it 24 hours a day.

Summary

In this chapter, you've learned about the business disciplines where cyberspace and information technology is making the biggest difference today. In Chapter 7, you'll learn about the business skills *you* need to lead these changes.

CHAPTER

7

Business Skills in Cybercareers

Now that you know what goals businesses are seeking to achieve with information technology, your next step is to understand the business skills you'll need in order to become an invaluable part of the process. Few technically-oriented people come by these skills naturally, but they can make all the difference between success and failure.

Planning

It's essential for both businesses and individuals to have a vision: a long-term goal to strive towards. But visions are useless without the ability to translate them into reality. The interface between vision and action is *planning*.

Good plans help you foresee the future, prepare for it, and take actions to achieve the future you desire. They provide a roadmap into the future, and offer guidance whenever choices must be made, or problems arise. As the old saying goes, "Good luck is the child of good planning!" Proper planning leaves one prepared to take advantage of good luck, and able to minimize the damage of bad luck.

Unlike fortune-telling and lucky amulets, there's no black art associated with planning. Proven planning techniques exist, and they can help you develop reasonable plans even if you lack desirable experience and knowledge.

Plans may be *long-term* or *short-term*. You'll sometimes hear long-term plans called *strategic*, and short-term plans called *tactical*. Notice the military metaphors. Long-term plans often deal with broad efforts to achieve competitive advantage, much as an army might plan a major offensive. In contrast, tactical plans often deal with solving specific problems or responding to immediate opportunities, much as an army might send a squadron to take a hill that has been left temporarily unguarded.

Financial plans may be associated with specific projects, or may apply to a group or department. In some organizations, they're indistinguishable from budgets.

To participate effectively in planning, you must *at least* learn how to

- Forecast future requirements (technical and financial) based on history and plans.
- Develop and use detailed knowledge of an application area.
- Develop and maintain financial budgets.
- Set up Gantt and PERT (Critical Path) charts.
- Negotiate for resources and requirements.

Developing and Maintaining a Strategy

Long-term, or strategic plans are the skeleton around which the functions of a project or department are built. Strategic plans are tied tightly to a vision: they are the first level of detail beneath the vision, showing how it will be implemented. Visions always tend to have a "pie-in-the-sky" element to them, where a goal is clearly described, but no path given to achieve that goal. The strategic plan provides the steps needed to get where the organization wants to go. These steps are still somewhat general, but are specific enough that no miracles will be required in order to move from one step to the next.

Let's consider an example. In reviewing his company's business vision, a Chief Information Officer (CIO) plans a strategy to implement this vision. After careful review, he concludes the company's computer systems must be completely overhauled.

His *strategic* direction will be to open systems, relational databases and client-server applications, because these offer his business improved flexibility and potentially lower costs. With an overall strategic direction established, he recognizes that this will be a massive task, requiring new hardware, operating system, databases and application programs. The company's proprietary computer hardware, operating systems, hierarchical database and terminal-oriented applications must all be replaced.

In developing his strategic plan, he chooses a technology platform: UNIX servers from Sun Microsystems running the Solaris operating system, along with Oracle Corporation's relational database management system and client-server applications software from SAP America. He will use Netscape products to enable user access via the web, and Electronic Data Interchange (EDI) software from Sterling Software to exchange orders, invoices and payments across the web.

Our CIO still does not know all the specifics of how these components will be implemented, but he now has both a clear vision and *a specific strategy* for implementing that vision.

Tactical Planning

Tactical planning is the bottom level of planning, where the nitty-gritty details are worked out. Tactical planning requires a detailed understanding of the area being planned. In the example discussed above, tactical planning would be handled by several experienced managers, each responsible for planning a specific part of the project.

Tactical plans must account for the inevitable day-to-day crises that will arise, even where it is not possible to predict exactly what these will be. (Of course, good plans help organizations avoid many crises entirely.) The easiest way to create a valid tactical plan is to be familiar with the normal challenges of the project you're undertaking. If you don't have that experience, you need to gather information. For example, you can review similar projects that have been completed before, interview people who have managed similar projects, review the literature, or brainstorm with outside experts.

There is no acceptable substitute for specific knowledge in working out a tactical plan.

If no other alternative is available, enlist a small group of trusted experts, present the strategic plan and vision to them, ask them to do some preparatory research on their own, and bring them together to help develop a suitable tactical plan. Depending on the project's size and complexity, this could take a few hours—or a few weeks. You still won't get a plan that's as solid as it would be if it were based on practical, hands-on expertise. But you will get a more reasonable estimate to work from.

Every tactical plan must have *contingencies* built into it: places where extra time, staff resources or money can be assigned to specific tasks if this proves necessary. The less you know for sure, the greater the contingencies should be.

In the project discussed earlier—converting an entire company to new systems and a new architecture—there will be a myriad of details. The detailed tactical plan may be dozens, or *hundreds* of pages thick. The CIO would delegate tactical planning to an experienced, project manager, ideally one who has previously performed similar conversions. The project manager will hire experts in each technology being implemented, e.g., Sun hardware and operating systems, Oracle databases, and SAP applications. He will also recruit key employees from each business area, to ensure that their specific business needs are being served by the new architecture and applications.

This combination will provide detailed knowledge of the overall project, the hardware, operating system, database software, applications software, and business processes. Since the overall project is still very risky, the CIO is also likely to contract with a major consulting firm that has had extensive experience in similar projects.

Developing a company-wide tactical plan like this could require as many as twenty-five people working full-time for two months. The business area representatives are knowledgeable of the details of the business requirements for their areas, and the technology experts can contribute their detailed knowledge of the specific technologies. The consultants should be familiar with what actually works and what doesn't. The project manager controls the entire process and makes sure the plan is as complete and accurate as possible.

In our example, the project's schedule is exceptionally tight. Every day the project remains unfinished, the company's competitors can gain more market share. Fortunately, the budget is relatively flexible, so the project manager can build in contingencies to avoid schedule slippages or other problems. For example, more servers can be ordered if necessary, in the event that performance proves insufficient in early prototypes.

Were both the schedule and budget tight, the success of the project would be at great risk.

Financial Forecasting or Budgeting

Financial forecasting, or budgeting, is a specific type of tactical planning. To budget accurately, you need to know the details. Typically, you'll encounter two types of budgeting: project-oriented budgeting and normal departmental budgeting.

Project-oriented budgeting seeks to determine how much money will be needed to complete a project. Departmental budgeting estimates how much money a department will spend during the next fiscal period: a year, a quarter, or even a month. (Occasionally, executives may require budgets that look two, three, or even five years into the future, but in today's fast-changing business climate, these can rarely be more than educated guesses.)

Departmental budgeting

Usually, the best place to start planning a departmental budget is to review and understand the previous period's *actual* expenditures.

Sometimes, in very stable organizations, the new period's expenditures will be virtually the same, and budgeting requires little additional effort. Most organizations will see change, however, so planners must project expected expenditures. Upcoming major projects or organizational changes can dramatically affect departmental budgets—and planners aren't always aware of them.

In extreme cases, where the department is changing significantly, or where the new budget is dominated by a few large projects, departmental budgeting begins to look more like project budgeting. Where the organization is changing, it's often possible to list the groups that will be part of the new organization, and review the expenditures they're currently making.

Many departmental expenditures are similar from period to period. For example, expenditures for salaries and fringe benefits will be similar, unless changes in the number of employees are expected. Even if "head-count" is changing, salary and fringe benefit information helps you understand what the department typically spends on people performing each role. Combine this information with knowledge of headcount changes, and you can accurately predict total salary and fringe benefits costs.

Facilities costs typically remain relatively constant, again unless a significant change is planned. Project costs will naturally vary significantly, but these can be incorporated from the financial planning done for each individual project.

Project budgeting

Project budgeting is a different animal. The scope of project budgets is usually more limited, so far fewer variables need be considered. Often, however, detailed historical information does not exist. If the project manager has previous experience with projects of this type, he or she can use those to make accurate estimates. If not, research will be needed.

Consultants can be found with experience implementing similar projects; colleagues at other companies are often willing to talk about their experiences; and some information is available in the literature. You may need to consult all these sources.

Then, of course, you'll need to modify this information based on specific details of your project and your organization. Business unit representatives, local technical experts, consultants and senior IS management all play a role in the project budget you create. For example, if you're told by the CIO that a project date simply *cannot* be missed, you're likely to assign more resources to the critical tasks that most affect delivery dates.

All this assumes that strategic planning is complete, and tactical planning is well underway—i.e., that you know what you're trying to achieve, and roughly how you intend to do so. Otherwise, there's no way to make reasonable financial estimates.

Before delivering a final budget, review it with major participants to make sure there have been no oversights, and that a sufficient contingency fund is in place to provide for the unexpected. In a well-planned project the contingency fund can be relatively small, perhaps two to five percent spread over the life of the project. In less well-defined projects, the contingency fund can become as large as 25 percent or even more. Where contingency funds are this high, it's often a danger sign that the project hasn't been planned well enough, and is at significant risk as a result.

Plan Maintenance

From reading the last few pages, you might imagine that plans are works of art, carefully crafted and then put in a case to be admired for the next several months or years. Not a chance. Even the most carefully-crafted plans need regular maintenance.

Many projects benefit from weekly reviews; some fast-moving projects need even more frequent reviews. Scheduling project reviews weekly ties in nicely with the idea that all project milestones should be no more than one week in length. This way, each project review can cover an entirely new set of milestones, and participants can more easily and accurately evaluate the progress they've made.

Inevitably, participants learn much more about the actual details of the project as the work progresses—requiring changes in plans, especially higher-level, less-specific plans.

However, don't change a plan without a good reason. Casually changing plans implies that nobody ever believed in the plan in the first place. If that's true, you created a very poor plan—or you have even deeper organizational problems.

Carefully review every potential change to determine if it's truly necessary, and how it impacts the rest of the project. Then, make an informed decision: do the advantages of the change outweigh its impacts? If you agree to the change, make sure it's reflected in both the overall plan and any subsidiary plans that may exist.

If the changes influence the project's cost, delivery date or scope, you'll need to obtain agreement from the project's eventual users, and any executives overseeing the project. Since that's not easy, you'll want to keep these changes to a minimum. (*None* is a very good minimum!) Make every effort to structure changes so they can be absorbed within the existing plan without affecting the "deliverables."

Project Planning

Now that you understand the basic ideas behind project planning, let's consider specific techniques for creating the plan.

Project plans are typically set up as a series of "tasks" and "milestones".

- *Tasks* are definable pieces of work that must be completed. Simple projects may have only three or four tasks, while complex projects may have hundreds or thousands of tasks.

- *Milestones* are signals that a task, or series of tasks, have been completed.

If you're in San Francisco, and your *project* is to visit Universal Studios in Hollywood, your *task* is to travel from San Francisco to Universal Studios. Your *milestones*, however, might include your arrival at the entrance ramp to Interstate 5, and finally your presence at the gates of Universal Studios.

Stories about projects falling behind schedule abound. The appropriate use of milestones can help reduce this problem. When projects are significantly behind schedule, it's usually because the project manager was not aware that progress had been slipping for quite a long time. Projects do not usually fall behind schedule as a result of missing the expected date on *one* task, but rather because of missing the dates on a *series* of tasks. By the time the project manager notices the problem, it has become too late to easily correct it. To avoid this, make sure your tasks are of relatively short duration—and have discrete, easily detected milestones.

Project management folklore claims the last five percent of a task takes eighty percent of the time. If so, the tasks weren't set up right. It's common for a project manager to inquire as to the status of a task and be told "it is 95 percent done". If the task requires three months to complete, it may be shown as "ninety-five percent done" for two months—and by then, the project is two months behind schedule. It's notoriously difficult to estimate what percentage of a task is *actually* complete, especially a large task that's being done for the first time. It's human nature to report the task as "almost done," rather than admitting you don't know.

If a large task gets in trouble, by the time the manager realizes it, the entire project may be in trouble. Again, the solution is to make all (or nearly all) the tasks very small, one week or less in duration. Then you never have to worry about whether a task is really seventy, eighty or ninety-five percent complete: *it's either done or it's not.* Of course, this will require you to understand the project in greater depth—but it'll be more than worth your time.

A good rule of thumb is to make all tasks no more than one week long.

Returning to our previous example, once a hardware platform was chosen, one general task was to acquire the computer systems. You could look at this as one task, but since it would take several weeks, you would be better off breaking it down further:

- The first task: determining the precise configurations of systems to be ordered. This task required numerous discussions with the vendor and internal experts, which were estimated to require four working days to complete. The milestone completing this task was receipt of a price quotation from the vendor, which arrived on the fifth day.

- The next task: actually ordering the systems. A Purchase Requisition (PR) was created on the first day and submitted for signatures. Since executive approvals had already been given, signatures were received quickly, and the PR arrived in Purchasing on the third working day. Purchasing held the PR for three more days before actually placing the Purchase Order (PO) with the vendor. The milestone for this task was the PO arriving at the vendor, which occurred one day late, since it was estimated for five working days and actually required six.

- The next task: receiving the systems. This task was not under the project manager's control, so he could only wait. It was estimated to take three weeks. Unfortunately, this task could not be broken down further, since the manager couldn't know the discrete steps the vendor would perform to build and ship the systems. The milestone on this task was receipt of the systems. Since the task was unusually long, the project manager compensated by regularly asking the vendor for status reports.

- The final task: setting up the systems and installing the software. This was estimated to require four days: the milestone was when the software was actually working and ready for people to use it.

Gantt chart

Simple projects can be planned and managed with simple tools, but more complex projects require better tools. Perhaps the single most important tool available to the project manager is the "Gantt chart", sometimes known as a "timeline". Each task is plotted on a horizontal bar graph, with tasks scheduled to complete *earlier* listed first on the graph, and *later* tasks at the bottom. Milestones are also shown—typically as tasks with a duration of "0" time, and with a diamond-shaped symbol. As tasks are completed and milestones met, the appropriate task lines are darkened on the graph to signify completion. It sounds complicated, but it's actually a very simple way to see a project's progress at a glance.

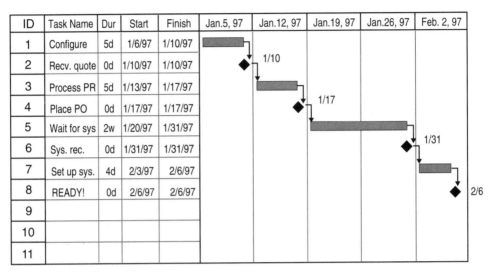

ID	Task Name	Dur	Start	Finish	Jan.5, 97	Jan.12, 97	Jan.19, 97	Jan.26, 97	Feb. 2, 97
1	Configure	5d	1/6/97	1/10/97					
2	Recv. quote	0d	1/10/97	1/10/97	1/10				
3	Process PR	5d	1/13/97	1/17/97					
4	Place PO	0d	1/17/97	1/17/97		1/17			
5	Wait for sys	2w	1/20/97	1/31/97					
6	Sys. rec.	0d	1/31/97	1/31/97				1/31	
7	Set up sys.	4d	2/3/97	2/6/97					
8	READY!	0d	2/6/97	2/6/97					2/6
9									
10									
11									

Figure 7–1   Gantt Chart

This chart corresponds to the example we've been discussing.

PERT (Critical Path) chart

Gantt charts are normally accompanied by another tool called a "PERT (Program Evaluation and Review Technique) chart," also known as a "Critical Path chart." Where the Gantt chart shows a project's progress through time, the PERT chart focuses on "task dependencies"—places where one task can't be completed (or started) until something else happens. A PERT chart shows the relationships among tasks, which is critical information for project managers, since if one task slips, many other tasks can slip as well—quickly placing the entire project in jeopardy.

In the following PERT chart, it's easy to see that none of the first three tasks can be started until the previous ones have been completed.

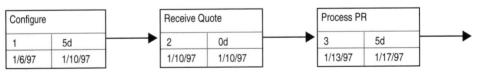

Figure 7–2   PERT Chart

PERT charts also show a project's "Critical Path": the route through the project's tasks which gets the job done as quickly as possible.

Most projects, and certainly all complex projects, have many tasks that can be done at the same time (in "parallel"), while other tasks must be done one after another (serially). A PERT chart helps managers make as many tasks parallel as possible, and analyze the amount of time required to complete serial tasks. It also helps managers squeeze out "slack time"—time spent waiting for other tasks to be completed. The result: a *shorter* critical path, and *faster* project completion.

As you shorten the critical path, it may change in other ways as well. Tasks that once had slack time may become critical: other tasks now must await *their* completion. The critical path may switch frequently from one area of the project to another, sometimes in surprising ways. It would be difficult or impossible to manage critical paths without a tool like the PERT chart—but *with* PERT charts, this becomes relatively easy.

In the accompanying example charts, another task has been added to the previous chart to show slack time and a parallel path. As the computer systems are ordered, the computer room is also prepared to accept them. This will only require one week—much less time than the three weeks required for the vendor to deliver the systems. As a result, there's significant slack time in this particular path. Since PERT charts are best at highlighting dependencies, and Gantt charts show slack time well, both are presented here.

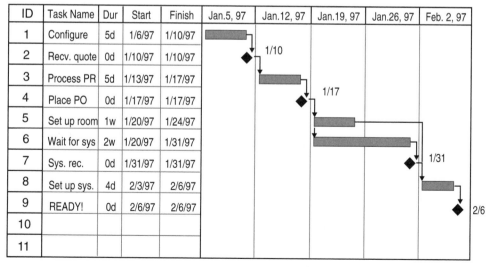

ID	Task Name	Dur	Start	Finish	Jan.5, 97	Jan.12, 97	Jan.19, 97	Jan.26, 97	Feb. 2, 97
1	Configure	5d	1/6/97	1/10/97					
2	Recv. quote	0d	1/10/97	1/10/97	1/10				
3	Process PR	5d	1/13/97	1/17/97					
4	Place PO	0d	1/17/97	1/17/97		1/17			
5	Set up room	1w	1/20/97	1/24/97					
6	Wait for sys	2w	1/20/97	1/31/97					
7	Sys. rec.	0d	1/31/97	1/31/97				1/31	
8	Set up sys.	4d	2/3/97	2/6/97					
9	READY!	0d	2/6/97	2/6/97					2/6
10									
11									

Figure 7–3 Gantt Chart

Resource balancing

Setting up all these timelines and dependencies is a complex process. Once it's complete, the project manager rightfully feels a glow of satisfaction for a job well done.

But the job isn't finished yet. All projects require resources, and resources are almost never unlimited. Will the resources you've assigned to your tasks really be *available* when you need them? *Resource balancing* makes sure they are. All too often overlooked by project managers, it's critical to making sure that your Gantt and PERT charts actually correspond to reality. If you don't balance your resources, you may be forced to rip apart your project plan and completely redo it.

Most often, the resources you need are *people*, but they also may be computers, networks, databases, or anything else. In the resource balancing process, you analyze your resources to make sure that none of them are overcommitted.

Let's revisit our example. In the first case, acquiring computer systems, there is no resource issue. In the second case, however, some tasks are done in parallel, and there's a potential for conflict. We've assumed both systems and database software will be configured at the same time. What if both tasks can only be done by one person, and that person cannot work on both at once? We have a resource conflict, and we must re-evaluate our plan.

Perhaps we can designate someone else to handle database configuration. Now, we can meet our original plan, but we need an extra resource. If one isn't available, we'll have to reschedule the configuration processes so they occur sequentially, not in parallel. Since there's slack time in the database procurement cycle, we can do so without adversely affecting the overall project schedule.

This is where understanding slack time and critical paths becomes especially important. By allocating our scarce resource first to the task in the critical path, and only secondly to the task with slack time, we've been able to "make do" with existing resources—without affecting the overall project schedule.

Software

Project planning may seem difficult, and one may wonder how complex projects can ever be successfully planned. Before computers were common, this was a major problem. Many hours were spent laboriously drawing and re-drawing charts, and project managers had their walls covered with them.

The advent of cheap computers, however, has removed all the drudgery from this process. Numerous software packages are available for only a few hundred dollars for PCs and Macs. These packages do all the work of actually drawing and re-drawing Gantt and PERT charts. The project manager is only required to enter the relevant information, such as task name, duration and resources, and the program does the rest. They will even balance resources and modify schedules when resources are found to be overcommitted. (The preceeding charts were drawn using Microsoft Project.)

Education

Many aspects of planning can and should be learned in a classroom setting, while others require experience. College business departments usually offer strategic planning courses, and they're almost always included in M.B.A. programs.

Financial planning is always available from colleges in the business department, usually beginning at the undergraduate level and continuing through the graduate level. The challenge is to sort out the information you need from the multitude of classes offered. An introductory accounting course may cover the basics.

Project management is also taught in most business departments, though it may be buried in another course. Tactical planning is rarely covered in colleges, although occasionally courses appear under various names.

Many large companies offer relevant in-house courses. Training companies and professional societies (American Management Association, for example) also offer courses in strategic planning, financial basics and project planning. These courses are tailored to efficiently provide the information non-finance professionals need, often in as little as three to five days.

Experience

Experience is useful in helping you develop better strategic plans, but if you have a good education and you understand the issues you're facing, it's not entirely necessary.

Experience is more critical when you're doing *tactical* planning. Courses are rare—and in any event, you need detailed knowledge of what you're planning to develop a good tactical plan. That knowledge can best be developed through experience.

Little experience is needed to do financial forecasting well. Some training in the basics and a healthy dose of common sense will usually suffice. Your best asset is a good understanding of the area you're creating a plan for.

In project planning, education can familiarize you with concepts and tools, but experience is needed to be effective. Since managing a small project can be similar to managing a large one (except for the scope and quantity of details), any experience managing projects will be quite useful.

Communication

Communication is among the most important business skills. No matter what you do or where you work, you're much more likely to succeed if you can communicate well.

Communications takes many forms, and depending on the particular circumstances different forms of communications may be the most important.

To communicate well in today's business environment, you must *at least* learn how to:

- Communicate in terms the audience understands and expects.

- Provide sufficient information but not too much.

- Know when to use verbal vs. written communications.

- Ensure all questions are answered.

Proposals

If you've got a great idea, you're not alone. Few businesses suffer from a shortage of suggestions on how to spend their money. How does the executive decide? By trying to identify the recommendations that can do the most for the business.

In the last chapter, you learned about Return on Investment (ROI) analysis. Now, you'll focus on the proposal documents where you'll make your case for your best ideas.

Some proposals are quite large, while others may be only a paragraph or two, but successful proposals have all attracted the attention of the right decision maker, by sharing certain important characteristics:

First and most important, successful proposals offer a *solution* to a problem. If the problem has not already been identified, the proposal must also clearly identify the problem and why it must be solved. While this seems trivial, it is repeatedly ignored even by large companies submitting huge proposals.

Business problems limit profitability, so many proposals focus on improving profitability in some way.

Second, a proposal must demonstrate clearly why the proposed solution is better than other approaches. Is it technically superior? Will it cost less, or can it be delivered faster? These questions become especially critical when your proposal is competing with others intended to solve the same problem.

In presenting your solution, make sure you've focused on solving the problems the business finds most serious. For example, if the business is most worried about getting its products to market faster, the winning approach will solve that problem *first*.

Finally, a proposal must be well written. It may not need to be a masterpiece of beautiful typesetting, with eye-catching graphics and gripping prose (though some of those things will certainly help). But it must have reasonable formatting, there must be *no* grammatical or spelling errors, and the text must be clear, concise and to the point. *Verbose proposals simply bore the reader.*

Presentations

Whenever you stand in front of one or more people to try to convince them of something, you're making a presentation. You can make a presentation about a project's current status, a new proposal, a recommended reorganization, or virtually anything else.

Most business presentations are done orally and utilize visual aids of some sort. Transparencies are currently the most common visual aid, because they look professional and are easy to create. Slides were once common, and are still used for very formal presentations where the highest level of graphics is critical. Computer-based presentations, where a computer display is projected onto a screen, are becoming more common. However, most are still of relatively low quality, not suitable for most formal presentations.

Making presentations is not difficult if you follow a few simple rules:

Each page should make one, and only one, point.

Make one major point on each page. If you attempt to convey several major points on the same page, you'll present more information than can be quickly assimilated—and *none* of your message will get across.

Each page should convey sufficient information that an oral explanation is not required. If your audience can't immediately understand the point of a page, you've failed. (Remember, many of your presentations will be viewed later by people who don't have the benefit of your personal presence.)

At the same time, take considerable care to deliver the maximum amount of information *with the fewest words possible*. As Blaise Pascal once said, more or less: "If I'd had more time, I'd have written a shorter letter." Invest the time to make it short.

Status Reports

Sooner or later, you'll have to write a status report, whether for a project or day-to-day departmental work. Some businesses have institutionalized these, with fixed formats that must always be followed. Even in such cases, however, there are useful status reports and worthless ones.

A status report (like virtually any document) should be as short and simple as possible while still conveying the essential information.

This begs an obvious question: what *is* the essential information?

Often, the writer and the reader may have very different ideas about this. Such differences guarantee failure, no matter how carefully a report is written. *Before you write a status report, find out what your audience wants you to cover.* (You might create a prototype report, ask how well it served the reader, and then make refinements.)

Once you know, you can decide how best to deliver that information. Sometimes all you need is a list of numbers showing the performance of a department; other times, a Gantt chart showing the current status of a project vs. the expected progress; still other times, a presentation or a prose document. In every case, the goal is to deliver necessary information in the simplest, clearest way possible. And if you're creating a status report *template*, make sure it's easy to work with and to read, since you'll probably be working with it frequently.

Ongoing Verbal Interactions

The literature tends to focus heavily on more formal aspects of communication, such as presentations, proposals and status reports. These are certainly important, but the most crucial form of communication is the day-to-day verbal interaction among co-workers. This continuous communication has far greater potential for influencing people than does more infrequent formal communications.

In government procurement, where proposal writing has been developed to a fine art, it's well known that the best way to win is to develop a personal relationship with the people who will receive and evaluate your proposal. This isn't so much because you will bias them in your favor (though that can happen). Rather, it's because you can pick up a vast amount of information through ongoing discussions that won't be available to your competitors: the subtleties and "hot buttons" that can really make a difference in your final proposal.

Virtually all formal communications are seriously limited in how much information they can transmit effectively. That means it's critical to focus on the most important information. The best way to do this is through ongoing, informal discussions with the people you're trying to influence.

No informal conversations will ever *fully* take the place of a well-done formal presentation. *But*, virtually every formal presentation will be more effective if preceded by informal conversations that help shape its content and form.

Everyone knows that many important deals are made on the golf course. What's the point? Not that you must learn how to play golf, but rather that many of the most important communications are carried on in an informal setting. Golf provides an avenue where executives can get together and discuss business informally. Vast amounts of useful information are conveyed in this arena, and this information is critical in making deals.

Informal conversations should remain focused on building useful business relationships, rather than just chatting with someone because they will listen. The real distinction that separates "relationship building" from "idle chatter" is probably more in the duration and frequency of the conversations, rather than the content.

Education

Written communications can usually best be learned in a classroom, and even verbal communications skills can be greatly enhanced by formal training. Communications classes are easy to find. Colleges offer a plethora of them. Many offer complete degree programs in communications, sometimes even sub-divided into types of communications.

Most cyberspace projects don't require quite this much communications training: many of these programs are reserved to people such as broadcasters, who devote their careers to communications. Information professionals, however, *do* need to write and speak well enough to clearly communicate ideas. College extension classes are frequently more useful for this purpose, since they're often more focused on business-related communications. Junior colleges or trade schools are yet another good source of business-related communications classes.

Many training companies offer classes focused directly on business communications. Large companies often provide such classes to their employees. These classes tend to be even more useful, since they focus directly on the types of communications required in businesses.

Experience

When it comes to communications, experience helps, but it's not a requirement for most cyberspace-related jobs. A notable exception is web content development, a writing and presentation job that requires sophisticated communications training and experience.

Where experience helps most is in helping you develop self-confidence. There are many good ways to gain this experience. Toastmasters is a well-known example. Making regular presentations to a group at work is excellent. Perhaps the best of all is teaching a class, since students are good at training their teachers to be "cool under fire."

People Management

Business relationships rarely flourish without effort on the part of those involved. Everyone in business has relationships with many other people, whether they're higher, lower or at the same level in the corporate hierarchy. Each of these relationships must be carefully managed for success, much as a farmer must carefully manage his or her crops to be successful.

While managing subordinates is very important, most of us have more managers and peers than we have staff to manage. Today, it's critical to master managing *upward* and *outward*, not just downward.

To succeed, you must *at least* learn how to:

- Ascertain the true needs of higher-level managers.
- Negotiate with peers—offer something they need.
- Stay out of court!
- Motivate and direct staff—get the work done.
- Resolve issues so all parties are satisfied.

Managing Upward

Except for company owners, almost everyone in business reports to *someone*. Even CEOs usually report to a Board of Directors. Your success in business will be determined in large part by how well you manage your relationships with those above you in the hierarchy.

General Motors is one of the world's largest corporations: few challenges could be as great as rising through the ranks at GM from an entry-level position to the Chairmanship. Roger Smith did so. While critics may debate how successfully he guided GM once he arrived, nobody can question his awesome achievement in *becoming* Chairman.

It's been claimed that his preeminent ability, exercised from the moment he joined GM, was to determine exactly what his manager wanted, and to deliver it. Smith was reputedly not exceptional at managing relationships with peers or staff, but superb at managing upward.

This isn't as easy as it seems. Few managers really make it clear to their staff exactly what they want. Some say nothing at all, others make their requests so vague that people are forced to guess; still others simply don't tell the truth.

Many lower-level managers don't really know what they want, or don't have the skills to express it. In these cases, it can help to speak informally with a manager. If it turns out they really do have a clear picture of what they're looking for, you'll eventually find out. If not, your suggestions will frequently be accepted. By making suggestions, you can both satisfy the manager's desires, and channel those desires into areas that are easier for you to satisfy.

Higher-level managers usually *do* have a clear picture of what they want. However, their goals often don't coincide with the company's stated goals. Many, if not most, high-level managers achieved their positions due to driving ambition and a willingness to sacrifice all else to achieve their ambitions. They may not be particularly concerned with the overall welfare of the company, but solely with their personal well-being. Of course, they can't say that, so they may resort to rather grandiose statements of what they want the group to do—when those goals are really peripheral to their actual desires.

Merely determining a senior manager's real agenda may be difficult, and fulfilling it may be virtually impossible. You can, however, look for patterns that gradually emerge over time, which demonstrate what they're really after. Carefully listen to their comments, observe which actions they reward and which they ignore, and you'll eventually get a relatively clear picture of their true priorities.

High-level managers motivated primarily by personal ambition will be oblivious to great deeds or projects, unless those deeds directly affect their personal success. When working for one of these people, the key to success is to arrange for *them* to reap personal glory.

Managing Peers

Managing your peers gets the least publicity, but it makes everything else much easier to achieve. As with managing upward, it's critical to determine what your peers really want and find a way to give it to them. While peers have less control over your future than your manager does, few projects can be completed successfully without their cooperation—and *all* projects will be completed more quickly and easily if peers are actively working together to make them successful.

The secret is to make your peers feel that they have an interest in the success of your project. It's basic human nature: people are more determined to see a project succeed if they feel some ownership in it.

Find out what your peer really wants. Once you know, you can shape the project so it provides at least some of that—either by making slight modifications, or simply by knowing how to present the project correctly. This is another area where communications ability is important.

Managing Staff

The ability to manage staff well is only necessary for those who have people reporting to them. Nonetheless, many people who never had management aspirations find themselves managing people, so it's always useful to know the basics for success.

Legal requirements

Managing people is rife with rules and regulations. Some are established by the Federal Government, and thus are uniform across the entire United States. Many are established by states, and can vary widely from state to state. Of course, other countries have their own set of rules and regulations, which frequently bear little or no resemblance to those of the U.S. Some are much more restrictive, while others are so loose, they're virtually non-existent.

You *must* become familiar with the specific rules of the country and state or province where your subordinates reside. There's no choice: the penalties for failing to comply with regulations can be devastating to both the company and the manager, and ignorance is rarely an acceptable excuse.

Many companies offer one- or two-day courses in the legal requirements of managing people in that area. If you don't understand the rules, these courses are of critical importance. If you're working independently, or if your company doesn't offer classes like these, seriously consider attending a class like this on your own.

Tip: the best of these classes are taught by practicing attorneys with labor law experience in the state or country you're dealing with.

First and foremost, treat people fairly. Don't discriminate for any reason. Some forms of discrimination are relatively well understood, such as the prohibition against refusing employment to a person of a particular race, sex or age. Others are not so well understood. For example, employers in the U.S. are required to make "reasonable accommodations" to allow disabled persons to perform a job. Essentially, the employer is not required to change the core characteristics of the job, but is required to make minor changes.

Second: document everything. Every decision regarding one's employees should be documented, together with the rationale behind it. You don't necessarily need to document *every* conversation, but you should document every decision, discussion or action that could be perceived by an employee as affecting his or her job or well-being.

Most attorneys feel that managers are on safe ground if their actions are fair and well-documented. Interestingly, it's usually *not* necessary to demonstrate that the decision taken was good for the business. For example, laying off one hundred employees may be very bad for the business, but it is acceptable as long as the people are chosen fairly and the process is documented. You'd want to have documentation explaining how these specific employees were chosen, to prove that they weren't discriminated against.

Another risk is unlawful termination, or firing. Some companies employ people "at will", which essentially means they can be terminated at any time for any reason. Many companies, however, have implied employment contracts with their employees. In these cases, a long and involved process must be followed before someone can be legally terminated.

Many companies that believed they were "at will" employers have discovered otherwise in court. Therefore, it's *always* best to have a well-documented and defensible procedure leading to the dismissal of an employee, based on grounds that are solely business related.

One controversial, poorly understood area is sexual harassment. The classic example of sexual harassment is a manager requiring sexual favors from an employee based on threats or promises surrounding the employee's job. But the real definition of sexual harassment is much broader.

Sexual harassment consists of creating or fostering an environment where a normal person would feel uncomfortable for sexual reasons. This can include an environment of obscene language, dirty jokes, suggestive posters or sexual innuendoes. The manager does not have to actually *do* these things: he can be held liable for allowing others to do them. If you see anything in the workplace that could be construed as sexual harassment, remove or eliminate it immediately.

Motivation

By definition, managers rely on their staffs to deliver the work and make them successful. Many managers fail because they can't motivate their subordinates. The right motivation can transform mediocre staffers into stars; poor management can turn stars into alienated, mediocre performers.

There are countless stories of brilliant executives who possessed vision, drive and charisma, yet failed miserably in implementation—often, because they couldn't motivate their staffs.

Motivating employees is really not difficult, so it is a mystery why many managers fail at it. Many managers act as though they've never been employees themselves, and don't remember how it felt to have a good or bad manager. Simply, treat employees fairly (which also helps avoid lawsuits), respect them, help them when they need help, and give them real responsibility.

Again and again, research has shown: people usually respond the way they're expected to. *Have great expectations.* Expect responsibility, decisiveness and effectiveness, reinforce your expectations at every opportunity, and you're much more likely to get what you're looking for. Conversely, if you expect laziness and incompetence, you'll get that, too.

Respect your employees, and demonstrate that respect. High expectations are impossible without respect. Delegate as much responsibility to your people as possible—which will also add to their motivation.

This does not mean you should abdicate your responsibility. You're still responsible for monitoring work progress, ensuring that employees can accomplish the tasks they've assumed, and providing support where needed. Be careful that your monitoring isn't viewed as a lack of confidence, but make sure to perform it nonetheless.

It's critical that you identify and fix problems quickly. If employees see that a manager is aware of problems and can resolve them, they'll be more motivated. Conversely, if you ignore or fail to resolve long-standing problems, those problems will become a cancer that saps motivation for your entire team.

Let's return to the SAP conversion project discussed before. Such a vast project can only succeed if employees are highly motivated. But managers can't afford to simply hand out assignments and walk away, assuming everything will be taken care of.

The solution: weekly project reviews that give every team member a chance to report on his or her progress. (Large projects may require several "layers" of these reviews, since there will be too many people to cover everything in one meeting.)

At these reviews, employees who are having problems can be identified, and managers can focus on providing assistance in resolving the problems. These are usually one-time issues that can be resolved relatively quickly. For example, an employee reports that he can't get cooperation from another organization; the manager agrees to call that organization's director.

Some employees will chronically have problems, however, and these employees will require closer, ongoing monitoring. If you're careful enough, they're more likely to perceive it as help rather than intrusion. You'll also maintain the motivation of other team members, who will see that problems are being monitored and fixed.

Handling crises as they arise

Thorough planning and careful management minimize the number of crises. But virtually every complex project, no matter how well planned, will encounter at least one crisis.

When your project's crisis arrives, move quickly. Fast action will reduce the impact of any crisis. This is not the time to set up a committee to study the issues in depth and make a report. On the contrary, some decision must be reached very quickly, often in hours, or at most, a few days.

Moving quickly doesn't mean making arbitrary, autocratic decisions. While a few crises can be resolved on the spot by an immediate decision, most will require some consultation and thought. It's best to have previously defined a small team of people chartered to resolve crises. Ideally, these people will be key project contributors who collectively have an in-depth understanding of the entire project. When a crisis arises, this team can be assembled in a few hours, review the problem, and quickly reach a conclusion. That decision must then be acted on immediately.

Many police departments have set up Special Weapons And Tactics (SWAT) teams that are called in to handle crises beyond the scope of typical law enforcement. Similar SWAT teams should be set up on major projects, and given the responsibility and authority to handle crises when they arise.

Education

Some classroom training on people management is essential. Legal issues, for example, must be covered in a classroom setting. This is not the time to be learning on the job!

It's quite easy to find courses on people management. Most colleges offer courses; many business departments have complete programs leading to a Bachelor's or Master's degree in management. Even junior colleges frequently cover this area. College classes (or a complete degree program) are best for developing a complete theoretical understanding of the field.

Training companies offer a wide range of classes, as do many professional societies. Most large companies offer an extensive list of "people management" classes to their employees. These deliver a focused look at the issues you're likely to encounter, and are ideal for covering issues that change quickly (legal rulings, for example).

Experience

Again, though, no amount of classroom training can fully substitute for experience. Many managers begin their first management job completely lacking in theoretical training, while others become overtrained before ever having a chance to practice what they've learned. A middle ground is best. Get some training before you start; then progressive levels of management responsibility should provide the experience you need.

It's rare for managers to have much experience managing cyberspace-related projects. But if you've managed groups of programmers or engineers, your experience will be directly relevant. Any management experience, even in a fast-food restaurant, is better than none. Many of the same issues arise regardless of the work being performed.

Leadership

Leadership: it's often discussed, rarely delivered. Many managers think they're leaders. Few of them really are.

A *manager* ensures that work gets done on time and within budget. He or she handles issues as they arise, hires and retains employees, and ensures that the work done supports the goals of the business.

A *leader*, on the other hand, steps out in front and shows the way. Leaders may or not be managers. Leaders may or may not be able to manage people and work, but they can guide the business into new areas. Leaders aren't needed in stagnant, "business-as-usual" companies: they will only be disruptive influences. Businesses that *want* to change, on the other hand, must have effective leaders to guide them through new changes and difficulties.

Leaders can be effective without being loved, but they must have a core of followers. The classic example: Adolf Hitler. Supported by a corps of unquestioning followers, Hitler led his country to slaughter and moral catastrophe with breathtaking effectiveness. A more positive example is Gandhi in India, who also transformed his nation, albeit in a more humanitarian direction.

I've chosen Hitler and Gandhi to demonstrate that leaders aren't necessarily correct about the directions they choose; nor are people with the right ideas necessarily leaders. If you have a vision, followers, and the capacity to convince your followers to help make your vision real, you're a leader.

To become a leader, you must learn how to:

- Communicate effectively with people at all levels.

- Build commitment to the vision.

- Sustain the commitment.

Transferring the Vision to Executives and Staff

Leaders must have a vision. But a vision alone isn't enough: not all visionaries are leaders. The difference is the ability to transfer your vision to followers, who adopt it as their own.

In business, your followers may be both decision-makers and rank-and-file employees. How do you get them to adopt your vision and take action? Obviously, you'll need to communicate well. But there's more: you need to present your vision in terms that are immediate and personal to your audience. *Each member of the audience must become emotionally committed to the vision.*

Business executives often have compensation packages tied directly to the company's revenue growth, profits and stock prices. If you can convince them your vision will improve their compensation, they may become your "followers"—even if they're higher on the totem pole than you. Conversely, it may be pointless to present a vision of improved staff working conditions to executives who don't much care about that.

People working on an assembly line, on the other hand, rarely have a direct link to the company's profitability. As long as the company stays in business and provides them with a job, nothing much will change in their life. Presenting your vision in terms of company profitability will be useless, since that doesn't directly affect them. Some other tie must be found that *does* directly affect them, such as higher pay-levels, reduced working hours, increased medical or vacation benefits, or more pleasant working conditions. That tie must be one that will have a deep emotional impact on the people, and not merely academic value.

The most successful leaders will be able to obtain followers from all levels. To do this, the leader must have and present a vision that benefits people at all those levels. Visions that only apply to one level will be less successful, the leader will get fewer followers, and therefore will be less successful. Some leaders can become great with a vision that benefits one group and has no effect (or may actually penalize) on another group. This is possible only if the groups being benefited are more powerful than those ignored or penalized.

An excellent recent example of business leadership is the story of Steve Jobs, Apple Computer, and the Macintosh. Jobs had a vision that he made into a huge success despite numerous obstacles and naysayers. The Macintosh vision had something for everyone. The Apple executives obtained a large and profitable company, which gave them rich compensation packages. The technical people indulged in exercising their creativity. The developers got a platform that was consistent and easy to write programs for. And the users got a computer that was simple to use.

The vision that Jobs led Apple to was so effective that it outlasted Jobs' tenure at Apple by several years. The strength of that vision probably also contributed to Apple's later troubles, since Apple's executives after Jobs were managers rather than leaders, and did not replace or update the original vision even when such changes were necessary for the company's survival.

Maintaining and Reinforcing the Vision

One great challenge of leadership is maintaining your vision—and your followers' focus—through adversity. Leaders are really only necessary when some great change or event must be accomplished. No leadership is required to maintain the status quo, nor even to make great changes that happen naturally and easily. Leaders are necessary to inspire changes, and to provide direction when difficulties arise—which they inevitably do.

Many people consider Franklin D. Roosevelt a great leader, but would he be considered so great if he hadn't been President during the Great Depression and the Second World War? Might other less well regarded Presidents have risen to the occasion given the same opportunity?

In times of adversity, many distractions will present themselves; the successful leader will successfully use his or her vision as a guide to determine how to handle (or ignore) them. Some apparently important issues will have to be completely ignored; others will have to be handled in a manner that appears blind or even cruel. All else must be subjugated to achieving the vision, even if that means making sacrifices that would be unthinkable in ordinary times. (Of course, your vision should be worthy of this sacrifice!)

Let's return to our example of a company-wide SAP conversion. To quickly achieve such a massive conversion will inevitably require numerous sacrifices. The company currently provides more reports than can quickly be converted; some groups will have to lose reports they've come to depend on, at least for several months. The leader must carefully assess which reports are truly essential, and sacrifice those that are only a convenience. This will not make the leader popular, but the willingness and ability to make unpopular decisions is central to leadership.

Presenting a Leadership Image

To succeed as a leader, you must always *look and act* like a leader. What does a leader look and act like? That's a difficult question, because leadership styles vary widely among organizations. But there are a few general guidelines. Leaders should exemplify what they expect their followers to become. If possible, they should project an image that each of their followers will work hard to emulate.

"Maintaining an image" sounds false, but doesn't have to be. The most successful leaders maintain an image that is relatively natural to them. Most of the time, they're just acting naturally. For those who aren't natural leaders, though, it'll take some effort, at least at first.

During World War II, General George Patton probably received more publicity for his carefully-cultivated image (pearl-handled revolvers, for example) than for his military victories. He would undoubtedly never have achieved the fame he did without that image. It is worth noting, however, that his public eccentricities never interfered with his ability to command troops. On the contrary, they made it easier, since troops were eager to follow someone with such a distinct character and personality.

Don't try to substitute image for results. If Patton had consistently lost battles, no amount of image polishing would have made him successful. Since he was consistently winning battles, however, his image enhanced his military victories, made new followers, and thus made successive military victories easier to achieve.

Leaders must appear effective. You can demonstrate this through quick, appropriate decisions. Leaders' images are usually better if they are perceived as fair and just, although that is (perhaps surprisingly) not crucial. Some eccentricities are useful in giving the leader a distinct character, although those eccentricities shouldn't interfere with the ability to lead.

Leaders must show conviction. It's inevitable to have doubts and fears, but carefully conceal them from your followers.

The leader must always project an image of absolute conviction and determination.

Education

Leadership *can* be taught, but useful classes are not easy to find. Some colleges offer courses on leadership, usually in the business department or in an M.B.A. program. Some are very well-done, while others are virtually useless.

Professional training companies frequently offer leadership courses to businesses. These are less variable: they tend to huddle more in the middle of the value scale. Some companies also offer in-house training courses. If these are taught by the right people they can be very useful, since they can offer examples that are directly relevant.

Many leadership courses focus on studying effective leaders throughout history, both in politics and business, to learn what made them so effective. If well done, this can be quite valuable.

Experience

There's an old saying: "Leaders are born, not made." While that's not necessarily true, it *is* true that classes can't substitute for real leadership experience. Experience leading a business project is best, although almost any leadership experience is better than none—even if it's only leading a club or sports team. Leadership can be manifested in many ways outside of business, and that experience is certainly useful.

Relationships

By nature, humans work best when they cooperate, and cooperation is based on relationships built with others over time. No matter what specific rules a company may have, most of the real work gets done based on the personal relationships among a company's executives, managers and staff. That's why so many deals are made on the golf course: the executives develop personal relationships there, which make it easier to flesh out the details later.

Strong business relationships aren't *all* you need, but without them, you're doomed to failure. To develop these relationships, learn how to:

- Understand what others need and want.

- Understand what *you* need and want.

- Balance between other people's needs and yours.

- Know how to find what you need.

Why Strong Relationships Are Needed

When you make a purchase in a supermarket, you rarely have a personal relationship with the supermarket checkout clerk. You don't need one. The goods are available for a specified price, and if you want them, you pay the price. No trust or relationships are involved.

Business deals are different, especially larger ones. They're typically one-of-a-kind arrangements, where trust is of paramount importance. Rarely if ever are products purchased at list price. Negotiations are an integral part of the process. Moreover, despite legal agreements, many details are often not locked in until long after the deal is signed. This can only work if the participants trust one another. Such trust isn't possible until a relationship has been developed that will allow it.

Relationships are critical to businesspeople at *every* level, for virtually every purpose. Imagine you need to purchase a new piece of software. Normally, it takes Purchasing two weeks to process your Purchase Order. But because you have a relationship of trust with a purchasing agent, you can convince them to process your Purchase Order immediately. Because you have a relationship of trust, *they* know you won't abuse the privilege by requesting expedited treatment when it isn't really needed. Without the relationship, you might well have missed your deadline.

Yes, standard procedures are followed most of the time by most people. To do otherwise would guarantee anarchy and the swift failure of the business. Nonetheless, to follow the procedures slavishly at all times will guarantee a rigidity and slowness that will quickly doom the business to failure. Moreover, it's impossible to write procedures so detailed that they account for all eventualities. (The Federal Government has tried, and the results are plain for all to see.)

How, then, are exceptions made, or new situations handled? With common sense (hopefully)—*and based on personal relationships, the stronger the better.*

Where to Look for Them

A relationship can be built almost anywhere, with almost anyone, as long as there's a sincere desire on the part of *both* parties to build it.

You absolutely must build relationships with your manager, peers, and staff (if any). If you have customers or suppliers, you need to build relationships with them, as well. There's really only one type of relationship to avoid: relationships with individuals or companies that *consistently* attempt to take advantage of you. Sometimes all relationships will be more advantageous to one party than the other, but over time, if the advantages don't roughly equalize, the relationship isn't working.

How to Build Them

There are no great secrets to building relationships. The first key ingredient is *fairness*. As we've said, nobody enjoys being taken advantage of.

Next comes *trust*. Both parties in a relationship must trust one another. Trust doesn't appear magically; it must be built over time. Further, great caution must be exercised in granting trust, since to trust someone false is to open oneself to betrayal.

Start by assessing the other party's intentions. Do they want a relationship? Do they appear fair and trustworthy? If so, test the relationship. Trust the other party in a transaction that's small enough that you won't be damaged seriously if it turns out your trust was misplaced. If this works, gradually build your relationship to the point where major risks can be taken without fear of betrayal.

Trust and risk are not one-way streets. The other party should also be taking actions demonstrating trust in you, and you should be delivering on that trust. Over a period of time, this give-and-take will result in a close relationship, one that can help you *both* achieve better results than either of you could achieve alone.

Vendors

One of the most common business relationships is the vendor-customer relationship. Traditionally, many American companies approach this as an adversarial relationship. They assume their vendors are planning to take advantage of them, so they attempt to take advantage of their vendors first, in self-defense. Imagine the classic relationship between a buyer and a car salesman: no trust exists, so both do their best to take advantage of the other.

This type of relationship is really not a relationship at all. It is thoroughly inappropriate for today's business environment.

One of the long-time strengths of Japanese corporations is that they have cultivated long-term relationships with their vendors. After such relationships have developed during several years, all parties can operate more as partners than as separate corporations. That's to everyone's advantage.

American corporations' adversarial vendor relationships are encouraged by the traditional bidding process. Selecting vendors on the basis of "lowest bid" can lower costs in the short-term, but it makes forming relationships difficult, and eliminates most of the advantages of those relationships. In the long-term, costs actually rise. It's a classic example of the short-term thinking that has plagued American businesses for many years.

If a business is to thrive over the long-term, it should form long-term relationships with its vendors. Instead of opening every procurement process up to all bidders, it is far better to have a small number of companies that are long-term partners. These companies will have a strong interest in ensuring their customer's success, and will therefore make sacrifices when necessary to ensure that success.

Customers

Few businesses succeed over the long term without repeat customers. It is equally important for businesses to form partnerships with their customers. These relationships may lower the profit associated with one individual sale (due to greater discounts or support requirements). However, they dramatically reduce the cost associated with sales and marketing.

Few business challenges are more difficult than finding a new customer. Countless businesses with superior products have failed because they couldn't find customers. Even those who succeed typically spend huge sums on finding and winning customers. There are also economies of scale associated with gaining or maintaining larger numbers of customers: profit margins can often grow dramatically as volumes increase, even if companies discount their products to gain the extra volume.

A customer is a priceless asset. A company willing to form a long-term partnership is a long-term customer, *easily* worth any additional costs. Of course, winning a customer to a long-term relationship is rarely easy. It frequently requires an initial sacrifice to establish goodwill. Is the sacrifice worth the loss? Only if you have reason to believe you have an opportunity to establish such a long-term relationship.

For example, assume your company has shipped a $100,000 item to another company. Somehow, the item was damaged in transit. The customer won't accept responsibility. There's no way to tell for sure whether the item was damaged before, during or after shipment, so it's not clear who's really responsible. If you're trying to establish a long-term relationship with your customer, and you believe there's a reasonable chance of success, you'll be more likely to accept responsibility, pay the damages, and free the customer of all liability.

Partners

Some relationships develop over time to become much more than just vendor-customer or peer-to-peer relationships. When both parties are working together to accomplish a goal, both parties invest equally, and both will benefit or lose equally, there's a true partnership. Many companies talk about forming partnerships, but most arrangements that are *called* partnerships really turn out otherwise.

In this era of downsizing, many companies are outsourcing major portions of their business. They often term such arrangements partnerships, but usually they're simply vendor-customer long-term relationships. It's rare for both companies to have equal investments and risks in the deal. Calling the arrangement a partnership gives the illusion of more equality than actually exists.

Two examples illustrate this point. Some years ago, Kodak decided to outsource their MIS operations. They found a large vendor willing and able to take over virtually the entire operation, signed a long-term contract, and transferred the majority of their MIS operations to this company. This deal was commonly termed a partnership, but it was really just a long-term vendor-customer relationship. For example, if the outsourced systems fail, the vendor will lose the revenue from the arrangement—but Kodak will be out of business. This is clearly not equal risk. Virtually all the investment was made by Kodak, not the vendor. While the vendor has major investments at stake, and significant risks if the deal fails, those investments and risks pale in comparison to Kodak's.

In contrast, a major Swiss bank recently set up a partnership with Perot Systems, Inc., an outsourcing vendor. This was truly a partnership, however, where the bank not only arranged for Perot Systems to take over all MIS activities, as had Kodak, but took many steps beyond that. They became part owner of Perot Systems, began joint development on new projects, and encouraged Perot Systems to market to other businesses products and services developed jointly by them. In this case the risk and investment are much more equal, as are the rewards or penalties at the end.

Partnerships need not be between companies. They can also be formed between peers in a company. Again, however, the rules are the same as before: both must share more or less equally in the risks, investments and rewards.

Education

The greatest challenge in learning about relationships is sorting the valuable information from the irrelevant. We're inundated today with books, TV programs, lectures and seminars on relationship-building, much of it only marginally useful.

One of the best places to learn about business relationships is in an M.B.A. program. Some have formal courses on the subject, but virtually all programs give you an opportunity to establish relationships with fellow students. Countless successful business careers have been founded on these relationships.

While most colleges offer courses on relationships, these are usually focused on personal relationships. Carefully search college catalogs: the courses you want are often found in the business department, with names like "Vendor/Supplier Management."

Short courses are also available from training companies, often focusing on Manufacturing or Purchasing issues. Again, the challenge is finding courses that are focused on the issues you want to learn about.

Experience

Experience won't necessarily help you learn how to build relationships. Many people go through their entire careers without ever learning how; others seem to understand it instinctively. Cultural or social training plays a major role; America's culture of independence sometimes devalues cooperate relationships, whereas many other cultures automatically assume them.

One way to learn about relationships is to watch your company's "power brokers," the people who appear to wield power effectively. Much of their influence is based on their relationships. Consequently, they spend most of their time cultivating existing relationships and making new ones.

Here's a real-life example. We'll call him Fred.

Fred didn't have a college degree; in fact, he barely finished high school. He had, however, worked for semiconductor companies such as Texas Instruments and Fairchild when they employed the people who later controlled many of the top companies in Silicon Valley.

Fred's one strong point was his ability to make and keep relationships. He had personal relationships with the CEOs of top firms such as Tandem Computer and Intel. Frankly, he wasn't good at much else. Still, he consistently found employment as a senior marketing executive. Why? He had an exceptional ability to generate sales by getting face-to-face meetings with top industry executives.

Whenever Fred wanted a new job, companies lined up to hire him— while other executives with far more abilities went begging for jobs. Those other executives, however, could not call the CEO of a large firm, immediately get a meeting and talk them into buying.

Carefully observe how relationships are built and used. Start putting those lessons into practice on a small scale: in a company department, a school class, a project, or wherever else you are. As you get more comfortable with relationship building, expand to a larger scale.

Awareness

Ever hear the saying: "business is a jungle"?

It may be a slight exaggeration—but only slight.

In business, careers and businesses *can* flourish or be destroyed in an instant. That's another reason your relationships are so important. They provide *some* protection against unforeseen disaster. Even lions and elephants (which can protect themselves against most threats) typically travel in groups and live much longer when associated with a group.

There's one thing jungle animals have that you need: "awareness." You always need to know what's *really* going on. Early awareness gives you more time to prepare for, and handle problems.

A primary distinction between wild and domesticated animals is their degree of awareness. A domesticated pig can be almost oblivious to its surroundings; a wild pig could never survive that way. In business, too, stupor is a prescription for disaster.

Awareness isn't paranoia, or even constant worry. That's not productive: it just makes you nervous. Rather, it's staying attentive to the signs that something significant is going on which you'll have to react to. Cultivate your awareness by:

- Monitoring your surroundings (business, people, and technologies).
- Learning which trends can be ignored and which are important.
- Developing a plan to react to important trends.

Current Business Conditions

Always be aware of how well your business is doing. Even at the lowest level, some information is available. You need that information to understand the company's prospects—and *yours*.

Is revenue up? Are profits up? Are more orders being booked than delivered? Is market share growing or declining? Are there new competitors? How is the competition doing? How are general economic conditions affecting your industry? What are the analysts who follow your company's stock saying?

Understanding your company's current business conditions can help you predict the likelihood of promotions or layoffs; new project opportunities; and the support and resources you can expect.

If the company is doing well, it might be a good time to propose introducing expensive new technology that can help improve market share. If the company is doing poorly, it may be a good time to propose a relatively inexpensive project to improve efficiency and cut costs. If the company is doing really poorly, the only projects that will get adequate support will be those that improve the chance of survival.

People Issues

To motivate people, it helps to be aware of what motivates them, and what's going on in their lives. A person in financial trouble can be offered a financial bonus to do extra work needed to get a project done on time. Another person might prefer to develop a new skill, and will work unusually hard on a project that helps develop that skill.

When it comes to personal matters, there's a fine line between awareness and prying. Don't cross it. *Listen, but don't ask, and never gossip.*

Technology Trends

Awareness of technology trends is essential to everyone, and obviously essential if you're involved in information technology or Cyberspace-related projects. It's not enough to know proven technology; you need to know what's on the leading edge. Both have a place.

Proven technology, even if dull, is commonly chosen for applications that can't fail. The state-of-the-art is applied where its special benefits are needed. Some projects may require you to work with technology still in development, if the benefits of that technology outweigh the risks.

Technology trends are driven by *what's hot* (fads) and *what's needed* (what must be done to keep businesses running). For example, few technologies are hotter than SAP. This complete suite of programs is designed to provide mainframe-level reliability and functionality in the client-server environment. Programmers skilled in installing and supporting SAP applications can command astronomical salaries (over US$100,000 annually) because its rapid adoption has led to a tremendous shortage of such programmers.

On the other hand, nobody would call COBOL a hot technology. A few years ago most COBOL programmers decided the language had little future, so they retrained themselves and moved on. Today, however, COBOL programmers are in great demand and are commanding high salaries. Companies have millions of lines of COBOL applications that are critical to their businesses and must be maintained, and not enough skilled COBOL programmers are left to do the job.

Programmers who followed these trends closely could have done very well. Other programmers could only have taken advantage of them through sheer luck—and luck is a notoriously fickle ally.

Most Cyberspace-related projects are heavily dependent on technology. Without a strong awareness of technology, it's easy to fail. You might, for example, fail because you proposed technology that was insufficiently advanced—or not yet mature enough.

There are several ways to stay on top of technology trends. The trade press is quite useful, as are the occasional users' group meeting or technology seminar. The best way is to become part of a project actually implementing advanced technology.

Today, so much technology is available, *nobody* can understand it all. You can, however, gain a working awareness of most areas of information technology through readings, seminars and meetings. Then you can learn one or two areas in depth, through participation in actual implementations.

Again, it's critical to be aware of what's going on in *your* organization. Projects that implement state-of-the-art technologies tend to be rare and difficult to become part of. You'll improve your odds if you know what's coming.

Education

Awareness means knowing what's going on *now*. Traditional college degree programs don't keep up, and may not be very useful for this. On the other hand, some progressive colleges offer courses that are even more advanced than most businesses. M.B.A. programs sometimes include excellent coverage of current and future business trends. Some Computer Science, Mathematics and Engineering departments are also current with, or ahead of, current technology.

Carefully review your prospective college's curriculum to see if it emphasizes old technologies like COBOL and FORTRAN, or newer technologies like Java, C++ and Oracle development. If you find state-of-the-art technology, you may have found the right college.

Experience

A few years of following current technology and business trends will make you aware of what you need to know, but only experience will make you sufficiently aware of the subtleties of motivating people.

Tactical Management

Volumes have been written on strategy, communications, and planning. But as a manager, you'll spend much of your time handling the multitude of small issues that must be resolved every day. These "tactical management" issues aren't written about much, but they're critical to your success. To succeed as a tactical manager, you must learn how to:

- Measure and track progress of local events.
- Correct little problems before they become big problems.
- Avoid common problems.
- Prioritize personal and group efforts.
- Ensure the group is always getting better at everything.

Managing Projects

Most managers will at some point have project(s) to manage. Earlier in this chapter, you learned basic project management techniques and tools; for example, you learned about Gantt and PERT charts and how to break down projects into small tasks. You also learned the importance of regular, typically weekly, project reviews.

In this section, you'll take a closer look at project reviews—and what to do if problems arise.

If a project is going well, your weekly review will show that the work for the preceding week was all completed. You can then review your Gantt and PERT charts to determine what tasks should be scheduled next.

However, if your review meeting reveals that last week's work *wasn't* completed as planned, corrective action must be taken immediately. You need to understand the reasons for the failure, and its impact on your schedule. Some failures are relatively simple: a key person may have been ill for a couple of days. These may be recovered during the following week just by having somebody work a few more hours.

Other failures may be more critical and require more drastic measures. They may reveal a failure in the planning process to account for some item. Or they may reveal a significant change in the project requirements or environment.

Such problems must be handled immediately and vigorously, whether by adding resources, reducing the scope of the project, re-allocating resources, changing the sequencing of the tasks, replacing some equipment or people, or some other action. The most dangerous time on a project is when a task (or group of tasks) has slipped behind schedule and stays there. If action isn't taken to remedy the matter, other tasks will quickly be affected, and the entire project will be placed in jeopardy.

Handling Day-to-Day Crises

Every manager faces day-to-day crises, some worse than others. If you're managing a long-term project, you may encounter fewer of them: your focus is usually weeks or months ahead. Conversely, operational or customer service management often seems to be nothing but a series of small crises.

Of course, the best way to handle crises is to avoid them, by improving your organization's structure, processes and procedures. Over time, see which areas seem most prone to crisis and take extra effort to improve those areas. Remember not to develop procedures that are so detailed and voluminous that nobody will use them. Keep things simple and easy to learn.

An issue is not a crisis if an effective procedure exists to handle it.

The other key component of avoiding crises is to build a group of people who are calm under pressure, think quickly and are resourceful. Using those attributes, they can extend your standard procedures to handle most situations that arise. Of course, you must also empower them to act on their own, and encourage them to resolve issues themselves.

When crises are unavoidable, however, your first task is to determine the risks and magnitude of the crisis. Hospital emergency rooms offer an excellent example. They first determine the condition of the patient. Those patients at most risk are handled first, regardless of when they came in. Patients at less risk must wait. While this system is unpleasant to the patient with a minor cold, it optimizes the limited resources available and minimizes the overall risk to all patients.

Once the risk is determined, you can choose a course of action. Where the risk is high and time is short, something must be done very quickly, even if the action is itself risky. Once the immediate risk has passed, another approach may be chosen as a long-term solution. In a crisis, the best solution is usually the one that quickly alleviates the risk, even if you'll have to revisit and replace that solution later.

When the risk is not so high, give more consideration to your course of action. You may be able to implement a long-term solution up front, without resorting to temporary solutions. You may even find that you're not facing a crisis at all, merely someone's momentary burst of impatience.

Time Management

Judging from the number of books on time management, plenty of people need help. Following a few simple rules can significantly improve most people's individual time management. (At the same time, no matter how skilled you are in time management, sometimes there's just too much work to do!)

The goal of time management is to spend the appropriate amount of time on each task. It's common for relatively minor tasks to expand, filling so much of your time that you have little left to handle the really important tasks.

To avoid this trap, first ascertain how you're spending your time now. Some time management courses advocate keeping a written log for several days of all activities that take more than five minutes. I prefer recording time spent in blocks of thirty minutes or one hour. It's sufficient to note that you spent two hours in staff meeting, one hour discussing a current project and one hour reading e-mail.

Once you've made the record, study it. You might discover you've only accounted for four hours of a ten-hour day. If so, you've spent much of your time on tasks too small to be recorded. Or you may find you've spent large chunks of time on a few relatively unimportant tasks.

Next, compare your actual priorities with those of your job requirements. If they don't match, you need to adjust your allocation of time to fit—reducing the amount of time you spend on unimportant or peripheral tasks. Once you've made the adjustments and given them time to become habit, make another record of your time. Are you closer? Are more adjustments necessary? Keep recording and comparing until time management is no longer an issue.

Short-Term Plans

Nearly all projects and activities can benefit from *some* planning, even small projects that don't merit detailed Gantt and PERT charts. Some plans are simply to-do lists written on the back of an envelope. Some people even find it's enough to keep those lists "in their head." Many executives use "day planners" to organize their day, plan their time, and review their short-term results.

Different approaches work for different people, but some things don't change. You always need to take into account resource constraints, the time you have available, scheduling and sequencing issues, your priorities, and the results you're after.

Prioritizing

Few managerial skills are as important as learning how to *set priorities*. Every new manager quickly realizes they're getting more requests than they have time to handle. If they try to do everything, they'll quickly be working twenty hours a day—and *still* be falling behind!

Setting your priorities straight isn't just a time management issue: it's a key to your entire career. If you can't do it, you won't give the appropriate attention to the projects that matter most to you and your organization.

Evaluate every request for time and resources to determine what will happen to your company, department, team (or you) if that request is deferred (or denied). Don't forget: every request you respond to takes time and resources you could have allocated elsewhere.

Also evaluate requests based on the amount of resources needed to fulfill them. Requests that require minimal resources can be scheduled ahead of those with major resource requirements. Sometimes you can quickly handle several requests that don't require much effort, gaining goodwill from several colleagues at minimal cost.

Process Improvement (TQM)

Total Quality Management (TQM) was a major corporate fad a few years ago. The faddish aspects of TQM have passed, but the solid aspects of TQM remain—and these ought to be embraced by every person and business.

Many TQM principles have been practiced for generations, but TQM is most closely associated with Dr. W. Edward Deming, who codified and articulated its philosophy after the Second World War. Deming's principles were embraced in Japan and are credited with a major role in the turn-around of Japanese manufacturing. In fact, Japan's most prestigious quality award is still named after Deming.

Deming's ideas were generally ignored in the US until the 1980s, when Japanese companies were suddenly perceived as a mortal threat to American manufacturing. As with most fads, his original principles were quickly modified, "improved," and often diluted by American firms who found them unpalatable in their original forms.

Do it right the first time!

Perhaps the most fundamental TQM idea is: "Do it right the first time!" Spend more time and effort getting things right from the outset: don't just throw together "any old garbage" and plan to fix it later.

The traditional American approach was epitomized by Detroit's automotive assembly lines in the 1960s. Cars would move down the line at a fixed speed. Every worker had a fixed amount of time to add their part to the car. Eventually the car would reach the end of the line, where it would (hopefully!) be inspected. Cars with major defects were taken off the line to be fixed, while those with minor defects were sent to the dealer, to be fixed there. Many were sold to consumers without ever being fixed.

Consumers discovered that Japanese cars generally worked, and American cars frequently didn't. No wonder Japanese car manufacturers took over a huge percentage of the American car market.

The American manufacturers' first response was more rigorous inspections by both the line inspectors and the car dealers. The result: lots full of cars that had to be fixed before being sold, and huge costs.

Eventually it became painfully obvious that it made more sense to build the cars right in the first place. The cost was immense. Every aspect of American car production had to be completely revamped: not just manufacturing, but also design, engineering, and many other areas.

American auto manufacturers created teams with representatives from all relevant areas, and gave those teams responsibility to design and engineer a car that would be easy to build well. Next, they empowered workers on the line with authority, responsibility and incentives to improve quality. The process has taken many years, and it's still not complete, but it has reduced overall costs significantly, and dramatically improved customer satisfaction. You can see the results at Chrysler and Saturn, to name only two examples.

Unfortunately, many American businesses still haven't gotten the message, perhaps because they haven't been faced with imminent demise—yet.

"Doing it right the first time" requires investing more time, effort and money at the beginning of the project. Few managers are willing to make that investment in an era of cost-cutting. Inevitably, projects take longer and cost more than they would have if initially allocated the appropriate resources up front.

Software projects abound that violate every aspect of TQM; not coincidentally, MIS is notorious for cost and time overruns. The statistics are appalling. Many projects are never completed, many more are completed but are never used, and still more are completed late and over budget. Only a very small percentage of MIS projects are completed on schedule, on budget, and are used as expected.

Why? In part, the blame lies with the executives approving the projects. Often, they would refuse to approve the project if they knew its true cost and schedule, yet are perfectly willing to accept continual cost and time overruns once the project is underway.

 Every project should have sufficient time and resources for both planning and delivery. If careful planning reveals the project can't be delivered with the time or money available, the project's scope should be reduced until it can be delivered. If that can't be done, the project should be postponed or canceled.

Rapid prototyping

Rapid prototyping has recently become popular in software development. On first glance, it may appear to contradict the "do it right the first time" approach, but if approached properly, it actually fits quite well with TQM.

One of the biggest problems with many software projects is that requirements change as the project progresses. This leads to cost and time overruns, and makes the finished software less useful. rapid prototyping is designed to avoid these problems.

With rapid prototyping tools, you can quickly assemble a "mock-up" of the finished system, so users can evaluate its appearance and functionality. The users can then evaluate the prototype and suggest changes. Since the mock-up was quick and cheap, so are changes to it. The actual project is only undertaken after final agreement has been reached on the appearance and functionality of the prototype.

Unfortunately, once the quick-and-dirty prototype is agreed upon, even its "quickest" and "dirtiest" elements may be enshrined in the finished design. Since they'll inevitably have to be changed later in the process, developers are back in the old trap of not "doing it right the first time."

To marry the two approaches properly, carefully define what parts of the prototype will be retained and what will be thrown away. Those parts that *will* become part of the eventual project need the most careful planning up front, while those that will certainly be discarded can be created with less care.

If it proves difficult to make this distinction, carefully construct the entire prototype. Since rapid prototyping tools are fast and efficient, you'll still save time in the long run. (If constructing the entire prototype is not possible, this may not be a good project for rapid prototyping.)

Focus on continuous improvement

Another basic principle of TQM is "continuous improvement." This simply means that every person, group and company should attempt to always improve everything. This should be done with thought, naturally, since investing a large amount to improve a system that will be removed in two months is obviously not wise.

Many Americans also have difficulty with the idea of continuous improvement. The American psyche seems to be geared toward quantum leaps forward, and doesn't readily accept that many small improvements can eventually equal one quantum leap. Japanese manufacturers have repeatedly demonstrated, however, that such an approach leads to huge improvements if followed carefully for a long period of time.

Many people claim they naturally always try to improve things. Perhaps. But even so, that's far different from institutionalizing continuous improvement, as the Japanese have. In many Japanese companies, *everyone* is encouraged to *always* look for improvements in *every* process. American companies tend to assign a few "experts" to be responsible for this. There's no way a few experts can equal the effectiveness of an entire company dedicated to continuous improvement.

To institutionalize a continuous improvement program, companies must publicize it widely, make it available to every employee, provide clear incentives, and show constant executive support. For example, a software company could have cash awards available to anyone who comes up with a product improvement, post signs widely to promote the program, and have regular meetings where the company president personally hands out the awards.

Such a program will only work if every suggestion is considered fairly and openly by evaluators who are motivated to accept all reasonable suggestions.

Removing the jargon from TQM

Many people find TQM a hotbed of incomprehensible jargon, and refuse to look beyond the jargon. This is unfortunate. Much of TQM's jargon is found in the field of Statistical Process Control (SPC), which focuses on manufacturing and other processes with inherent variability. With SPC, companies can determine whether variability (defects) is due to failures of an individual worker or in a process. However, SPC only applies when a process is repeated enough times to have statistical significance. Cyberspace processes rarely have this characteristic, so SPC isn't applicable. But other aspects of TQM *are* applicable, and much good can be derived from TQM with absolutely *no* knowledge of SPC.

When TQM became popular, many consultants appeared, with widely varying credentials and expertise. Many of them created or adapted new names they could claim for their own. This led to several major schools of TQM, each with its own jargon. You can cut through anyone's TQM jargon if you understand Dr. Deming's basic principles.

Applying Dr. Deming's principles to cyberspace

The following fourteen points are taken from *The Deming Management Method*, by Mary Walton. Deming's methods deserve more space than is available here, so the entire book is recommended reading.

1. **Create constancy of purpose for improvement of product and service**. This applies equally to any endeavor in life, not just to manufacturing. Unless a company and *all* of its employees focus on continuous improvement, it will not happen. This focus must be clear from the dock workers to the CEO.

   Constancy of purpose does not happen by accident. It requires a continual effort and focus. Once, TQM became so popular that all bidders on certain Federal contracts were required to have active TQM programs. One company promptly decided to create a strategic plan for its TQM program. The executive in charge set a due date, and informed his staff that the date must be met, *regardless of how poorly the plan was done*. It was immediately clear to all present (except the executive) that the company really had no interest in TQM, but merely wanted to bid on the Federal contracts. Such a program is obviously doomed.

2. **Adopt the new philosophy**. The focus on continual improvement must become like a religion: poor workmanship and service must simply become unacceptable.

3. **Cease dependence on mass inspection**. At first glance this seems only applicable to manufacturing, but it can equally well be applied to software development and most other activities. "Do it right the first time": don't plan on fixing things later.

4. **Cease awarding business on price tag alone**.

5. **Improve constantly and forever the system of production and service.** Focus on continual improvement *forever*, not just for a short time or until one project is completed.

6. **Institute training**. The people doing the work must be properly trained. They have usually learned their job from another worker, which may or may not be a good source. A small investment in training will pay off many times in improved productivity and quality.

7. **Institute leadership**. As we've discussed, leaders are hard to find. It's easy to tell people what to do and punish them if they fail, but leaders will actually help people do a better job, by effectively instituting positive changes.

8. **Drive out fear**. The American corporation is based on a hierarchical model where the person at the bottom must fear everyone higher. This is wrong. Fear has no place in a productive organization. Peo-

ple should feel free to ask questions and make mistakes occasionally, or they will stop trying.

9.   **Break down barriers between staff areas**. The American way of life is founded on competition, not cooperation. In the business world, every department competes with the others. Better to have all departments *cooperate*, so that all can succeed.

10.   **Eliminate slogans, exhortations and quotas**. This strikes fear in the heart of most American managers, who would normally *start* an improvement program with new slogans and exhortations. In fact, the workers in question have usually seen this many times before and recognize it for what it is—another manager trying to avoid making the fundamental changes that are really necessary.

11.   **Eliminate numerical quotas**. If you improve the quality and the process, the *quantity* will improve by itself.

12.   **Remove barriers to pride of workmanship**. People like to feel proud of what they have accomplished, but it is all too easy for management to make that impossible. Managers cannot instill motivation just by waving a wand. Individuals motivate themselves. Managers merely make it possible. One of the best ways to accomplish that is by encouraging people to have pride in their work, and then to make it possible for them to do quality work.

13.   **Institute a vigorous program of education and retraining**. All too often, American companies moving to a new technology dump the old employees and hire new ones with current skills. It is almost always more economical in the long run to retrain the existing staff. Hire a few new employees and seed them into key areas, but focus on handling most new requirements with existing staff. This greatly increases motivation and leverages knowledge about the company that these employees have built up over years.

14.   **Take action to accomplish the transformation**. A transition of this nature is so major it can only succeed if spearheaded by the top management of the company and supported by the entire company. Anything less will doom TQM to failure.

You can't implement TQM if you're focused purely on short-term profits. But if you implement TQM properly, you set the stage for making customer loyalty—and long-term profitability—much easier to achieve and maintain.

TQM also teaches companies to avoid annual reviews. Virtually every Human Resources manager in America would be appalled at that prospect, but annual reviews do seem tailor-made to destroy employee motivations. At best, after an annual review, a motivated employee will remain motivated. More often, a formerly motivated employee suddenly becomes unhappy, and his or her work suffers accordingly.

Annual reviews destroy teamwork, since by their nature they put people in competition with one another for a limited number of highest evaluations. They instill fear and leave people depressed and unmotivated. And they are often performed by individuals that the employee neither respects nor trusts to take an honest look at their performance.

Most American executives feel that a well-rounded executive should have experience managing a number of different areas, and thus rotate managers frequently between areas. They believe that knowledge of the company and job area are relatively insignificant. In extreme cases, they're even willing to outsource major functions.

TQM teaches otherwise. While outsourcing has a role, it's overutilized. Why? An executive put in charge of that piece of the business didn't understand how to run it effectively, so they contracted it out to another company.

It won't take long to find dozens of examples of major business mistakes made simply because the manager didn't understand the work being done. Not only won't anyone admit it, when it becomes impossible to avoid, they'll call it a strategic decision.

As Mary Walton concludes, "It would be good to have Dr. Deming's ideas applied in the workplace. But it would take a miracle from God if they were." True enough, but if *you* fully understand and apply Dr. Deming's principles, you'll find yourself leading one of the most efficient areas of the company, with a staff that is slavishly devoted to you.

Education

Some areas of tactical management are easily addressed with education. It would be brutally painful to learn all of them the hard way, through experience. Project management, time management and process improvement should be learned in a classroom. It's possible to learn them on-the-job, but it can be difficult.

Two- and three-day classes abound on project management, usually offered by groups such as the American Management Association. Project management classes can also be found in the business or management section of many colleges. These classes will vary in length, focus and quality, but most will do the job.

Crisis management is rarely taught formally, though some information may be buried in classes on planning.

Time management classes are perhaps the most popular of all. Most management schools offer them, and short courses are everywhere. Most of these courses are good, if not taken too seriously. If nothing else, make sure a class teaches you how to set better priorities.

Most colleges will offer some training on TQM in their business or management section. Several training companies have become quite successful offering little other than TQM training, although it is sometimes called by other names. The best bet is to find a course that remains relatively close to Dr. Deming's original teachings. Most courses like this are offered in colleges, not by dedicated training companies.

Experience

In general, only experience will teach the importance of planning. Classes can teach some of the techniques, but rarely with the detail you'll need. Experience is essential in short-term planning and crisis management. As we've said, project planning, time management and TQM should first be learned in a classroom, and then put into practice in actual projects.

You'll ultimately need both experience with project management and experience with the technology you're managing. If, for example, you've managed a construction project, you'll know quite a bit about basic project management techniques. But if you're called upon to manage a software development project, you'll still have a lot to learn about software technologies.

Summary

A successful Cybercareer requires a well-rounded set of experience and abilities. The field is so new and has been growing so quickly that many people with limited experience and abilities have been able to make significant contributions. As with most new fields, the early pioneers have not been held to standards as high as those who come later.

As Cyberspace rapidly matures, strong technical skills will increasingly not be enough: strong business and management skills will also be necessary. In this chapter, you've had a glimpse of the non-technical skills you will certainly need to meet your potential.

CHAPTER

8

Change Management

I live in terror, that's what keeps me current. I mean that sincerely.

—Mike Troiano, CEO/President, Ogilvy & Mather Interactive

By now you know that change, constant and unremitting, will be the central reality of your business life. Whether you're technical or non-technical, you know you can't expect a job for life—and you can't expect to learn in school even a small fraction of what you'll need to know during the course of your career.

Imagine you're 55. Your world includes the PC, photocopier machine, pocket calculator, fax, and Federal Express. How many of these were around when you started your career? ***None.*** You used a dictaphone and sent your memos to the typing pool. You made copies with carbon paper. You used a slide rule instead of a calculator. And if you wanted a message delivered, there was the Post Office—period.

The first computer I used didn't have a monitor—it typed onto paper. And I worked with IBM cards. Today I am Manager Of Intranet Operations. That may change in a week, but that's what I am today.
—Debra Winters, Manager of Intranet Operations, SunIR

You can't stop change. You can't ignore it. You can't avoid it (unless you're one of the few people wealthy enough to retire early). And there's no way around it: even good change is stressful.

To be successful, to stay healthy and productive, you must make change manageable. How? By preparing for it, anticipating its arrival, and moving with it, not against it.

Prepare for Change

Fortune favors the prepared mind.

When we know a baby is coming, we:

- Fix up a nursery,
- Prepare to restructure our lives around a different rhythm,
- Discuss possible problems with the doctor,
- Take birth preparation classes to learn how to breathe under the stress of child birth, and
- Pack a suitcase for the hospital.

You can make the same kinds of preparations for every other kind of change, too:

- Store your energy
- Free up time
- Prepare to move responsibilities around
- Plan for worst case scenarios
- Practice the drill

Stay Rested and Fresh

The best way to deal with the stress of change is to be rested and fresh. Living on the edge of burnout *seriously* reduces your ability to cope with *any* stress, change-related or otherwise.

I'm not talking about taking a once-a-year vacation. You can't become an athlete in a two-week crash course: you can barely begin the process. It takes months of steady development. It's the same with learning to manage change.

What's more, who can predict change so well that we can schedule two weeks of vacation before it happens, when we'd need it most?

If you burn your candle at both ends, this section is for you. If you're chronically overworked, irritable and sluggish, this section is for you. Because if you want to be successful at managing change, you simply *must* have energy reserves at your disposal.

Automate Anything and Everything

One of the *best* ways to prepare for change is to work yourself out of a job. As long as you are capable of making a transition to new skills, you won't be out of work, no matter how many jobs you work yourself out of.

Debra Winters on Automation

I've always been an automater. Every time I've come across a manual process, I've tried to find a way to have the computer do it for me.

That frees me up to learn more things. That's how I became a programmer. I automated myself out of every job I could. And if I had nothing to do, I read a book, or went down to the corporate library and *found* things to do. That was one way I kept getting promoted: I was constantly finding ways to improve a process, and to add value to my job by doing things I otherwise wouldn't have time to do.

My objective has *always* been to automate myself out of a job. And I think that should be everyone's goal, personally.

Debra Winters, Manager of Internet Operations, SunIR

Many people have made themselves so essential they miss out on opportunities to grow. Their management can't afford to spare them. These people mistakenly call this *security*. In reality, there's a better word for it: *denial*. Unfortunately, they awaken too late. A few years before retirement, they feel secure enough to start coasting, and *bang!* They're downsized, without the skills they need to survive.

The best way to advance yourself is to make yourself available for new opportunities. This means jettisoning your current responsibilities without dumping them on someone else. Usually there's only one place to dump them: on the computer. That's where automation comes in.

Anything you do regularly is a candidate for automation. There's only one thing better than automating a process: determining the process isn't needed, and eliminating it altogether.

Standardize Processes and Document Them

Many processes can't be automated—*yet*. Information may come to you in various forms. Your procedures may all require custom handling. If you want to move forward, it's critical that you can transfer your knowledge and responsibilities to others in an orderly way. If you can't automate a procedure yet, then document it, and standardize it as much as possible. Once you've done all that, you may find the procedure now *can* be automated.

To prepare for change, eliminate the work that prevents you from preparing.

I'm not saying you should return to the industrial-age era of constant, repetitive, mundane work. Your best asset is your unique human mind, which can deal with near-infinite variety and all manner of unique situations. By streamlining or jettisoning those repetitive mundane tasks, you make yourself available for far more challenging work.

Prepare for Important or Probable Contingencies

Anything that can go wrong; will.—Murphy's Law

Murphy lives. Or at least his spirit does. Problems occur, usually at the least opportune moment. *The middle of a crisis is not the time to start thinking about how to solve it.* Details get missed, good alternatives aren't considered or tried. In group situations, people aren't always clear on their roles.

For example, the day you suffer a network break-in is *not* the day to start planning how you'll handle one. To respond appropriately, you should *already* know every door and window in your network. You should have clean versions of software, uncontaminated with backdoors, to replace software that may be contaminated. In a large-scale environment, your team should be coordinated well enough to seal all the entryways simultaneously.

These things need to be planned. In reality, *disaster recovery* rarely works smoothly even when planned. *Without* planning however, a break-in can cause days of lost work for entire corporations, and cost millions of dollars.

The more likely an event is to occur, the more important the planning.

If you suspect your company may be planning a layoff, you and your colleagues should be polishing up account termination procedures, virus scanning and protection procedures, and general system security—because security breaches are often created by disgruntled ex-employees.

If your company is bidding on a contract you can't complete with current staff, you should have recruiting plans in place, potential candidates in quick reference form, and hiring approvals secured.

The firefighting mentality pervades many modern businesses. It is the most costly mistake many companies could ever make.

Firefighting—where companies react to crisis instead of anticipating and planning for them—is virtually impossible to audit. Nobody knows how much it costs, or who's accountable. As a result, firefighting just may be the biggest financial black hole a company has. There's only one antidote for the firefighting mentality: *planning*.

Practice Changing Things: Habits and Attitudes

Debra Winters the Neophile

I embrace change. When things get mundane and "same-old," I get bored and my performance slips. So I challenge the process and go searching for change. For me, change is like an injection of B vitamins.

Major corporate re-orgs usually terrify people. I look at them with completely different eyes: they *fascinate* me. It's like, *now* who am I working for? For me it's an opportunity to build another working relationship.

Debra Winters, Manager of Intranet Operations, SunIR

Only one person in 20 is *neophillic: a lover of change or novelty.* The rest of us have some degree of *neophobia*, or fear of change. Few people learn to embrace change in school. At least, business schools teach methods for mitigating the risk of the unknown, using statistics, formal processes, historical data, or third party authentication. Even this, however, can lull people into a false sense of security.

Change is scary. However, as with anything else, you'll get better with practice. If you routinely practice changing things in a controlled environment, you're likely to improve at managing even the changes you can't control.

To change the world you must first change your mind. Thus, practice changing something regularly to get into the appropriate mindset. This is the core tenet of neurolinguistic programming, which is one way people overcome phobias. Some examples of practicing change can be as simple as:

* Changing your route to work
* Identifying a phrase you always say and changing it
* Eating a new type of food you haven't tried before

- Attending association meetings

- Reading books on different topics

- Defending the opposite point of view from the one you usually take

Anticipate Change

If I have seen farther than other men, it is because I have stood on the shoulders of giants.—Albert Einstein

Change doesn't appear out of the blue. We just *think* it does, because we didn't see it coming. Change usually sends all kinds of annoying little warning signs that people prefer to ignore.

To anticipate change, first locate its sources. Change happens because someone needs it to happen. *You* may not need it to happen, but *someone* does—or more likely, a whole lot of "someones." *Your first tool for anticipating change is to find out what needs exist and are going unfulfilled.*

Second, change happens when all of the tools are in place to make it possible. James Burke spent an entire season on PBS telling us about the *Connections* that had to occur to make possible our greatest technological revolutions. (If you missed the series, go read the book: it's worth your time.)

To anticipate change, you must be aware of the tools, techniques, and technologies available to facilitate it. Some people think *staying current* is futile: there's no way one lowly human being can handle an exponentially growing knowledge base. But our own communication and technology advances can allow us to stay current better than our predecessors ever could.

We have at our disposal a network of people around the world to share technological innovations with; a network of knowledge repositories to store this information in; and a growing set of tools to help us search this "knowledge space" for relevant information. *Use them.*

The most significant change doesn't happen in a linear fashion. More often than not, it takes a novel perspective to see the connections, as James Burke demonstrated in his book and BBC TV series *Connections*. (As an example, Burke showed the connections that led from an excess of undergarments to general literacy.)

To discover these "non-linear" changes, you have to think differently: become open to seeing new possibilities for current materials and techniques. The cognitive term for this is *brainstorming*.

Lynne T. Keener says

No matter how well you can handle change, you still need to know how to read the public's expectations and signs of acceptance.

Read, learn, listen - did I say *learn*?

Lynne T. Keener, Director, Internet Services,
Keener Information Design Group

Needs Analysis

Project developers obviously need to decide what their projects should accomplish. This "needs analysis" is usually done when determining which new project to take on, or defining the scope of a project in development. You can do your own personal needs analysis virtually every day.

Be observant. Notice your own small frustrations and those of others. Don't say "live with it." Instead, ask: "what's *wrong* with this picture?" When you do your needs analysis, remember your best information comes straight from the source: the people experiencing the problems and frustration on a day-to-day basis.

Don't assume those "on the outside looking in" really understand the problems. This is why the Japanese developed Quality Circles. A Quality Assurance Engineer visiting for a day can't replace the experience of those on the assembly lines.

Needs analysis doesn't have to be a formal process. Often the most impressive needs lists come from just jotting down ideas when they happen and then looking them over a few days later to see if they still make sense.

Stay Current

Nobody can learn *everything*: there are too many new facts, technologies, products and services. Think about how you study for an exam. You:

- Scan headings, pullquotes, graphics, and captions.

- Identify and define new terminology.

- Read the material.

- Attempt to assimilate the material by posing and answering questions about it or developing one's own structure for the material.

- Take formal quizzes or tests to prove your competence.

Now extend those skills to everything else you need to learn:

- Scan the knowledge stream (books, magazines, conferences, e-mail lists, newsgroups, and e-zines).

- Use agents to filter out irrelevant data.

- Read what's *pertinent*.

- Assimilate the material by trying it out.

An important corollary: dedicate some time each year to formal education that helps you add structure to the knowledge you've acquired informally.

Use "Agents" to Scan

The stream of knowledge is flowing faster than ever. There are an unprecedented number of sources, both on-line and off.

On-line information is usually more current, but has less structure and depth. That's because the editorial role of adding formatting, creating structure and adding depth *costs money*. Most on-line information sources don't charge yet, so they can't afford to offer the same quality as off-line sources. On-line magazines with advertising revenues are changing this, but they represent less than one percent of the on-line knowledge stream.

On the other hand, off-line sources face all the mundane tasks (and costs) associated with paper, shipping and warehousing. Books don't move at the speed of light the way bits of information can. It may be a year, or much longer, between when I write these words and when you read them.

Table 8-1 On-line vs. Off-line Information Flow

On-line	Off-line
More current	Less current
Less Depth	More Depth (more so in books than in magazines)
More data—less structure	More structure
Scanning can be automated	Automation tools are not available

Another problem with on-line sources is the vast amount of raw data available. Nobody can read it all. But there are technological solutions: *agents*, computer programs that can do the scanning for you.

Scan for relevance: don't even try *to read it all.*

Read some

Once you have identified *potentially* good sources, read them, absorb them. At this point, scanning isn't enough.

Get some background so that you can understand the theory and issues. Build a mental picture or structure in your head. Don't just passively let the words fly by. Actively read to understand and assimilate knowledge.

Try a little

If you input something without processing or "outputting" it, you'll never remember it for long. Act on what you have read. Discuss it with others. Try it out. If it's software, download it and test it. Write your own commentary.

There's no substitute for experience. Not only are today's new Internet, intranet and Web technologies different from what's come before, they operate in a new paradigm. They're part of an experience unlike anything the cyberspace "newbie" has ever experienced.

You can't learn about the Internet. You have to live it. It's on-the-job training for everybody involved.—Tim Brady

Learn every year

Learning never stops. Budget some structured learning into your schedule every year. A good rule of thumb is to plan for 80–100 hours per year. That's equivalent to

- Six college semester hours per year.

  or

- Two weeks of all day training in professional education courses.

  or

- Three three-day conferences.

Unstructured learning can teach you plenty, but it rarely gives you the opportunity to sit back and look at the big picture—and you need to understand the big picture to get to the next level. *Formal structured learning can help you turn trivia into knowledge.*

Brainstorm and Dream

Your head is round so your thinking can change direction.
—Anonymous

Critical, analytical, reductionist thinking tells us what we *can't* do far more often than what we *can* do. Critical thinking is necessary, but it rarely initiates innovation.

Brainstorming is *uncensored* thinking. It's much like dreaming: you turn reality off, and free your mind to create what it wants. Brainstorming is the breeding ground of innovation.

Just as you keep your brain supplied with new information, keep your mind supplied with new ideas. Just as structured *learning* time should be in the time budget, so should unstructured *dream* time.

Practice your brainstorming and dreaming! An author may write a thousand pages before the first good one. A dreamer may need to generate a thousand ideas before he or she finds a *keeper*.

Execute Change in an Orderly Fashion

Change does not have to mean chaos.

Imagine the emergency evacuation of an airplane. People can leave at a controlled, but rapid pace. Or they can stampede, and possibly get hurt or killed in the process. The difference? Knowing clearly how to proceed.

It's the same for change: you can take steps to make it happen in an orderly fashion. Those steps put you in control. You can sometimes stop the change, or alter its direction if you see trouble ahead.

To execute change in an orderly fashion

- Try it out in a safe environment.
- Make sure your investment is worth the effort.
- Get feedback early and often.
- Use experience to build upon training.

Prototype and Test before Implementing

Few people ever get anything right on the first try.

Few babies learn to walk without falls. Few 1.0 software releases work as advertised. If you do tests and trial runs before you create the "finished product," you'll learn many lessons—and build a better product.

This goes for everything from building a web site and testing it on a focus group, to implementing reengineering, to excelling at your next interview.

Nicola Tesla, the real father of alternating current, routinely built models in his head and tested them out. Few people saw those mental models, so they believed he created everything from scratch, almost perfectly, the first time. Most of us don't have Tesla's savant visualization skills. Thus we must build our prototypes in the real world—and, equally important, *test* them there.

Rachel Borden of Sun Microsystems comments that a good tester is very detail oriented, trying every option—and at the same time, a creative type who envisions situations that "couldn't possibly happen," but often *do*. The real world contains an almost infinite number of variables, and the most infinite of all is the human brain, which can dream up hundreds of ways to use something that the designer never intended or prepared for.

Evaluate the Risks, Benefits, Lifespan and Strategic Value of Your Tactics

There's such a thing as pointless change "for its own sake." Why bother, when there are so many things that really *need* to be changed?

You've already learned that senior managers often make decisions based on return on investment (ROI): at bare minimum, ROI must exceed the time and resources invested. Sometimes the hassle of achieving a goal just isn't worth the benefits.

You have to have the discipline to take the risk, and you have to have the discipline to think the risks through.
—*Bill Prouty, Chief Webmaster, SunIR*

For example, if it costs you $2 to get a new customer, their business is only worth 50¢ including repeat business, and only one in five will generate additional business, you're losing money. By the same token, downsizing by cutting benefits and encouraging attrition may achieve the goal of reducing staff, but you're often left with the least productive staff members, who can't afford to leave—and can't keep up with your additional workload.

Sometimes change isn't worth the cost of the transition. Many companies upgrade software or hardware simply because new products exist, instead of making a business case for the upgrade. When planning the cost of a product or service, take into account its useful lifespan. If you won't recoup the money spent on the product *plus* the human cost of installing, configuring and learning it, again you're losing money.

Always Involve the Victim

Victimized by Change? Debra Winters Has Been!

I went through several corporate layoffs in the mainframe days. I never got laid off but—it was awful, horrible. Everything changed, friends had to leave, and it was all sad change.

That's what brought me to Sun. I volunteered to leave Amdahl because I just didn't want to go through it again.
—*Debra Winters, Manager of Intranet Operations, SunIR*

Inflicting change on anyone without their buy-in and participation makes them a helpless victim. People are much more responsive to change and novelty when they feel that they have control over the situation.

Whether it's a new computer system, a reengineered process, or a new workspace, management often imposes changes on workers without involving them. Sometimes management solicits feedback but ignores it and doesn't even explain why it was disregarded. That leaves workers feeling that management is only "going through the motions" to appease the workforce, and doesn't really care.

Sometimes management believes there isn't enough time to solicit and truly consider employees' feedback. If the staff has confidence in management's decisions, this can work out—sometimes. But most of the time it's a symptom of a company operating in expensive, ineffective "firefighting" mode.

As the old saying goes, if you don't have time to do the work right in the first place, where will you find time to do it over? Doing something right does mean prototyping and testing systems with the people who will actually use them. These are the people most likely to find the problems you've missed—or the opportunities for improvement.

Never forget that your people are your largest cost—and your most valuable asset. Optimizing programs, web sites or processes without optimizing their most costly element is a waste of resources. In cyberspace, the demand for quality people outstrips their availability, and will for many years to come. If you neglect your best people, you'll alienate them, lose out on their insights, and ultimately, lose them altogether.

Roll Out Change with a Trained Team in Place

In most cases, until a new product or technique is widely used, its full range of uses won't be apparent. As a result, you can't provide truly comprehensive training in advance.

But you can and should provide *some* training. Change works best when the 'changee' is in control, and the best way to be in control is to be knowledgeable about the situation you're in.

Train people up front in the core theoretical concepts they'll need to know, and in the basic standard procedures. That will give them a framework for learning new ways to use your product or service, and it'll minimize the number of "blind alleys" they'll need to follow. Some people are less curious and don't care to experiment. Advance training will at least keep them from feeling lost, confused and unproductive.

Skill List for Change Management

The skills associated with change management include:

- Standardize and Document

- Automate

- Contingency Planning

- Needs Analysis

- Trend Analysis

- Continuous Learning

- Brainstorming

- Prototyping

- Risk/Benefit Analysis

- Strategic Value Analysis

- Mentored Rollout

Sources of Education

The change management strategies you've learned in this chapter aren't formally taught anywhere—but they *work*.

The closest thing you'll find to "education for change" is the formal continuous process improvement or reengineering courses now offered at some universities and colleges.

Sources of Experience

If you really want to become exceptionally good at managing change, find and participate in projects intended to catalyze major changes, such as reengineering projects, new technology roll-outs, corporate restructuring, or forays into new markets.

Summary

In this chapter, you've learned about the importance of *managing* change, so it won't steamroll you.

Change is a constant on both the business and technology sides of cyberspace. In the next section, we'll introduce the technical skills you need to complement your business and "change management" skills.

PART IV

Technical Skills

- Technical Skills for Your Cybercareer

- Technical Development Skills

As a phenomenon, cyberspace may have transcended technology. But without people who have a sophisticated understanding of information technology, it would collapse in no time.

In the next two chapters, you'll take a look at the two major types of technical careers now available to cyberspace professionals: *support*, and *development*. You'll learn what companies are looking for, and what skills you'll need -- both specific *technical* skills and transferable *knowledge* skills.

CHAPTER

Technical Support Cybercareers

Cyberspace is often viewed as the realm of the *hacker* or *techie*—the technical person. Many non-technical people have shied away from it as a result of that reputation. However, for those who are technical, today's cyberspace offers unprecedented career opportunities and choices.

When mainframes ruled the world, young people were typically told they could be in "hardware" or "software." Conceivably those interested in software might be allowed to choose between "applications" and "systems" software. These choices offered little insight or direction to the aspiring computer professional.

The world has changed dramatically since then. In this chapter, you'll consider the choices now available to the technical professional, and the skills you need to take advantage of them.

Hardware

Hardware doesn't go away: there's still no way to run software without it. But the nature of working with hardware has changed dramatically. Once, legions of electronics repair technicians found work fixing expensive hardware. While these *bench techs* are still at work in some places, more people are being educated for this work than there are jobs available. As the economics of hardware manufacturing have improved, most repair is handled by simply replacing broken boards with new ones.

Engineers are still at work creating new hardware, though even in this work, most of the interesting work is software-related. Most new hardware products contain their own inexpensive CPUs, which run software that handles the functions they perform. In fact, most peripheral controller cards today contain more software than ran on entire first-generation personal computer systems.

The critical "pure hardware" challenges that remain are largely physics-based: how can more miniaturized circuits be placed on the same chip without causing overheating or timing delays?

Software

For software, the reverse is true: a narrow set of choices has blossomed into a wide variety of options. Today's highly diverse software doesn't always fit neatly into "system" or "applications" categories. Moreover, with the advent of personal computers, the field of software *support* has grown explosively. We'll discuss the evolution of software support next.

Support Evolution

In the mainframe world, there were systems analysts who *designed* systems, programmers who *implemented* them and computer operators who *supported* them. Today, the administrator or computer support person requires the same level of knowledge as the programmer (albeit not the same *type* of knowledge).

Their ranks have also grown. Once, a few people would support a hulking beast of a mainframe. Now, dozens (or hundreds) of personal computers and workstations must be supported, and there are almost as many system administrators as programmers. The change hasn't shown up in official statistics. In fact, the U.S. Bureau of Labor Statistics won't include system administrators in its widely-used occupational listings until 1998 or 1999, even though they have been around for more than ten years.

Software Diversity

Software has become far more diverse, as individual computers have become more complex—and especially as those computers have been networked.

Operating systems (system software) have evolved to meet this growing complexity. Today's computers may utilize multiple processors. They nearly all multi-task and multi-process, running several tasks at once. They're often multi-user, serving more than one user at a time. They may "thread" and "parallel process": they can break tasks into smaller units and outsource part of the work to other CPUs working concurrently.

It's no longer acceptable for computers to force humans to adapt to them, so computers have become more user-friendly and intuitive. Operating systems are giving way to operating environments which comprise both the operating system that keeps the computer running, as well as a "user-centered" environment.

Applications, too, have become more sophisticated. They reach out and touch other applications, other computers, other users. Software-to-software communications, called *protocols,* have grown in importance.

How *Cybercareers* Covers Technical Skills

Since yesterday's skill definitions don't reflect the new, more complex world of software and hardware, they're not used in this book. Instead, this book's coverage is built around the major distinction that exists in today's world of PCs, workstations, client/server environments, intranets and the Internet.

This distinction is between *development* and *support.*

These are separate but equal skill sets. For example, the development environment requires the same perfectionism and attention to detail it always has. Some aspects of development are changing to reflect an increased focus on "the big picture," but relatively few jobs focus heavily on issues like design, planning, maintainability, and reusability.

Support professionals have no choice *but* to consider design, planning, maintainability and reusability, as they face integrating dozens, hundreds or thousands of variables. Support roles require a *managed chaos* mindset.

In this chapter, you'll also learn about technology differences that will impact your career options, such as the difference between standalone and networked operating systems and applications.

In Cybercareers, technical skills mean *transferable* skills, not just specific areas of knowledge like Windows NT or C++ expertise. If you focus on a single area of knowledge without developing transferable skills, you'll likely find yourself obsolete early in your career.

Technical Support Skillsets

Until recently, technical support skills haven't had the attention and prestige of technical development skills. No technical support career path existed: it doesn't take many people or a complex organization to support a mainframe. But with PCs, workstations and complex networks, that's changed. It takes more people with more skills to support such an environment. Today, the biggest hurdles in preparing for a technical support career are:

- **Lack of Formal Education:** While technical development careers have the Electrical Engineer (EE) and Computer Science (CS) degrees, and technical management has the Management of Information Services (MIS) degree as a career path, technical support still doesn't have a formal degree program. To this day, universities and colleges don't offer 4-year technical support degree programs. They usually *do* offer certificates and two year degree programs. This obstacle hasn't seemed to harm many technical support people though. A SANS salary survey has shown that UNIX system administrators with no college or a two year degree are actually paid *better* than their peers with a 4-year degree or even more formal education.

*People may have succeeded without a formal degree but **not** without education or experience. Technical support positions require very highly trained personnel.*

Long-term, lack of education is not an option for success.

- **Lack of Equivalent Pay:** Compared with developers, technical support people were traditionally underpaid. One significant reason: many technical support roles have been held disproportionately by women. In some circles, support jobs have been called "pink-collar" work. This, too, is changing. The SANS salary survey now shows that UNIX system administrators are now equal or slightly higher in pay than equivalent programmers.

- **Lack of a Formal Career Path:** Once, technical support wasn't a career: it was a waystation towards becoming a programmer or MIS manager. Now, technical support *can be* a career. It can take many years to advance from entry-level administrator or operator work to senior-level support positions that handle only the complex problems front-line personnel can't resolve. Even senior-level support staff have career options. They can follow the classic management path that has existed for decades. Or they may remain technically-focused, by pursuing an *architect* role where they design elements of a company's computing infrastructure.

- **Lack of Specialty:** Technical support positions aren't specialty positions. While developers might work in only a few languages and technologies, e.g., C++ and databases, companies generally have many hardware and software combinations to support. The number of possible combinations and interactions can be overwhelming.

In my ten years in technical support, I worked on twenty different hardware platforms, more than ten different operating systems (more than twenty if you count variants of UNIX as individual operating systems), and over ninety different applications and services. That's slightly broader experience than my typical peer. *But those just starting out today will encounter even more diverse systems and will need even broader experience.* It's impossible for the non-savant to support environments this diverse through rigid procedures and rote learning: you'll need strong broader, transferable "principle-based" skills as well.

In the rest of this chapter, you'll learn about both the specific technologies you may encounter as you're getting started, *and* the principle-based skills you'll need to assimilate new technologies as they come along.

A Closer Look at Technical Support Skills

Technical support jobs have a patchwork quilt of skill requirements. There's no way to formally declare that a person with *X* title will use *Y* set of skills in their daily work. However, there are general skillset categories you can use to train and plan for technical support work.

You can also think of support skills as having two levels of sophistication: support for standalone systems, and network support. These are similar in many respects, but network support work tends to be more complex.

Here are the primary skill categories for system-level and network-level technical support:

System Level Skills

- Hardware Support Skills
- Operating System (OS) Support Skills
- Application Support Skills

Network Level Skills

- Network Infrastructure Support Skills
- Network Operating System (NOS) Support Skills
- Service Support Skills

Hardware Support Skills

As hardware has changed, so has hardware support. Twenty years ago, virtually every computer had its own operating system, and virtually every operating system ran on only one computer or family of computers. Hardware manufacturers supplied buyers with both the hardware and the operating system.

The PC changed all that. Hardware rapidly became interchangeable. If, a decade ago, you wanted to upgrade your PC's 20 megabyte hard disk to a 40 megabyte model, you could choose your supplier—as long as your new drive used the "MFM" standard most PCs supported at the time.

This new *openness* drove down prices, and led to the extraordinary growth of the personal computer marketplace. Companies like Sun Microsystems extended this "open systems" philosophy to high-powered workstations. Sun built its systems with off-the-shelf components—not products manufactured specifically for one hardware platform.

Today, a wide range of hardware can be used with a wide range of software. For example, systems built with PowerPC microprocessors can run a couple variants of the UNIX operating system, a few variants of the Windows operating environment and the Macintosh operating system.

Nowadays, companies rarely maintain a separate hardware support staff. Therefore, all computer support people must have *some* basic hardware support skills. Knowledge of hardware is also required for those who make equipment purchasing decisions.

Much has changed, but computers are still comprised of central processing units (CPUs), input/output (I/O) buses, peripheral device controllers, peripheral devices and memory—regardless of who makes them. These devices are typically standardized. The specific technical knowledge you may need corresponds to the standards in use where you want to work.

Specific Areas of Technical Knowledge

There are literally hundreds of areas of hardware knowledge; those listed here are the most important *today*, and those expected to have a significant future.

CPUs

A company's choice of CPUs is often a useful "shorthand" that helps you understand the type of computers it uses. This choice limits the other technology choices a company is likely to make. For example, knowing that a company has built its computing infrastructure around Intel 80x86 systems tells you it makes heavy use of one of the Windows operating systems; likely uses business "office suite" applications like Microsoft Office, and quite possibly utilizes custom development software like Microsoft's Visual Basic, Visual C++, or comparable Borland products.

- **Intel/80x86 CPUs:** The most popular CPU line was invented by Intel, which still dominates its market. This line began with the 8086 chip and has progressed through the Pentium Pro and Pentium II chips. Since the first four generations of these chips were named 8086, 80286, 80386 and 80486, this line is widely known as the 80x86 line. IBM chose a slower version of the 8086, the 8088, for its first IBM PC systems. When IBM PCs were cloned, the clone systems used the same chips, so they could run the same software. You'll sometimes encounter the terms Intel-compatible or IBM-compatible; all these terms refer to the same types of systems. In combination with the Microsoft Windows family of operating systems, these are sometimes called "Wintel" systems.

- **PowerPC CPUs:**   The PowerPC chip was created in a joint project between IBM and Apple, and is used in several newer computer systems, notably the Power Macintosh line of Apple computers.

- **SPARC CPUs:**   SPARC chips were developed by Sun Microsystems and are used in Sun workstations and servers, and in Sun clone computers.

- **Alpha CPUs:**   The Alpha chip was developed by Digital Equipment Corporation (DEC). It is the fastest CPU now available, though this may not always translate into the fastest real-world system performance. Alpha CPUs may be found in Digital workstations running Digital UNIX or Windows NT, and in a small number of third-party systems.

CPU buses

CPU buses handle the communications between CPUs and the other devices on the system; they can dramatically impact system performance. Add-in cards created for one bus generally cannot be used on systems that use another bus.

- **PCI:**   PCI was developed by Intel and is now used widely on both Intel and PowerPC platforms.

- **ISA:**   ISA is the original PC bus standard that dates back to IBM's "PC AT." ISA slots can still be found in virtually all PCs today, though IBM and Microsoft's NetPC initiative promises to eliminate it in some business PCs.

- **SBUS:**   Sbus is used on RISC workstations, notably Sun Sparc systems.

I/O buses

- **SCSI:**   SCSI is a generic I/O bus that allows easy, fast connections among multiple devices, including disks, CD-ROMs, printers, and scanners. SCSI is used by all major computer platforms.

- **IDE:**   IDE is a PC I/O bus standard, used primarily for low-cost hard disks and CD-ROM drives.

- **VME:**   VME is a dinosaur of a standard, previously used in UNIX systems and still in use in some locations.

Skills Needed in Hardware Support

Apprentice level skills

- **Install cards, chips and cabling**—Installing parts is fairly easy. Most boards and cables are designed to go together in only one way. Many people can learn the basics of assembling hardware in a few days.

Journeyman level skills

- **Configure addressing on hardware**—PC support often requires an understanding of how to make many devices "cooperate" in the same computer. This can mean manually configuring DMA, I/O addresses, IRQs and SCSI addresses to ensure that devices don't conflict with each other. Even recent "plug-and-play" technologies leave much to be desired. Technicians find they must often override automatic settings, in part due to the incredible diversity of hardware on the market. One can argue that plug-and-play may even make life harder for the professionals who now must know how to override it.

- **Resolve addressing conflicts on hardware**—Just as configuring hardware is important, it's equally important to know how to resolve conflicts others may have introduced.

- **Resolve common problems**—Addressing conflicts aren't the only problem. Isolating problems brought on by common (and sometimes uncommon) wear and tear represents a considerable portion of the troubleshooting effort.

- **Test system configuration**—It's important to know how to test computers to determine whether they're working properly—or why they may not be.

- **Specify system configuration requirements**—Knowing what parts go with what other parts is very important when specifying system configurations. This is much an art as a science at this point, due to the complexity of combining hardware from multiple vendors into a single system that will work as a coherent unit.

Master level skills

- **Troubleshoot novel problems**—Many problems are common. If you've seen it fixed once, you can easily fix it again yourself. But finding and fixing a problem for the first time is much harder. It takes a good grasp of theory, *and* a logical problem solving approach. Often, the best approach is isolate a problem into smaller and smaller sections, and eventually to a single component. This requires practical reasoning skills that not everyone has mastered.

Hardware Educational Requirements

Several training vendors offer "PC" troubleshooting and repair courses. Some junior colleges and vocational schools offer old-fashioned, "board-level" troubleshooting and configuration courses, which teach how to isolate problems that can be solved by replacing boards. Unfortunately, most junior colleges and vocational schools still offer "component-level" training, which teaches how to replace electronic components such as chips, resistors and capacitors. Since it is now almost always more cost-effective to replace a board rather than repair it, component-level training is of little use to most computer support professionals today.

Training to support 80x86-based systems is offered by many sources. Training on other CPU lines is typically available only from the manufacturer, though this may change.

Some examples of vendor training to use as a guideline are:

- Data-Tech Institute—Data-Tech offers seminars, video training and computer-based training (CBT) including *Troubleshooting and Maintaining PC's.*

- Learning Tree International—Learning Tree offers a couple of PC hardware seminars *including Hands-On PC Configuration and Troubleshooting*. (This course can be transferred to some colleges for credit. It is also a preparatory class for the A+ Certification exam, discussed in more detail shortly.)

Certification is Available Too

Sylvan Prometric offers exams for several certification programs:

- Level 2 Certification—Level 2 certification, a hardware-only certification program, is offered by the National Association of Personal Computer Owners (NAPCO). Information can be acquired from NAPCO in the U.S. at 1-800 962-7261 or from Sylvan Prometric at 1-800-967-1100.

- A+ Certification—A+ certification, a hardware and operating system certification program, is offered by the Computing Technology Industry Association (CompTIA). Information can be acquired from CompTIA at (708) 268-1818 ext. 301, or from Sylvan Prometric at 1-800-967-1100.

- Vendor Certification—AST, Compaq and Epson have certification programs specifically for their hardware. Again, call Sylvan Prometric for information.

Experience

- Experience can be gained on the job at many companies.

- Some large computer stores hire people to assemble new computers and troubleshoot customer problems.

- Experience can also be gained through volunteer work with agencies like CompuMentor.

Hot Areas

The main areas that will continue to have needs long term are:

- **Computers based upon the 80x86 CPU line:**   As of 1996, almost 200 million 80x86-compatible computers are in use; by 1999, this number should grow to over 300 million.

- **PCI peripheral bus:**   While PCI was invented by Intel for 80x86 systems, it's becoming the accepted standard bus for many hardware vendors using many types of processors.

- **A new type of computers, often referred to as "network appliances" or "network computers" is on the horizon:**   This is a type of computer that may replace the diskless workstations and X-terminals of today. Notwithstanding the hype, relatively few network computers are now in place, and many industry analysts believe there will be no more than 1-2 million network computers running by the Year 2000. Still, there is good reason to expect this to be a growing portion of the business workplace within five years. Keep an eye out for this.

Operating System Support Skills

Operating system (OS) support is the heart of many technical support positions. The operating system, sometimes referred to as the system software, is the intermediary that controls a computer's hardware. Most application software is written to run on specific operating systems, not specific hardware. Operating systems are far more standardized now than even ten years ago; however, several aggressive competitors still exist.

If you understand the basic principles of operating systems and OS support, it's much easier to deliver support regardless of the OS your organization uses. For example, once you know how most operating systems handle printing, it's easy to learn how to print from a Microsoft Windows 3.x system even if you've rarely used one.

Specific Areas of Technical Knowledge

Many operating systems have been around for decades, and are dying a slow death, to be replaced by one of a few families of modern operating systems.

Two operating system families will continue to grow into the 21st century: UNIX and Microsoft Windows. The Macintosh computer will hold its own for the measurable future, but jobs for people who only know the Mac environment won't be that common.

On the horizon are the network appliances. Their operating systems are still in the dreaming and defining stages for the moment. They are likely to be a significant area to learn in the mid-term future, but not a contender for the short-term future.

Keep an eye on the Network Computer trend.

UNIX Operating System family

UNIX is more complex than Windows, and not surprisingly, UNIX technical support people usually make more money than Windows support people. UNIX isn't as widespread as Windows, so fewer UNIX support positions are available. Nonetheless, there is a significant and growing demand for UNIX personnel.

UNIX is coming to fill the "mission-critical" role that mainframes once held exclusively. In today's corporation, UNIX is commonly the server

OS in a client-server environment. Many people also use UNIX as a desktop operating system for scientific and high-end CAD (Computer-Assisted Drafting) work.

The history of UNIX

UNIX was developed at Bell Laboratories in the early 1970's. It has a long and colorful history and many variations. Bell Labs chose to license the UNIX OS to many colleges and universities throughout the 70's, and to extend the OS in-house. This in-house version went through many revisions and eventually became known as UNIX *System V.* Meanwhile, the University of California at Berkeley developed a variant that also became very popular, called *BSD* (Berkeley Standard Distribution).

In the early 1980's, UNIX was used on many vendors' platforms. Most vendors either licensed System V directly from AT&T (Bell Labs' parent at the time), or the BSD version from Berkeley. People became very attached to the version of UNIX they ran, and were often known as "System five bigots" or "BSD bigots."

This schism caused concern in the UNIX community. AT&T and Sun Microsystems, then the largest BSD reseller, partnered to develop UNIX System V Release 4, or SVR4. Many other UNIX vendors worried that this partnership could lead to favoritism in license pricing, and set out to create their own next-generation UNIX, called OSF/1. Thus UNIX remained split into two main camps.

In response to Microsoft's introduction of the powerful Windows NT, UNIX vendors formed another consortium to merge the differences in their UNIX variants. This alliance became known as COSE.

To date, COSE has had little impact: most UNIX variants are still based on System V, BSD, SVR4, or OSF. While UNIX system administration is fairly consistent among variants, transitions among different flavors of UNIX can still be very difficult. Sun Microsystems has found that almost half of its customers have been unwilling to switch to SVR4, forcing Sun to continue supporting a BSD variant.

UNIX Futures

The future of the UNIX support person is bright. Demand continues to outstrip supply, and the Internet's rapid growth may exacerbate this for at least a few more years. A total growth rate of about 60% is expected between 1996 and 1999.

UNIX Professional Associations

These major UNIX professional associations offer venues to share experience, as well as extensive training opportunities:

USENIX—(UNIX and Advanced Computing Systems Technical and Professional Association) `http://www.usenix.org/`

SAGE (System Administrator's Guild), a subgroup of USENIX— `http://www.usenix.org/sage/`

There are also many vendor-specific user's groups. Contact individual UNIX vendors for more information about groups in your area.

Windows Operating System Family

In the early 1980s, Microsoft developed an operating system for IBM and compatible PCs, called Disk Operating System (DOS). DOS still exists, but in the late 1980's Microsoft recognized the need for a graphical user interface (GUI) that would make its operating system easier to use.

To meet this need, Microsoft created Windows. Windows went through several incarnations; by the early 1990's it had evolved to Windows 3.1, the version that still predominates on corporate desktops today.

In the long run, people were moving away from command line based operating systems. To meet that need, Microsoft developed the Windows NT operating system. NT is both an operating system and a GUI together which makes it an *operating environment*.

While NT provided many server features, NT did not replace the DOS/Windows 3.1x combination as the primary choice for the desktop. Microsoft then created a client operating environment called Windows 95 as the low-end "client" solution for Windows-based infrastructures. Both Windows NT and Windows 95 are "32-bit" environments, and they run much of the same 32-bit software.

Windows Futures

The DOS/Windows 3.1x combination is still common and won't die out for a few more years. Nonetheless, the future is in the true 32-bit Windows environments, Windows NT and Windows 95. Demand for Windows NT trained professionals should rise by more than 50% between 1996 and 1999.

Microsoft Professional Association

There are many different Microsoft user groups. Visit (`http://www.microsoft.com/usa/`) to find one close to you. Also visit `www.microsoft.com/syspro`, the home page for Microsoft system professionals, and `www.microsoft.com/msdn`, the Microsoft Developer's Network.

Primary Skills Required in Tech Support

Operating system technical support skills may be divided into classes of procedures, or by the level of experience you're likely to need.

Classes of procedures

- **Install**—Install system software

- **Install**—Install network access on client systems

- **Install**—Add peripheral device software

- **Configure**—Configure network access on client system

- **Configure**—Configure system software

- **Disk or Filesystem Management**—Manage file permissions. Most single-user computer systems have file permissions that can restrict a user's ability to access or delete files—even DOS. Because only one person typically uses a DOS or Windows 3.x system, permissions are almost irrelevant. Nonetheless, system files must sometimes be protected from the novice user who might inadvertently damage them.

- **Disk or Filesystem Management**—Manage disk/filesystem preparation, usage, repair and archiving where appropriate. Archiving and backing up data are critical tasks, even though they're often considered menial, and done poorly. Disaster recovery is also critical: it's estimated that over 50 percent of all companies don't have adequate disaster recovery plans, and are at risk of bankruptcy in the event of a serious natural disaster.

- **Theory**—Demonstrate knowledge of standards and basic operations that operating systems are based upon.

- **Troubleshoot**—Resolve common operating system problems.

- **Troubleshoot**—Test setup and troubleshoot novel problems with system software. As noted earlier, senior technical support people must know how to break a system down into elements and isolate problems—and to do so, they must have substantial practical reasoning and problem solving skills.

- **Architect**—Plan capacity requirements for client systems: At most companies, the need for computing power, disk space, and software tools grows constantly—while budgets don't. Forecasting hardware and software requirements is critical. An architect must be able to deliver accurate short and long-term forecasts of requirements and features growth.

- **Architect**—Architect the infrastructure for the client systems: Anticipating the components you'll need is only half the battle. The other half is knowing how (and whether) those components will fit together.

- **Architect**—Develop disaster recovery plans: Disaster recovery is far more than maintaining regular backups. It involves planning for contingencies, and having an action plan available when the worst happens.

Experience Levels

Apprentice Level Skills

- Install system software
- Install network access on client systems
- Configure network access on client system
- Manage file permissions

Journeyman Level Skills

- Add peripheral device software
- Configure system software
- Manage disk/filesystem preparation, usage, repair and archiving where used
- Resolve common operating system problems

Master Level Skills

- Plan capacity requirements for client systems
- Architect the infrastructure for the client systems
- Demonstrate knowledge of standards and basic operations that the operating system is based upon
- Test setup and troubleshoot novel problems with system software
- Develop disaster recovery plans

Education

Some colleges and universities are starting to offer UNIX system administration and Windows support training. You can use the following examples as "benchmarks" to help identify what kind of training you need:

- Examine the training offered for the UNIX System Administrator certificate program at the University of California at Santa Cruz Extension training. (`http://www.ucsc-extension.edu/unex/ certs/unixadchart.html`). This is excellent core training that you can measure other programs against.

- Examine the requirements for the Microsoft Certified Systems Engineer certification program for the core set of courses recommended. (`http://www.microsoft.com/Train_Cert/mcp/ certstep/mcse.htm`)

Most vendors offer UNIX operating system support training for their specific variant of UNIX. Many independent training companies offer UNIX and Windows courses including:

- Learning Tree International
- American Research Group

Certification

Certification is available for many programs including:

- A+ Certification—A+ certification, a hardware and operating system certification program offered by the Computing Technology Industry Association (CompTIA). For information, call CompTIA at (708) 268-1818 ext. 301, or contact Sylvan Prometric.

- IBM AIX System Administrator or AIX Support Professional—For information, call IBM in the U.S. at 1-800 426-8322, or (`http://www.austin.ibm.com/services/aixcert`) or contact Sylvan Prometric.

- UNIX Systems Certified Professional or Certified PC Service and Support Professional from Learning Tree International—For information, call Learning Tree International, or contact Sylvan Prometric.

- Microsoft Certified Systems Engineer—For information, call Microsoft at 1-800-636-7544 or visit (`http://www.microsoft.com/ Train_Cert/mcp/certstep/mcse.htm`)

- SCO ACE or ACE+ Certification—For information, call SCO at 1-800-726-8649 or (`http://www.sco.com/ Training/ace/acenotes.html`)

- Certified Solaris System Administrator
  —For information, call Sun at 1-800-422-8020 or
  (http://www.sun.com/sunservice/suned/catalog/csa.html)
- PCA (PC Administrator)—PCA certification is offered from WIFI, the educational division of the Austrian Chamber of Commerce. The test is given in German. Ask about the availability of the test in French and English. For information, call Drake Testing in Germany 49 (0)211 500 99-0

Experience

At many companies, you can gain on-the-job experience you can use to work yourself into operating system support:

- Interns or temporary employees are hired for special projects such as operating system upgrades or system moves. Contact temporary employment agencies or professional associations to find these jobs.
- Start as a backup operator—a person who runs backups on computer systems and networks. (However, backup operator positions are becoming less common. And try not to be offended if someone calls you a *tape ape*.)
- Start in a telephone support (a.k.a. *help desk*) position. At first, you may simply be answering phone calls and typing contact information into the call tracking database. As you become more familiar with the OS, you can answer more questions; if you're also taking courses, you can develop your knowledge very rapidly.
- Many students have acquired experience working in their school computer labs.
- Many women have worked their way up from secretarial or administrative assistant roles. (I haven't heard of any guys doing this, but tell me if you know any.) It's common for an administrative assistant to create a user account for a new employee as part of the new hire process, or to fix a printer problem when no one else is available.

- Trainees are more likely to be hired in companies where there's already a senior level person available to train them. Since there are typically 50-100 computers per system support person, don't expect small companies to hire you as a trainee or "junior" support staffer.
- You can also get experience through volunteer work with agencies like CompuMentor, or in your local schools.

Hot Areas

Windows: For technical support staff, Windows 95 and Windows NT are very good long-term opportunities.
UNIX: There are dozens of UNIX vendors, and opportunities with many different variants of UNIX.

- Sun Microsystems stands out as the number one Internet UNIX server company. Experience with Sun's Solaris operating system is very valuable; Solaris system administrations are in high demand, especially on both coasts.

- HP is another large UNIX company. Demand for HP UNIX System Administrators is second only to demand for Solaris System Administrators. Demand is higher on the west coast of the US than on the east coast.

- Silicon Graphics (SGI) is making major inroads at multimedia companies that use UNIX.

- Surprisingly, shareware versions of UNIX, especially Linux and BSDI, have become extremely popular, especially as Internet servers.

- If you can demonstrate expertise in *multiple* versions of UNIX, you'll be preferred over those with experience in only one UNIX variant.

Keep an eye out for network appliances and their associated operating systems.

Applications Support Skills

The operating system is only one small element of the software that people use. Thousands of applications are available. Most companies will need to support at least a word processor, a spreadsheet, and one or two software packages devoted to workflow, such as a billing or a manufacturing tracking package.

Specific Areas of Technical Knowledge

Applications can be grouped into several general categories. While dozens of vendors may offer applications in each category, this section will focus on the most popular offerings, the ones with the greatest market share.

Word processing/publishing applications

Word processing is a core competency for *everyone* working in cyberspace.

Beyond basic word processing, some professional level skills are required for anyone that writes or in some way publishes for a living. Desktop publishing is an extension of word processing that adds layout control not traditionally found in word processing programs (though this distinction is blurring as word processing software improves).

A third area of interest is HTML publishing tools: both HTML editors and HTML conversion tools.

The most common word processing and desktop publishing applications are Microsoft Word, Adobe Framemaker, Corel WordPerfect, and Quark Xpress. Dozens of HTML authoring and conversion tools exist, for users of widely varying experience.

Spreadsheet applications

Spreadsheets are flexible tools for a wide variety of financial tracking, processing and forecasting applications. Companies use spreadsheets for everything from sales reporting and expense reports to complex custom applications. Microsoft Excel, Lotus 1-2-3, Wingz and Quattro Pro are among the preeminent spreadsheets.

Graphics/presentation applications

Presentation programs are often used by management, sales people and trainers. They provide an efficient way to create and modify slide shows, overheads, and even simple multimedia programs.

Microsoft PowerPoint is the leading presentation program; others include Freelance Graphics and Harvard Graphics. However, the Web itself is fast becoming a presentation medium. Presenters now have access to presentations built on HTML pages, and can even deliver presentations stored on the Internet rather than a notebook PC hard drive.

Additional business applications (accounting, project management, decision making)

Many other business-specific software tools are available. Project management software, discussed earlier in this book, enables managers to plan and track the status of their projects. Accounting software is used to maintain books and track account information. Executives use decision support software that helps analyze the company's raw data, identify trends, and support strategic decision-making.

In project management software, "shrink-wrapped" packages like Microsoft Project and Symantec TimeLine are common. However, for mission-critical financial, planning and human resources software, most large companies use highly customized solutions. These may be based on expensive packages like Oracle Financials or SAP R/3.

Local Helper applications or plug-in accessories

Increasingly, Web browsers are becoming a dominant desktop application; they can provide integrated access to a wide variety of applications on both intranets and the Internet. Today's Web browsers have "open" architectures: their features can be extended with "helper" or "plug-in" accessories from a variety of software developers. For example, plug-ins may be used to increase the number of media types a browser can view. (Plug-ins are sometimes also used to extend the capabilities of photo editing and desktop publishing software.) Dozens of helper/plug-in applications are available, varying widely among OS and hardware platforms.

Personal information management applications

Contact management software is critical to sales forces, and to other employees who must maintain extensive relationships with people outside the company. Calendaring and task management packages are becoming common, as well. Many programs are available, notably Lotus Organizer and Microsoft Outlook for the PC

Department or enterprise-wide phonebooks are becoming a network services tool. They're maintained not by individual users, but through corporate Name and Directory Services mentioned in Network Opersating System Support.

Communications applications

The World Wide Web and e-mail are becoming the core communications tools of the intranet. You'll learn about these later in this chapter, when we discuss networked applications.

Standalone system communications tools include modem communications software, fax and fax-back programs, voicemail and voice response systems, and bulletin boards. In these categories, market leaders tend to change frequently, and the Internet will eventually obsolete many of these tools.

Custom applications

Companies often write their own custom applications for various business requirements. Each is largely unique, though they may be based on common development or database platforms.

Skills

Apprentice Level Skills

- Install application

Journeyman Level Skills

- Configure application
- Demonstrate in-depth usage by mentoring users

Master Level Skills

- Troubleshoot novel problems
- Evaluate new products

Education

Education is available for many standard applications at community colleges, vocational schools, continuing education departments of colleges and universities, and education vendors, including many stores where the applications are sold. There are also hundreds of books, self-paced and CBT (Computer-Based Training) classes available for the leading applications.

Certification

Microsoft offers the Microsoft Certified Product Specialist program for its applications. For information, contact Microsoft on the web at
`http://www.microsoft.com/Train_Cert/mcp/`
`certstep/mcse.htm`

Experience

Experience is usually gained by using the tools, or by providing front-line support via a phone support line or helpdesk.

Hot Areas

Word processing programs are and will continue to be a core application area. HTML authoring and conversion are here to stay. For your own personal development, consider learning to use scheduling tools to manage your work day. You may not have to support other users with these tools, but they can help you manage your own task load, create your personal work history, and track your experiences.

Network Infrastructure Support Skills

A network has many different elements. There are the cables that physically connect it. There are also the network devices that join various network segments together, including hubs, switches, routers and bridges. Each piece of hardware speaks specific protocols or communications languages. In most cases, all you need is basic knowledge of the protocols these devices use to communicate with each other.

Network communications is a complex field. For convenience, network protocols have been organized into "layers," or areas of responsibility. The most widely-used model for understanding network communications is called Open Systems Interconnection; it divides communication into seven distinct layers.

Application
Presentation
Session
Transport
Network
Data Link
Physical

Figure 9–1 Open Sysems Interconnection

In reality, few networking technologies map perfectly to the seven-layer model, and there are many other important factors you'll need to understand. But you'll encounter this model constantly, so now's a good time to learn it.

Each layer has a different role and utilizes different protocols and standards. (For example, FTP communications might be layered atop Ethernet networks built on coaxial cable.) The most important networking standards include:

- Ethernet with twisted pair cable based on the IEEE 802.4 standard 802.4, which combines the Physical and Data Link layers.

- The IP standard of TCP/IP (handled at the Network layer)

- The TCP standard of TCP/IP (handled at the Transport layer)
- RPC or Remote Procedure Calls, a session layer standard that serves as "traffic controller" for all network services, including Web, FTP and disk sharing
- File Transfer Protocol (FTP), an application layer protocol standard.

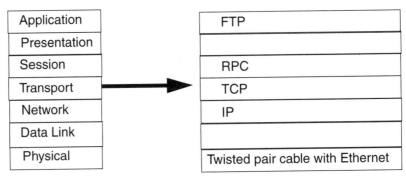

Figure 9–2 Network protocols

As you can see, understanding network protocols means diving into acronym soup. Start by reviewing some case studies describing how the protocols are used, and which tools are available to test and troubleshoot networks that use them.

Nowadays, TCP/IP (the combination of TCP at the Transport layer and IP at the Network Layer) is the most popular network protocol. It's the basis for the Internet, and rapidly becoming the defacto standard for most If you expect to support Windows 3.x environments as well, you need to understand the basics of working with "multiple protocol stacks" on the same computer. This is a tricky area, where expertise is of real value.

Specific Areas of Technical Expertise

Standards and Protocols include:

- Ethernet
- Token Ring
- Wireless
- ISDN–ISDN is a digital service provided by telephone companies which allows for higher-speed communication than typical analog modems; the ISDN protocols cover the bottom 3 layers, physical, data link and network protocols.

- FDDI–FDDI is a 100 mb (megabit) fiber-based LAN protocol that's been widely used for the past several years in engineering and technical applications, but is now facing significant competition from Fast Ethernet, Gigabit Ethernet and ATM. The FDDI protocol covers the physical layer with a token ring datalink layer running at a speed of 100 mb (megabit).

- T-1–T-1 was originally a phone company standard for transmitting multiple channels of information across a single 2-pair copper cable. This was adapted to send a stream of data at 1.5M (megabit). Since then, T-1 lines have also been widely used by companies that need to connect local area networks into wide area networks.

- X.25 has increasingly been supplanted by faster technologies such as frame relay, which gain much of their speed by relying on external hardware for error checking instead of providing it themselves. However, X.25 is still widely used in international applications where faster alternatives may not be available.

- PPP–PPP is similar to IP except that it is usually used on low-end computers for phone/modem communications.

- ATM is a set of protocols that are designed to provide high-speed communications. The physical layer is referred to as SONET in many cases, however, this standard is evolving.

Network devices:

- Modems
- Routers
- Bridges
- Hubs
- Switches

Skills

Apprentice Level Skills

- Install and terminate cable
- Test cables
- Monitor network for performance

Journeyman Level Skills

- Install communications hardware
- Configure communications hardware including modems, routers, gateways, repeaters and bridges
- Resolve common network problems
- Configure and evaluate results from network analyzer
- Monitor security reports and respond to incidents

Master Level Skills

- Demonstrate knowledge of protocol architecture
- Test configurations and troubleshoot novel problems
- Develop disaster recovery plans
- Design network topology

Education

It isn't hard to learn how to make and connect cables. After that, it's essential to learn some theory, even for common tasks like configuring a router. Starting with a couple of good basic network or data communications theory courses will pay big dividends when you go on to learn about specific technologies and protocols.

Networking education at institutions of higher learning varies widely in quality and relevance. Among the better courses are those offered at the University of California at Santa Cruz extension
(http://www.ucsc-extension.edu/unex/network/net.html)

The router, bridge and other network hardware vendors also offer training, of varying quality. One program is especially worth noting: the Cisco Certified Internetwork Expert (CCIE) program, offered by Cisco Systems, Inc., a market leader in networking equipment. For information, call Cisco at 1 (800) 553-6387 or
(http://www.cisco.com/warp/public/331/1.shtml).

Experience

You can get network infrastructure support experience from several sources:

- With the downsizing or reengineering of many voice telecommunications departments, there are opportunities in computer networking for some of the better people who are already familiar with cabling and telephone exchange hardware.

- Moving up from a cable contracting company is an option. It tends to work best if you have a lot of cable troubleshooting experience and can demonstrate the use of cable test equipment. If you can learn about cable troubleshooting and test equipment, you'll be more prepared for work at a major corporation. Once there, you can learn other skills to broaden your expertise and increase your value.

- As with other technical support skills, volunteer work benefits everyone. In addition to CompuMentor, there are several NetDay projects that need people who know how to lay cable, or are willing to learn. There's also a long tradition of using volunteers at Interop (now called Networld+Interop), the most fascinating networking trade show. This event's goal is to demonstrate that many network vendors' hardware can work together. The highlight of the show in the past has been the Connectithon which has tied together toasters, Coke machines, and spy-cam balloon camera combinations among its more unusual components. You can call Networld+Interop to volunteer to help string and connect the hundreds of miles of cable this major networking event requires. Of course, it doesn't hurt to volunteer for other computer related tradeshows either.

Hot Areas

There are several hot areas in network infrastructure:

- **Nomadic and Telecommuting:** Consider focusing on the technologies that are enabling the rapid increases in nomadic computing and telecommuting and the rapid growth of ISPs (Internet Service Providers), including ISDN, PPP, and modem skills.

- **Internet:** The Internet is based upon a wide range of network hardware and cabling. T-1 (E-1), T-3 (E-3) and Frame Relay will be good areas to get into for the measurable future.

- **Metropolitan Area Networks (MANs):** Corporate campus wide networks require high-speed connections today. ATM, FDDI, CDDI, and 100 megabit "Fast" Ethernet are all good areas to gain experience. These technologies are valuable now and may streamline the transition to tomorrow's next-generation Internet connections.

Network Operating System Support Skills

A Network Operating System or NOS is simply an operating system that controls hardware and schedules software on a network, so it can be used by multiple people. NOSes consist of:

- **Protocols for underlying communication**—As you've learned, computers communicate using protocols, and all computers on the same network must share the same protocols. You've learned that lower-level protocols handle the "physical" aspects of how bits get from Point A to Point B. Network operating systems work at higher levels, especially the transport and application layer.

- **Network services**—In addition to controlling the communication between computers, Network Operating Systems also provide resources to clients: the computers and humans using the network. For example, NOSes may provide shared disk space, manage the use of shared printers, or enable shared Internet or modem connections. Since resources often must be restricted to authorized users, NOSes keep track of users requesting resources, either via lists of names on each server, or through a central Name Services or Directory Services repository.

- **Operating System software**—Like any other computer, a server must have an operating system that controls its hardware.

To support a network operating system, you need to become familiar with:

- Procedures for managing name and directory services.
- Resource sharing.
- How to design a client-server environment where resources can be optimally managed.
- User authentication and security—not just on individual servers, but throughout the enterprise.

You'll need a basic understanding of underlying protocols to troubleshoot problems and eliminate performance bottlenecks.

These basic skills are common across many different Network Operating Systems (NOS). Once you know the theory, you can look up the specific procedures in a manual, as you would with a desktop OS. The primary difference between desktop and network OSes is their breadth and complexity. While desktop OSes deal only with one system and its resources, NOSes deal with the client, the server, the interaction between the two, identification of specific users, *and* the management of common and user-specific resources.

At present, PC clients tend to use simple local operating systems plus a few extra programs to speak to the servers. Servers tend to run network operating systems which may use a different language or interface.

In the UNIX world there is little if any difference between a client and server OS: starting a few more programs at "boot time" easily turns a client into a server. Traditional PC OSes didn't have these innate abilities, though this is changing. Most Windows NT systems can become a server at will. Even Windows 95 provides peer-to-peer networking, though it isn't well-suited to act as a server.

Specific Areas of Technical Knowledge

To support network operating systems, you will need to understand many or all of the following technologies, protocols and standards:

- **TCP/IP**—The Internet runs on TCP/IP. TCP/IP will significantly change in the next few years as IPv6 or IPNG are introduced to support rapid growth in IP addresses. The most widely-discussed is Simple Network Management Protocol (SNMP), which helps companies manage multivendor networks.

- **Novell NetWare**—Still the market leading local area network operating system, but declining NetWare uses a proprietary transport level protocol called IPX. With new leadership, however, Novell's long-term strategic direction is also TCP/IP.

- **Microsoft Network**—Microsoft designed its network solution to be independent of underlying protocols. Microsoft's application level protocol, SMB, can run atop TCP/IP, IPX, Microsoft's NETBios, and other less common protocols.

- **Appletalk**— This is an Apple network protocol. Since Macintoshes are a minority, this area isn't destined to grow much.

- **Firewalls**—Firewalls provide network security by filtering network traffic, allowing only approved packets through. Firewalls are usually placed on a company's connection to the Internet to prevent public access of private corporate data.

- **Domain Name Service (DNS)**—DNS is a hierarchical name service that manages (only) IP addresses and names for TCP/IP networks. It's the Internet's core naming service. More complete naming services are being proposed such as X.500, DAP and LDAP.

- **Network Information Services (NIS)**—Sun Microsystems' NIS, sometimes informally referred to as "yellow pages," is a multipurpose name service that can store user names, user groupings, system names, and customized data. NIS can only work within one TCP/IP subdomain, a significant limitation. When Sun recognized a need for a hierarchical name service, Sun created NIS+. Unlike NIS, which spread widely to third-party products, NIS+ has not been widely integrated. The Lightweight Directory Access Protocol (LDAP) is more widely hailed.

- **LDAP**— Lightweight Directory Access Protocol is a simplified version of DAP (Directory Access Protocol). Netscape is implementing it as part of its suite of network support items. Microsoft is also moving quickly to support this. LDAP performs many of the functions of NIS, and even some beyond NIS, because it overcomes NIS' hierarchical limitations.

- **Simple Network Management Protocol (SNMP)**—SNMP is an application protocol that enables network administrators to manage components of a network (bridges, routers, systems, etc.) remotely, so they can manage a wide area network centrally.

Skills

Apprentice Level Skills

- Install server operating system
- Install network access on client system
- Configure network access on client system
- Control access to resources
- Manage server contents (including archives)
- Log server activity and generate reports of activity

Journeyman Level Skills

- Configure server operating system
- Add peripheral device software
- Integrate network gateways with other protocols

- Monitor performance of server
- Manage security on server
- Manage user accounts, authorization and data access on server
- Resolve common network operating system problems
- Manage naming and directory services

Master Level Skills

- Plan capacity requirements for server
- Define processing requirements for server
- Architect the infrastructure for the server
- Demonstrate knowledge of standards that the network operating system and network topology are based upon
- Test setup and troubleshoot novel problems with network and server software
- Develop disaster recovery plans

Education

Junior colleges and vocational schools offer more NOS-related programs than four-year colleges and universities, but some colleges and universities do offer network management certificates through their continuing education programs.

Most vendors offer courses or authorize others to provide training for their NOS products. and support certificate programs for their NOS products. The best way to find out about these courses is to contact your NOS vendor. Independent training vendors also offer courses on a wide range of NOSes.

Certification

- Certified Banyan Specialist (CBS) and Certified Banyan Engineer (CBE) programs are offered by Banyan for its network products. For more information, call Banyan in the U.S. at 1(508) 898-1795.
- Certified Local Area Network Professional, Certified Wide Area Network Professional and Certified Internetworking Professional programs are offered by Learning Tree International.

- Certified Novell Administrator (CNA), Certified Novell Engineer (CNE), and Master Certified Novell Engineer (Master CNE) programs are offered by Novell. For more information, visit `http://education.novell.com/`

- Netware Certified Professional program is offered by Learning Tree International.

Novell was the first vendor to provide certification, and has offered the CNE (Certified Novell Engineer) program for many years. Nowadays, "CNE" isn't just a certificate—it's a job title. Obtaining other Novell certification often isn't considered equivalent.

- TCP/IP Certified Professional program is offered by Learning Tree International.

- Windows NT Systems and Networks Certified Professional programs are offered by Learning Tree International.

- Microsoft Certified Systems Engineer program is offered from Microsoft. For information, visit `http://www.microsoft.com/Train_Cert/mcp/certstep/mcse.htm`

Experience

- Network support people tend to work their way up from system support roles, taking courses and passing certification tests along the way.

- A few people start out doing network cabling and work their way into network support roles.

- Some students get experience in the networked computer labs at their schools.

- You can gain experience through volunteer work with agencies like CompuMentor, or at your local schools.

Hot Areas

Novell's NetWare has been the preeminent PC network NOS for many years. It will continue to be popular, but its influence will shrink. Today, customers prefer TCP/IP-based single protocol solutions that easily accommodate generic intranet products. The change will happen slowly: less than 40 percent of MIS managers expect to move to a single network plan before the end of 1998.

Microsoft designed its NOS to be independent of underlying transport layer protocols. This was smart strategy: now Microsoft's resource sharing and name and directory services can run in conjunction with whatever underlying network is already in place. This makes Microsoft's network a good long-term option for network professionals.

TCP/IP is the winning transport protocol. Its penetration will increase significantly in the next few years with the advent of widespread intranets. Some companies will move entirely to TCP/IP; others will maintain TCP/IP and one other protocol.

You'll have the most options if you understand TCP/IP. You'll be even better off if you're trained in both UNIX and Microsoft network implementations of TCP/IP, so you can handle the inherent idiosyncrasies of multiple protocol stacks.

Service Support Skills

As networks evolved, multi-user applications arose. These applications separated the client and server components, and made for more complex administration.

Specific Areas of Technical Knowledge

On first glance, there are several types of multi-user applications, each requiring specialized technical knowledge. These include databases, intranets, e-mail systems, groupware, and other types of software.

When you look under the hood, however, they're all very much alike.

The core element of a database is data. It is input, stored, retrieved for reports and maintained by administrative personnel.

The core element of a first generation intranet Web is the hypertext or multimedia file. It is input by a document owner, stored by a gatekeeper, retrieved by an end user and maintained by an administrative person.

A posting or file is the core element of both e-mail and netnews. The posting is input by the user, stored and forwarded by computer programs, retrieved by end users and maintained by an administrative staff.

Various types of files are the core element of groupware. These files are input by one or more people. This input can be simultaneous if they are collaborating in real time, or in sequence if they are working offline. The files are stored; then retrieved, modified and reinput by co-workers. Maintenance is performed by an administrative staff.

As you can see, while the types of information may be different, and the individuals who can access it may be different, the overall processes, concepts and principles are largely the same.

Let's take a closer look at each type of network service.

E-Mail

The World Wide Web (WWW) may be the most popular service on the Internet and many intranets, but e-mail is the bread and butter of virtually every network. It's been around for years. Now, however, corporate e-mail systems have been extended to the Internet, and the same systems are being used increasingly for enhanced services such as complete "messaging solutions" a la Lotus Notes or Microsoft Exchange, which can do more than just route a message, but can also manage the entire "workflow" associated with forms processing.

Most corporate e-mail systems have been based on proprietary software such as:

- cc:Mail from Lotus

- Microsoft Mail from Microsoft

- Eudora as the client for Internet mail

There are three main e-mail application protocols:

- **Simple Mail Transfer Protocol (SMTP)**—SMTP has been used for many years for UNIX and general Internet e-mail. Sendmail is the core UNIX program for handling and forwarding e-mail. For years, it's been a running joke that you need an advanced degree to use and configure sendmail. However, a monumental tome from O'Reilly and several vendor classes have made sendmail somewhat less taxing.

- **Post Office Protocol (POP3)**—POP3 is an e-mail application protocol that enables clients who aren't always connected to the network (usually PCs) to connect to a server and retrieve e-mail. POP3 has been around for a while and many e-mail packages use it.

- **Internet Message Access Protocol (IMAP)**—IMAP is a newer Internet standard for e-mail.

Modern e-mail software does more than just send, receive and forward e-mail:

- Gateways convert e-mail from one type to another (i.e., from cc:Mail, a proprietary format, to SMTP e-mail).

- E-mail lists are automatically managed with e-mail list software. The main list management software packages are LISTSERV and Major-domo.

- *Autoresponders* return specific information when an e-mail is received.

E-mail administrators must be able to work with these tools as well as the basic mail system.

World Wide Web

The World Wide Web (WWW) is the most widely recognized service on the Internet. It is also the cornerstone of most intranets. The Web is composed of web servers; web clients (browsers and robots); gateways between web servers and internal databases or groupware; and often custom software.

Dozens of additional applications support web and intranet development, including:

- Document Management Tools: version control for documents, workflow for documents.

- Web Site Testing/Verification Tools.

- Web Replication Tools: Proxy servers, cache servers, and mirror servers.

- Web Administration Tools: logfile management, user management, performance tuning.

It's critical to understand that the Web's success is based upon its *transparency.* The most successful web server administrator will be the one who makes all server-related activities equally transparent and intuitive. Those who publish to the server shouldn't need to know what the docroot path is. Gatekeepers who review content shouldn't have to understand cryptic lint checking error files, or debug "Java class file not found" server log error message.

Databases

Databases hearken back to mainframe days. They have mission-critical roles in nearly all large companies, and a growing number of smaller companies.

Nonetheless, the core database support tasks are the same as they've always been. Administrators install the databases. Developers create applications for them. Data is routinely entered by end-users. Reports are routinely generated by managers. An administrator or support person handles maintenance functions, such as granting user accounts and access; backing up data; archiving old data; tuning the server for performance; and troubleshooting.

Netnews

Netnews is a communication tool. It is fast becoming just one of many ways of replicating common communication across the Internet or an intranet. By the year 2000 the average user won't need to know if their communication is being sent via netnews, a web chat program, or some other means. Netnews will simply become one of many collaborative technologies.

Workgroup or Groupware tools

Workgroup and groupware tools are the cornerstone of second generation intranet applications that streamline workflow. These tools include: live collaboration tools, time-shifted collaboration tools, archive tools, and workflow processing tools.

Live collaboration tools include video and audio conferencing, group whiteboards and other group authoring environments. These provide a real-time, immediate connection among people, using special technology that eliminates lags and time delays.

Time-shifted collaboration tools are similar, but files are stored, so collaborators can work on them at different times.

Archive tools allow users to archive works in progress as people collaborate on them. Archive tools might seem to be more important for time-shifted collaboration, but few collaborative endeavors are momentary gestalts. Archive tools allow all collaboration to be saved as part of the community memory.

All of these tools assume people are working together even if they aren't in the same place, or working at the same time. However, not all business has evolved to the point where work can be done in parallel. Often, work has a flow. It starts with one person and is passed to another. Task flow control, tracking the stages of a process, determining who should get work next, and warning the employee that the task is "on the way" can all be streamlined through workflow processing software.

Two software products currently offer the infrastructure to create groupware. They are Lotus Notes and Microsoft BackOffice. Neither of these products offers true workflow "out-of-the-box"; program development is required. But few true workflow products are available, so Notes and BackOffice are likely to hold sizable market share for the next few years. Vendors for both products offer training and certification.

A third product offers a more complete, ready-to-use solution: Remedy's Action Request System. This product offers easy-to-implement solutions for help desk automation, customer report tracking, and several other functions.

Skills

Almost all these applications operate on the same principles, use the same elements, perform the same processes, and allow you to leverage the same skills. This means you can get plenty of "bang for the buck" by learning the transferable skills that apply to all of them:

Apprentice Level Skills

- Install service
- Manage contents of service (including archiving)
- Log activity of service and generate reports of activity

Journeyman Level Skills

- Configure service
- Monitor performance of service
- Manage security on service
- Manage user accounts, authorization and data access on service
- Configure gateways between this service and another
- Resolve common problems with service

Master Level Skills

- Capacity planning for service
- Define requirements for service

- Architect the infrastructure for the service
- Demonstrate knowledge of standards that the service is based upon
- Test setup and troubleshoot novel problems with service
- Develop disaster recovery plans

Education

You have a number of options for learning about these network services and applications.

Since databases have been around the longest, they have the broadest and deepest educational support. Many colleges and universities teach database technology. Many computer related vocational schools, community colleges and education vendors offer database training. Database-related degree paths are rare, but many certification programs are available.

E-mail, groupware and older Internet tools are rarely taught in the college or university setting. Some education vendors offer classes.

The exponential growth of the Web has spawned many educational opportunities in all forms of education. Colleges and universities often offer continuing education courses. Junior or community colleges, vocational schools and education vendors offer many classes.

Unfortunately, many of these educational programs suffer from the naive perspective that webmasters should try to be masters of all trades. While the education is broad, it's often superficial, focused on specific procedures rather than transferable skills.

Visit the Cybercareers web site (`http://www.cybercareers.com`) to learn about the best sources of higher level education as they become available.

Certification

- Lotus offers a variety of certification programs for their Notes products, including Lotus Certified Notes System Administrator, Lotus Certified Notes Consultant (LCNC), Lotus Certified Notes Specialist (LCNS) and Certified Lotus Professional. Information and worldwide contact phone numbers can be obtained at (`http://www.lotus.com/laec/16a.htm`).
- Lotus Certified cc:Mail Specialist and Certified Lotus Professional for Lotus cc:Mail (CLP for Lotus cc:Mail) certification programs are offered from Lotus. Information and contact phone numbers worldwide can be obtained at: (`http://www.lotus.com/laec/16a.htm`).

- Microsoft Certified Systems Engineer is a certification program that offers certification in BackOffice and Microsoft SQL products. For information, visit: (`http://www.microsoft.com/Train_Cert/mcp/certstep/mcse.htm`).

- Certified Sybase Professional (CSP) Database Administrator and CSP Performance and Tuning Specialist programs are offered from Sybase. For information, visit: (`http://www.sybase.com/services/education/ csp_overview.html`).

- Internet/intranet Certified Professional program is offered by Learning Tree International. This certification program is oriented towards the web server administrator role.

- Oracle 7 DBA Certified Professional program is offered by Learning Tree International.

Web certification suffers the same current fate as web education. While offered by many sources, it's often superficial and not directly supported by the industry at large. Two industry associations are currently working towards a realistic certification program. Visit the Cybercareers website (`http://www.cybercareers.com/`) to learn what they come up with.

Experience

You can often get experience by setting up network services or applications for yourself or for a small, needy organization. In many companies, some web servers aren't controlled by the MIS organization. Departments often build their own databases, and may give you an opportunity to get involved. Hundreds of non-profit groups need these services as well.

In some cases, a junior-level person can start out by administering backups and user account management for one service, and work into upper levels of support. These junior level people may be entry level system administrators, or even administrative assistants and secretaries. As with many other areas, experience without previous or at least concurrent education has far less value.

Hot Areas

The Web is hot, and it's going to stay hot for a long time. As organizations move from first generation intranets based upon publishing and dataflow to second generation intranets that support workflow, databases and groupware will also be hot topics. E-mail will probably continue to be an "unsung hero" in many organizations—everyone will depend on it, but management will rarely recognize its contribution.

Summary

In this chapter, you've reviewed the technical areas that will be most critical to a successful cyberspace *support* career—and the transferable technical skills you'll need to take full advantage of them. In the next section, you'll take a close look at the other major information technology career option: *development*.

CHAPTER

10

Technical Development Skills

Software development may be facing the most significant changes in its history—changes that will dramatically affect anyone who intends to make a career as a developer or programmer.

We've been raised on the stories of one or two or five people making it big after starting a software company in their garage, basement or dorm room. Who *are* those people? Most people think first of programmers. What do those companies do as they grow? Hire more programmers, maybe a manager or two, and if they're especially intelligent, perhaps an architect or designer to think about long-term planning issues. That's the sum total of software engineering at most companies today. What's wrong with this approach? It scales very poorly when grown to the size of today's programming organizations, which may have hundreds or even thousands of technical staff members.

The core problem is complexity. Brooks described the phenomenon well in the "Mythical Man Month." The more code you add to a program the more complex it becomes. As it becomes more complex, more communication (for example, specifications documentation, requirements documentation, API documentation) is needed. As it becomes more complex, there's a tendency to add more people. Then you need more meetings, memos, reports... and you're right back where you started.

A few thoughtful people have taken time to step back from the coding firefight and evaluate this situation. They have proposed methodologies for adding high-level organization and structure to the development process. They have created technologies such as CASE (Computer Assisted Software Engineering) that can automate elements of software development. In certain best-case scenarios, when these methodologies and technologies have been applied, they've reduced staffs of 100 programmers to staffs of five.

This type of software engineering isn't easy to implement. It forces structure on the free-spirited programmer. It forces the business to plan in advance. It forces people to learn new skills. It can't be made to happen overnight. It's a long-term investment, one that isn't readily accepted by managers with short-term mindsets. It isn't even taught in many computer science curriculums.

However, as businesses are driven to reengineer and downsize, they can't avoid revisiting the way they develop software. In this chapter, you'll take a look at the entire process of software development: both how it's done today, and how it's *going* to be done.

Then you can choose for yourself whether to be part of the past or the future.

Software Engineering

Software engineering consists of analysis, design, implementation, testing and maintenance.

Analysis: In the analysis stage, developers attempt to clearly define the real-world goal they're trying to achieve, or the problem they're trying to solve. They then prepare a set of requirements: essentially, a *target* for the rest of the development process.

Design: In the design stage, a solution to the problem is formally described in a *design document*. Especially in large projects, the design document will also cover the application programming interfaces (APIs) chosen to allow different logical blocks of code to work with each other.

During the design process, a prototype of a proposed solution should be developed and presented to people who are representative of the system's ultimate users. Their feedback should be solicited *and acted upon.* Obviously, projects shouldn't proceed if the analysis hasn't identified the right problem, or if the prototype hasn't solved it. All too often, however, these "reality checks" are bypassed in the name of saving time, and the results can be disastrous.

Sometimes analysis is skipped because the problems are perceived to be obvious. Sometimes, analysis is performed by marketers without the contributions of technical design professionals. Scott Adams' *Dilbert* has exquisitely lampooned the results of *this* approach. For projects of any real significance, there's simply no substitute for rigorous analysis.

Some post-secondary schools do teach *software engineering:* the entire software development process. Many, however, persist in teaching Computer Science as little more than a combination of program language syntax, algorithms and sometimes technologies.

Why? For one thing, it's *easier* to simply teach programming. And there *is* a large demand for people that can write code, so colleges and universities are admittedly meeting a business need by teaching core programming skills. Fewer people are currently required to perform the analysis and design work—so principle-based analysis and design can be left for the schools more interested in teaching it. However, with the rise of RAD (Rapid Application Development), this is changing quickly. Many analysis and design experts will be needed in the near future.

Finally, some Computer Science programs see themselves as focusing on the "science" of computers; analysis skills that involve interviewing potential users and understanding business processes are seen as business or marketing related.

These reasons may seem reasonable, but colleges and vocational counselors who don't tell students that there's more to software development than programming are not serving their students well.

Implementation: Once a prototype has shown that the design is on the right track, implementation begins: programmers can begin serious programming.

Configuration Management: Software is best created in small modular blocks or modules. It is important to manage the coordination and version control of these modules, and create an infrastructure that allows these modules to be easily combined when needed. As software projects grow, this role becomes more important.

Testing: Nothing's perfect on the first try—especially software. To identify problems, software is tested. Large scale software testing involves many levels of testing, just as the development of a web site does. Testing can be as simple as making sure a program actually runs, and as complex as making sure all of the software modules communicate with appropriate timing in a multi-threaded program.

Maintenance: If programs were perfect and the world never changed, maintenance wouldn't be necessary. But we don't live in such a world. It's common for programs to be released as soon as the worst ("show stopper") bugs have been fixed. That leaves plenty of refinement for later. In addition, business needs change. One year, a company may have customers in one country; the next year, a *dozen* countries. On the simplest level, this could require changes to the way shipping databases handle mailing address. It might also require the need for entirely new cash management modules that can help with handling foreign currencies.

Maintenance is the least glamorous part of software development. But every programmer would benefit from experiencing it

Few programmers have to face the long term consequences of their programming. Some take short cuts. For example, they may "hard code" elements that should have been coded in a way that made them easier to adjust or expand later. Or they may scrimp on documentation. All these expediencies help the developer get the job done faster, but cause additional work for the organization in the long term.

Maintenance programming doesn't involve unique skills. But designing code that is reusable and easy to maintain *does*. You'll learn about those skills later, in the Design and Implementation Skills section of this chapter.

The Difference Between Maintenance and Development According to Ken Erickson

Maintenance and new development skills are very different. Those who maintain systems must think logically, put aside any pre-conceived notions of how something is "supposed" to work (as opposed to how it is actually working), have a thorough understanding of their systems, and be able to *remember* things in excruciating detail.

People doing new development, on the other hand, need a great breadth of experience in the field—that's the only way to reliably know what works and what doesn't work in practice. Developing new systems requires imagination and creativity.

—*Ken Erickson, Developer, SunSoft*

Analysis and Design

As you've learned, analysis creates a set of requirements that define what a program is supposed to do; design specifies how the program accomplishes these goals. Now, let's take a closer look.

Among the decisions that are often part of the analysis stage are: whether to build the program in-house or purchase it from a vendor; and whether the project is even feasible. To reach decisions like these, extensive interviewing and research may be necessary: the analyst must understand both the *data* and *processes* that will be reflected in the finished program.

During the *design* phase, strategic decisions are made about how the program will be structured, and how the module interfaces will work together. Some high-level performance issues will be addressed. This phase rarely looks at specific coding techniques. It focuses heavily on implementation strategy: how the parts will fit together, and how to divide them so they can be delegated to a team of developers.

Domains of Knowledge

To perform analysis and design well, you need to understand at least one, preferably multiple strategies for approaching and solving problems; techniques and methodologies for modeling problems and solutions; and how to clearly document your findings so developers can implement them.

Process-oriented analysis and design strategies

Process-oriented analysis and design strategies are based upon general systems theory, which in turn resembles some current theories of how the brain works. Inputs are defined (*input*); actions are taken on those inputs (*processing*); and outputs are produced (*output*). Specific approaches to analysis and design include the *Yourdon method* and the *DeMarco method*.

Typically, analysts develop *data flow diagrams* (DFDs) or flowcharts that demonstrate the input, processing and output of various processes. *Data dictionaries* are used to hold information about each piece of data. All of this information is carefully documented. Before the analysis phase is complete, these diagrams and data dictionaries must be verified to make sure all loose ends have been eliminated. Verification includes:

- Correctness checking: making sure all DFDs and data dictionary elements are correct and reasonable.

- Completeness checking: making sure all items, both data and processes, have been completely defined.

- Consistency checking: making sure all data and processes are accounted for from beginning to end, and none are lost along the way.

In the design phase, processes are reviewed. In the design phase, the designers take a step back and view the project from the "50,000 foot" level. At this point, most of the details are "hidden," or too small to be visible. That's fine: at this point the focus should be on large concepts, not trivia. Careful high-level design allows common processes to be modularized. This leads to generic, reusable code and standard interfaces between modules, which are both elements of good programming design and practice.

Data-oriented analysis and design strategies

Data-oriented analysis and design strategies are referred to as *Information Engineering*. The philosophy behind these strategies is that data structures stay constant for long periods of time, but processes change. In organizations that routinely reorganize, this is often a very accurate assessment. Data-oriented strategies and methodologies are often used with databases and the extensive *data warehouses* that are becoming popular.

Data-oriented analysis begins by analyzing relationships between entities in *entity relationship diagrams* (ERDs). This activity is also called *data modeling*. Next, the entities' structures are analyzed to define the processes that are associated with them.

At this point, the model is *normalized*: refined to eliminate duplicate data and references. This enhances performance. It also helps to create standard entities and processes, which can be modularized and then implemented with code that's easy to reuse—significantly reducing costs. Finally, process dependency diagrams (PDDs) are created.

In data-oriented design, the development work often includes developing the dialogs between the user and the computer, and the interface screens that provide that dialog and administration procedures—and having real users evaluate them. These dialogs may include granting or preventing access to data, auditing, and problem or disaster recovery procedures. *Information engineering is likely to be one of the hottest methodologies for the next several years.*

Object-oriented analysis and design strategies

Object-oriented methodologies borrow many features from both process- and data-oriented methodologies. This is because the core element of object-oriented design, namely the object itself, is comprised of both *data* and the *processes* that affect that data.

Object-oriented analysis extends the data modeling done in data-oriented analysis. It doesn't just identify commonalities (attributes) of *data*, but also commonalities of *methods*, which are actions performed on the data. With this information, analysts can create *classes*: generic units that combine data and action. Specific data entities then become *instances* of those classes or *objects*—complete with the actions that can be performed on that data.

Once you have all this information, you document it, through table-type diagrams commonly called *Booch* diagrams, or via graphical diagrams, as in the *Coad/Yourdon* and *Rumbaugh* methods. Some people prefer to mix-and-match methods to accomplish their specific goals.

Object-oriented analysis has become increasingly hot, especially with the growth of Java. The next step is likely to be large-scale Java development, which will require even more attention to analysis.

Skills

The analysis and design skills we've discussed are master-level software engineering skills. They can be learned by programmers skilled in practical reasoning. They can also be used in combination with 4GL programming tools such as Rapid Application Development (RAD) and CASE tools, even without learning specific programming languages. The skills you'll need include:

- Defining the problem to be solved
- Identifying constraints
- Defining requirements
- Identifying the methodology to be used
- Modeling the problem in a methodology
- Documenting an implementation plan

Education

To learn about analysis and design, you'll have to actively seek out the courses you need. Some schools offer them, others don't. Many training vendors also offer courses, as do the originators of many of the specific methodologies you've learned about.

Experience

Analysis and design experience is difficult to come by, because few companies formally use analysis and design yet, though the field is rapidly growing. You can best find opportunities to perform analysis and design by networking with people that practice it.

Hot Areas

With the increased interest in both data warehousing and object-oriented techniques, data-oriented and object-oriented methodologies are now in greater demand than process-oriented methodologies.

Implementation (Programming)

Programming means creating instructions that, when carried out, will lead to a specific result.

According to Ken Ericskon, A Programmer Is...

Years ago, a fairly accurate description of a programmer would be: someone who implements X algorithms in Y language. The line's been blurred since the PC arrived. Now, the role of a programmer depends a great deal on a company's organizational structure.

In older, traditionally mainframe-dominated shops (insurance, banking, airlines, etc.) you still find a sharp division between the "analyst" and "programmer." The analyst writes specifications, the programmer writes code, and neither is well suited to do the other's job.

However, in the software industry, especially in Unix, you will typically find "software engineers," programmers trained to think as *engineers*. There, it's common for the same person to handle requirements analysis, design, *and* implementation.

On top of that, with the easy availability of powerful software for PCs, people who would have once been considered "users" are now often programmers, in that they develop *their own* databases, reports, etc.

—Ken Erickson, Developer, SunSoft

Understanding Programming

Machine code

Once, all software was created in arcane languages of zeroes and ones (or in some cases hexadecimal numbers) called *machine code*. Machine code was, and still is, system-specific: every processor has its own. As you can imagine, machine code was exceptionally difficult and susceptible to error, and there were few tools available to streamline it. Fortunately, very little software is created this way nowadays.

Functional

After machine code, high-level "functional" programming languages such as COBOL, Fortran, Basic, Pascal and C evolved. They're called "high-level" because the programmer can write in a language much closer to human speech than machine code. The programmer then runs a special program which takes the high-level language (*source code)* and translates (*compiles*) it into machine code that the computer can understand and execute. This type of software development has been common for many years, and most colleges and universities teach it.

Object-oriented

Original programming languages were a quantum leap forward, but they still had to reflect the serious limitations of the computers they ran on. Put simply, people still had to think much like computers—and few human activities naturally resemble computer processing.

As computers became more powerful, it became feasible to develop software that mimicked human activities rather than forcing people to become automatons. Humans tend to think in terms of things and what can be done with them. As children we explore our environment, picking up objects and seeing whether they can be eaten, thrown, shaken, and so on. We separate their intrinsic characteristics or *attributes* (red, soft, noisy) from their actions or *methods*. This thought process is mimicked by *object-oriented* software development.

Object-oriented software development, done correctly, requires a very different perspective than functional programming. Many people skilled in functional languages have a hard time making the transition. Some object-oriented programming (OOP) languages, such as C++, can use functional programming constructs. This sometimes helps, but more often it prevents people from fully making the transition.

Ken Erickson says OO Requires Different Thinking

[In switching to object-oriented development] the biggest change is learning to think of a problem in terms of its *data*, rather than in terms of a computer language. With OO, you spend a lot more time in the design phase—you can't start implementing until you understand the data relationships.

Of course, you really shouldn't *need* a programming methodology to force you to *think* before coding...

—*Ken Erickson, Developer, SunSoft*

OOP and functional programming still share much in common. Source code is generated by a programmer in a high-level, "sort-of-human" language, which is then compiled into machine code for the computer.

OOP has been around for about 20 years. The concepts are now relatively mature, and OOP is finally making the transition from a specialized niche to a mainstream skill. There will be significant growth in the market for OOP programmers in the next 5–10 years, especially those who know C++ and Java.

Some colleges and universities teach specific object-oriented programming languages. Few colleges and universities teach the entire skillset of object-oriented analysis (OOA), object-oriented design (OOD), and object-oriented programming (OOP). Many computer and software vendors have a more effective curriculum than classical post-secondary institutions. Make sure your educational institution's curriculum meets *your* needs, both for training in a specific language and for learning the entire process of OO analysis, design and programming.

There's much to be said for learning the basics of programming in the classroom, then gaining practical experience in the workplace, and returning to school to study formal analysis and design.

Fourth Generation Languages (*4GLs*)

The latest trend in software development is to automate the creation of source code wherever possible, just as the task of creating machine code was automated by compilers. Tools to automate source code generation are referred to as fourth generation languages or *4GLs*. These include:

- CASE (Computer Assisted Software Engineering) tools
- RAD (Rapid Application Development) tools
- Visual programming systems

It's no small feat to represent knowledge in a structure and format that a computer can generate source code from.

Traditionally, systems analysts did this work, and programmers could interpret their instructions, making adjustments as needed. With CASE and RAD, the role of the programmer can be delegated to the computer. But computers are very literal beasts. If you tell them to put peanut butter on the bread before you tell them to open the package of bread and remove a slice, you may get some very interesting sandwiches. Few computers are capable of verifying whether their results make sense in the real world.

Therefore, anyone working with 4GL tools must be exceptionally precise. They must intimately understand the process they are modeling. They'll stop speaking in terms of algorithms and source code. Instead, they'll work with data and information modeling structures, using terms like *entity-relationship modeling*, as discussed earlier.

Databases

When programming originated, program logic was separate from the data being acted upon. Originally, data was generic and homogeneous. Then, people discovered that by adding order and structure to the data, they could apply program logic to it much more efficiently. Databases were born.

Meanwhile, programs were created to assist with standard database maintenance, saving programmers more time with each new application. Thus, data storage and maintenance was also separated from the program logic that analyzed it. This freed the programmer from recreating these maintenance functions in every program they wrote. It also enabled modularity, so that data could be used by different people with programs written in multiple languages. This "modular" strategy has been key to the dramatic success of both PCs and the Internet.

Scripting languages

As you've learned, most modern programs are written in a high-level language and then converted to machine code. But there's a major exception: *scripting languages*. Here, source code is left in the high-level language; a special *interpreter* program reads the source code and executes the program directly. Programming skill is still needed for writing code in scripting languages.

Scripting languages are very important for cross-platform programs, where the program would need to be recompiled for every computer platform. Secondarily, scripts are commonly used for small items that the administrator is likely to need to change. Thus, administrators tend to be more fluent at scripting.

Specialty languages

Some applications provide a general framework for accomplishing tasks, and allow users or developers to build a custom environment on that framework. For example, applications such as spreadsheets and word processing programs use *macros*. These may be nothing more than recordings of keystrokes within an application to repeat common operations; they may also be much more complex. Macros tend to be widely used by power users.

Domains of Knowledge

Of course, each computer language has its own algorithms, syntax and procedures: its own domain of knowledge. You'll take a closer look at the most prominent languages shortly. But programming has another dimension beyond this. Much as a human language contains not just syntax, but also colloquialisms and jargon, programmers can specialize in different areas of development.

For example, some programmers specialize in GUI development: they create the *graphical user interface* that allows users to communicate with the program. Other programmers may specialize in the interaction between clients and servers. Still others may specialize in writing programs that manipulate data in a database.

A formal title may not express either the languages or specialties you're experienced with, but that's the information a manager or hiring professional will need to know about you.

Programming languages

There are dozens of different programming languages, each with its own uses, strengths and weaknesses. Ideally, the development team defines the problem, specifies the requirements, develops a general design, and based upon that design, chooses a language. In reality, many companies focus on one or a few languages that meet most of their needs acceptably.

- **C/C++**   C is a functional programming language and is often very abstract. C is a complex language that requires a skilled programmer who can think clearly in abstract terms.

     C++ is an extension of the C language that supports, *but does not enforce*, the use of objects. It is possible to write almost pure C code that many C++ compilers can successfully compile. In other words, just because a C++ program works doesn't mean it's object-oriented. But it is becoming more important that programmers actually learn how to write good object-oriented code, instead of just slightly modifying their C coding style.

C and C++ are used almost interchangeably on job descriptions. It's hard to differentiate between the true demand for C and C++. Together, however, C and C++ account for more than half the programming jobs advertised. All programming students should become acquainted with the C language and its C++ extensions.

- **Java/JavaScript/JScript**   Java is an object-oriented programming language developed at Sun Microsystems, Inc. The language is platform independent, which is to say that code written for a UNIX system should run without changes on a 32-bit Windows system as well—if developers are cautious not to take platform-specific "shortcuts." Java also includes *classes*, or generic object-oriented code libraries for many common *frameworks*, or general programming technologies.

  These features have made Java a big hit with the developer community. So far, Java accounts for a small fraction of the development jobs offered. However, it's been less than two years since Java was formally introduced, so it's remarkable that Java is being requested at all. It took much longer for C and C++ to become popular in business. Currently, the demand for Java programmers is significantly higher than the supply. In some high-tech centers such as California's Bay Area and New York, it's said that *"Java programmers don't need jobs—they need agents."* If you plan to be a developer for the next several years, make sure you learn Java.

  Often, when Java is discussed, you'll also hear about two scripting languages, Netscape's JavaScript and Microsoft's JScript.

  Netscape developed JavaScript for use in its Internet and intranet server and browser products. JavaScript is an object-oriented scripting language similar to Java with some hooks into Java classes. JavaScript is designed to be small and quick, with limited GUI capabilities and no capabilities beyond the Web browser and server. This contrasts with Java, a full-fledged programming language with extensive GUI features and many applications beyond.Web browsers and servers.

Meanwhile, Microsoft created JScript, a version of JavaScript for its own use and for licensing to third parties. JScript performs the same functions as JavaScript, but also supports Microsoft technologies like ActiveX™.

- **Visual Basic/VBscript** Years ago, Microsoft extended the entry-level Basic programming language, creating a complete visual programming environment called Visual Basic. Visual Basic isn't quite as easy as Basic; it's a full-fledged programming language. Just as Netscape created a scripting language similar to Java, Microsoft has created a scripting variant to Visual Basic, called VBScript. The main drawback to Visual Basic and VBscript is the fact that they are oriented towards Microsoft operating systems (Windows 3.1/NT/95) and products (such as Microsoft's Internet Explorer Web browser and its IIS Web server). While Microsoft and Windows have large market share now, there is no guarantee their leadership will remain unchallenged. Moreover, many companies have heterogeneous, *mixed-platform* configurations. If they choose Visual Basic or VBScript instead of a platform-independent language like Java, they will have to use additional languages when they work in non-Windows environments. While Visual Basic appears to be a "hot" language today, it isn't likely to boost your career over the long-term.

- **Perl** Perl is an abstract scripting language developed several years ago. Variants of Perl exist for most platforms, but scripts must be adapted to each platform's specifics; Perl isn't as interchangeable as Java or JavaScript. Many early Web gateway scripts were created in Perl, so there are extensive libraries of Perl code to work from. Jobs requesting Perl experience are roughly as common as Java positions. Perl knowledge is especially valuable in UNIX system administration.

- **Other** Many other languages exist; demand for them is smaller but not insignificant. Two languages, Basic and Pascal, are often used to introduce students to the fundamentals of programming, due to their simplicity and resemblance to "human language." The following table lists *some* of the languages you might encounter:

ADA	**APL**	**Assembler**	**Basic**
Cobol	**LISP**	**Fortran**	**Pascal**
Prolog	**RPG**	**Smalltalk**	**TCL**

Database systems

Database systems combine programming with the development and management of a structured data organization, often called a *schema*. The development and management of this schema varies among database products.

SQL, or Structured Query Language, (pronounced "see-qual") is the standard language used for writing programs that access, update, and store information in a database. Most multi-user database products use SQL. Therefore, if you plan to work with databases even occasionally, you need to learn it. In fact, SQL knowledge is second only to C/C++ knowledge in programming job descriptions.

Some databases are platform-specific. Others are cross-platform. Several of the leading database products will be discussed below.

- **Mainframe**   IBM's DB2 is the dominant mainframe database. Knowing DB2 is important primarily for those who need to create interfaces with older mainframe-based "legacy systems." Many IBM shops are migrating to data warehouses based on Oracle or Sybase.

- **PC/Microsoft Windows**   Several databases are only found on Windows-based PCs, including Paradox and Access. (Two older database products, Foxbase and dBASE, exist for DOS, Windows and the Macintosh.) These databases are primarily for single-user or workgroup environments. They generally don't scale well; which is to say they can't handle corporate-wide "enterprise" applications.

- **Enterprise**   For today's enterprise applications, most companies choose database products from Oracle, Sybase or Informix, running on either UNIX or Windows NT platforms. Other choices exist; for example, Microsoft offers Microsoft SQL Server for Windows NT, and as mentioned earlier, IBM offers DB2.

4GLs and RAD

Earlier, you learned that 4GLs attempt to automate coding wherever possible. Such languages are necessarily quite abstract. To use them, it's more important to have sophisticated reasoning, analysis and design skills than to have traditional programming skills.

Delphi: Borland's Delphi and the newly released IntraBuilder have gained considerable acclaim for their ease of use, though demand for Delphi skills still falls into the niche category.

Powerbuilder: Sybase's Powerbuilder offers extensive RAD (Rapid Application Development) capabilities. For Web developers, its claim to fame is its Web interface, which delivers platform-independence. This makes it possible to develop for multiple platforms at once. Experienced Powerbuilder developers, especially those familiar with versions 5.0 and above, are in high demand and expected to stay that way for the foreseeable future.

Sapphire Web: Sapphire Web from Bluestone is a rapidly growing RAD tool devoted exclusively to the Web. The ease and speed of development on this platform is making it a very popular alternative to learning Java.

Code libraries, frameworks, APIs

Why reinvent the wheel?

Traditionally, software developers spent an inordinate amount of time recreating code that was created before for other purposes. They wondered: *couldn't we simply reuse the original code? We'd be much more efficient, and we'd be able to deliver our new projects much faster.*

To this end, reusable code was created.

In the early days, companies purchased *code libraries* that performed common functions like sorting data according to a specific algorithm, or looking up data in a linked list, or displaying items on a screen.

Groups of common code libraries related to specific parts of the system became known as *application-program interfaces* or APIs. Early APIs were used to simplify programming of graphical user interfaces. Now, APIs are used in many ways: for example, Netscape's proprietary web gateway, NSAPI (Netscape API) provides simple access to functions on a Netscape server.

Meanwhile, programmers have begun to realize that most programs are based upon some business or technical process. Most of those processes have a limited number of reasonable solutions that follow common patterns. Thus, developing common code libraries to mimic entire business or technical processes can again shorten the development time. These code libraries of processes are called *frameworks*. Some general definitions of frameworks include *semi-complete applications*, and *integrated sets of domain-specific functionality.*

The most well-known and often requested API knowledge is the *Microsoft Foundation Classes* or *MFC*. People choosing to specialize in Microsoft based development are advised to become acquainted with this toolset. Between five and ten percent of the programming job descriptions now request MFC experience.

Programming technologies

When enough people do something the same way, there can be powerful economies of scale. For example, it's cheaper to build software, because there's a bigger market. Hardware manufacturers can be confident that their devices will work everyone else's. People can learn new technologies with more confidence that their knowledge will be valuable to employers.

These common approaches are often defined as *standards*.

There are standards for virtually every aspect of computing; they help provide structure to the entire industry (and to everyone trying to make a career in it). Let's take a closer look at some of the most important technologies you'll encounter, organized by category:

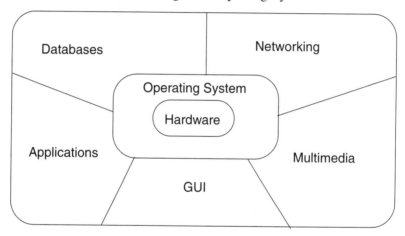

Figure 10–1   Relationship of Technology Areas

Hardware Interfaces: It takes software to receive, interpret, and send electrical signals to a computer's various components. These hardware interfaces are often called *BIOS* and *device drivers*. The BIOS or Basic Input/Output System is the lowest level interface to peripheral devices. Device drivers are elements of the operating system that communicate with the BIOS or the peripheral device directly. Those who develop BIOSes and device drivers need an in-depth knowledge of hardware standards; an electronic or electrical engineering background can help. This work falls under the general category of systems programming.

Operating System: The operating system (OS) controls hardware, schedules all processing tasks and provides an interface through which the user can control the computer. In UNIX, and increasingly in other OSes, the OS is separated into a *kernel* and higher level programs which perform specific functions. The kernel is the core of the operating system, sometimes referred to as the *master control program. If you plan to become involved in the specialized field of OS programming, start by learning the strategies and techniques that have been used to implement today's operating systems. One key technology to focus on is multi-threading.* Multi-threading means breaking down a program into small pieces that can be executed concurrently in cases where a computer has more than one CPU (central processing unit). OS development also falls under the general category of systems programming. Roughly 10-20% of programmers are involved in systems programming; most of the others are application programmers.

Graphical User Interface: Graphical User Interface or GUI programming deals with either the creation of the GUI itself (systems-level programming), or more commonly, the creation of user interfaces for specific applications (application programming). Most GUI programming is specific to one operating system and/or windowing system.

The Macintosh platform has one standard GUI. There are variations among the various Microsoft Windows products, but few are significant. UNIX systems, on the other hand, have multiple windowing systems. These are built on X-Windows, developed at MIT. X-Windows programming is sometimes referred to as X11 programming.

Building on X-Windows, Sun Microsystems created a windowing system called Open Windows. Competitors agreed on a different standard called *Motif.* Motif has become the most popular UNIX GUI; even Sun offers a version of it now.

In UNIX, Windows and Macintosh environments, GUI programming has been streamlined by visual programming environments that offer "paint-like" programs which allow you to draw the GUI elements you want, and then generate the source code for you.

Networking: For a more detailed look at networking, refer to Chapter 13's discussion about protocols and the OSI seven-layer network model. To become a network programmer, it's likely you'll need to understand TCP/IP and the use of Remote Procedure Calls (RPCs). With some exceptions, programming focused on the network's *application layer* is often considered to be application-specific programming; you'll learn more about this later. Programming of lower network layers is usually considered systems level programming.

Database: Databases often comprise both technologies and programming languages, and most database training deals with both. Three standards are especially important to database developers: SQL, Microsoft's Open Database Connector (ODBC) and Sun's Java Database Connector (JDBC).

Multimedia: There are a few dozen different multimedia standards. These include GIF and JPEG for static graphics; and MPEG and Quicktime for digital movies. Sound standards are starting to emerge, as well. For more information on multimedia standards, see Chapter 15.

Applications: There are a wide variety of applications, and each has its own set of standards. For example:

- **Electronic Commerce** has EDI (electronic data interchange) standards; encryption standards such as SSL (Secure Sockets Library); a common encryption algorithm, RSA (Rivest-Shamir-Adelman, named after its creators); and payment protocols such as SET (Secured Electronic Transaction).

- **Client/Server applications** have become widespread, and increasingly these make use of new object-based standards such as CORBA (Common Object Request Broker Architecture). Several standards exist for creating programs that communicate with objects. The most popular current technologies include CORBA, ORB, DCOM and ActiveX.

- **Web-based applications** are growing rapidly with the intranet's popularity. The majority of new web-based applications are database oriented, so if you can combine web and database skillsets, you'll be in hot demand. One of the most asked-for web standards is CGI. The funny thing about CGI is that it simply uses three common programming techniques: environment variables, writing to standard output, and reading from standard input. Any good programmer should be able to learn CGI in an hour or two.

- **GUI development** is becoming very automated by screen painters and visual development environments. Learning GUI technologies is becoming less of a priority.

Embedded Systems: Today, many devices are programmed, not just computers. Your car, your VCR, your microwave oven and cellular phone all have internal programming, typically built into one or more chips. that store and execute the entire repertoire of routines. People who work on these *embedded systems typically* have substantial hardware interface experience and somewhat more limited applications development experience. Embedded systems aren't glamorous, but their programmers are in considerable demand.

Distributed Object Methodologies: Several standards exist for creating programs that communicate with objects. The most popular current technologies include CORBA, ORB, DCOM, and ActiveX.

Skills

To succeed in these development areas, learn how to

- Create and modify software programs from supplied specifications, using agreed standards and tools.

- Research errors and problems, and revise programs to resolve them.

Education

For programmers, formal education is critical. Since students have limited time, it's important to choose the appropriate course of study. It usually makes sense to learn the languages, technologies and frameworks most in demand, especially those that are growing in demand.

For developers, the importance of software platforms like Windows and UNIX is diminishing somewhat. Platform-specific knowledge will be a priority primarily for those who wish to specialize in systems programming.

Make sure you develop the transferable skills you need to adapt to new platforms and technologies as they become prominent.

No matter what you may hear, the future of programming is not in any single language. Those who can't learn to use at least three, perhaps as many as eight languages, will have a rocky career.

I'm not a programmer by title, but my programming/scripting skillset includes assembler, Basic, Fortran, Java, Perl, csh, Bourne shell, Korn shell, DCL and REXX.

Some schools, usually 2-year schools, attempt to pass off a person with one language as a programmer. For quick, little jobs, they may be. However, those that expect to stay in the industry long-term can't afford the arrogance of being a "Johnny One-Note." Languages come and go: if you can't evolve to the next language, you'll become extinct.

Those who only know a single language don't develop the higher-level skills that a programmer needs to mature to senior level. Their perspective is often too narrow to solve many problems. Thus, it is reasonable to expect someone who wants to work in the industry long-term to learn many languages. In fact, it is this breadth of knowledge that leads to real skills— and that is the premise of this book.

Based upon current demands and growth trends, a recommended course of language study is as follows:

1. **Training language**—Pascal or Basic.

2. **C/C++**—Since C/C++ is a requirement for over 50 percent of all programming openings, all new programmers should learn it.

3. **SQL** —As many as 20 percent of programming jobs require SQL experience, and databases continue to grow in importance.

4. **Java**—New students should learn some form of object-oriented programming. Java is a true object-oriented language, it's growing dramatically in popularity, and it's a relatively easy environment for learning proper object-oriented techniques.

5. **Visual Basic**—While Visual Basic is currently in high demand, Java is growing much faster. You *can* be considered well-rounded without learning Visual Basic. But Visual Basic is an excellent training environment for learning visual programming environments.

In addition to the languages listed above, make sure to get some technology training. Most post-secondary schools offer valuable introductions to operating systems, system level programming, and programming language theory. Institutions vary widely in their commitment to application level training. This is unfortunate, since application-level programming accounts for roughly 70 to 80 percent of available programming jobs. If you're interested in application-level programming, make sure to explore students database programming, network application programing (often referred to as client/server or distributed programming), and web technologies.

Certification

In many MIS organizations, you must have a four-year Computer Science degree to be considered for many job titles. However, it is possible to break into programming with a two-year degree, if you develop specialized knowledge by supporting or testing a product that's in demand.

Certificates and certification won't be sufficient to help you get your first job. But they can help establish competence in a particular technology or language, especially one that's too new to be taught in post-secondary schools.

Most computing education vendors offer programming courses; the leaders include:

- Learning Tree International
- American Research Group

There are several certification programs available.

- Java Certification—Sun Microsystems, Inc., has developed 'Sun Java Programmer' and 'Sun Java Developer' certification programs.
- Learning Tree International offers the following certification programs:

    —Certified Oracle7 Application Development Professional

    —Certified C and C++ Programming Professional

    —Certified UNIX Programming Professional

    —Certified Software Development Professional

- Microsoft offers the 'Microsoft Certified Solution Developer' program.
- Sybase offers:

    —Certified PowerBuilder Developer Associate

    —Certified PowerBuilder Developer Professional

    —Certified SYBASE Professional Open Interfaces Developer

- Software Publishers Association offers the Certified Software Manager.

Experience

There's only one way to get programming experience: write programs!

Of course, school and home programming projects carry less weight than programming done for business. Nonetheless, the more experience you have solving real world problems—preferably *complex* ones—the better off you'll be.

Some people work their way into development roles from testing or product support positions.

Hot Areas

Right now, the hottest languages and technologies include C/C++, Java and SQL. In many cases, the strongest demand is for people who can combine a variety of new technologies. For example, today's mainstream client/server programming involves GUI development, networking and 4GLs, among other technologies. Most intranets integrate web and database technologies; the demand for people who can do this is soaring.

There's one short-term trend to be aware of: the *Year 2000* problem. Many computer programs cannot accurately handle dates starting with the year 2000. Among these programs are many mainframe-based COBOL programs that are critical to day-to-day business. The need to fix this problem has created an enormous short-term demand for experienced COBOL programmers. Don't bet your entire career on COBOL, but if you have the right experience, now's a great time to cash in.

Of course, no matter what kind of application programming you do, you'll be much more effective if you have a strong understanding of business.

As you've learned already, your career depends on your ability to anticipate emerging trends. Every year or so, examine the job listings to see what skill sets are hot. You might even keep a log of numbers and compare them from year to year. It's a quick and easy way of discovering trends that might not always be obvious in your personal experience, or even in the trade press.

Configuration Management

The larger and more complex a software development operation is, the more management overhead is needed. Software is best created in small *modules*, which must be closely coordinated. Since these modules may often be revised, it's equally important to manage the revisions process, using *version control* software. Let's take a closer look at how modular software is created and how its evolution is managed.

Building Software

Software is combined together during the compilation stage with the use of `makefiles`. Makefiles are files that define *how to make* a program. Makefiles specify the files or file libraries to be included; the order in which they should be added; and any compiler options that must be set. They're a fundamental tool for all C and C++ programmers. Other programming languages also use (but don't require) makefiles. In fact, Borland has designed a GUI-based make program that the average new programmer wouldn't even recognize as make.

Since UNIX comes in dozens of "flavors," a meta-make tool called `imake` can be used to coordinate instructions for each version of UNIX. *Make* and *imake* are themselves scripting languages.

Version Control Data

Since software changes so often, and the changes can easily introduce new problems, or "break" the software altogether, it's critical that software versions be carefully tracked. Version control is also essential for many other files that change frequently, notably web files. Most large software development organizations use special software that creates version records and track software changes.

Typically, every developer is responsible for "checking in" and "checking out" each file they wish to use. Many development environments can make the routine updating of versions nearly transparent to the programmer or developer.

Skills

- Create scripts in `make` and `imake` languages to combine modules and libraries into software programs.
- Create and modify compiler options within make and imake files.
- Set up version control workspaces.
- Check data in and out of version control workspaces.

Education/Experience

You won't find courses in `make` files, compiler options, or version control. These skills are learned on the job, or with books. But if you're a developer (or, in many cases, a UNIX system administrator), these are skills you'll need to have.

Testing

Once a product is created, it should be tested to make sure that it does what it is supposed to do, and it *doesn't* do what it *isn't* supposed to do. (Occasionally, the term *quality assurance* is used in place of testing. Quality assurance ought to be broader than testing, however. It ought to include practices that prevent the introduction of errors throughout the development cycle—not just finding them once they're there.)

Testing is a methodical process. It involves knowing what the product was originally specified to do, developing ways of exercising the product, comparing the actual results to expectations, and documenting the discrepancies. The best testers don't just find failures: they document ways to reproduce the failures consistently, so programmers can more easily find solutions.

Formal testing is as critical as formal analysis and design (and unfortunately, sometimes it's equally neglected).

Testing Stages, Strategies, Documentation and Tools

Let's take a closer look at the various stages of testing, testing strategies, test cycle documentation, and testing tools.

Stages of testing

Unit Test: A unit is the smallest component of the product. The smallest unit may be a single module, library or class,. In more complex software, containing hundreds of thousands of modules, libraries or classes, the unit may be defined as the smallest *logical* element of the product. However the unit is defined, this definition should appear in a test plan. Unit testing can then be performed by a testing specialist, or a set of automated software routines. In some cases, the programmer who wrote the unit will be called upon to test it. This isn't ideal, because the author of the code is so close to it that he or she may fail to see problems that someone else *would* notice.

Integration Test: Units of code are assembled into subsystems, which must also be tested to make their component units communicate properly with each other, and that messages passed between them are consistent.

System Test: System testing tests the product *as a whole,* to make sure it acts as specified.

Regression Test: Working software can develop problems as changes are made to it. "Regression" testing is performed after changes are made, to ensure the software hasn't "regressed" in quality.

Acceptance Test: In the world of shrink-wrapped software (i.e., software sold in shrink-wrapped boxes at software outlets) acceptance testing has little meaning. However, most large organizations commission software products either from other departments within their company or from external vendors. When software is created according to a specific commission, the recipient of the software can and usually does perform tests to make sure that what they receive matches what they wanted, as spelled out in their initial design plan or performance contract. These tests are called acceptance tests because if the software passes these tests, it is accepted.

Performance Test: Performance testing determines how quickly or efficiently a piece of software works. Since performance varies with a variety of hardware and software factors, performance testing often requires sophisticated knowledge of system tuning and optimization. Performance testing results are often used by marketing and sales forces to promote their product over another vendor's.

Tests that compare competing products are called *benchmarks*. These tests are often developed by third-party testing or certification organizations. Knowledge of the specific benchmarks that apply to a specific product is essential to the performance tester.

Testing strategies

Black Box Test—Black box testing is based upon the idea that it doesn't matter what is *inside* of a box: given certain inputs, the box (or in this case, software) should produce specific outputs. Most unit, system and regression testing is black box testing.

White Box Test—In white box testing, the tester evaluates the code itself for appropriate algorithm logic implementation and mathematical correctness.

Test cycle documentation

Test Plan—Testing should be carefully planned and documented in a *test plan*. This document outlines test strategies, what testing will be done at each level, what will be tested, and what outcomes are expected.

Test Cases—Test cases are the individual situations that are tested.

Test Matrix—The test matrix lists the testing *variables*. Often, these are many and complex. For example, different hardware options, system and software configurations, and quantities of data can all dramatically affect a program's performance—or whether it works at all. Of course, in the real world, not *every* option can be tested. A test matrix defines sets of variables that can be combined to meaningfully test sets of variables—minimizing the number of tests needed, while maximizing the reliability of the results.

Testing tools

Harness—In many cases, a program requires a clean environment where the program can be executed by the test routines (scripts, programs and macros), and the outcomes can be recorded. Ideally this entire process is done automatically. This environment is called a *harness*. Ideally, harnesses should not interfere with the testing itself, or alter its results.

Test Routines—Some testing is performed manually, by testers who sit in front of the computer and execute steps, one by one. Wherever possible, however, software routines are written to execute the tests automatically. These routines may be programs, scripts, or even (in the case of many GUI applications) mouse and keyboard macros.

Test Logging and Report Generation—Testing produces two forms of paperwork. First and foremost, bug reports or reports describe specific failures, document the state of the system when it failed, and ideally show how the failure can be reproduced. Secondly, status reports outline the tests that have been performed, areas of success and failure, and comparisons with earlier versions. These status reports can often be automatically generated if tests are automatically logged—saving considerable time (and preventing paper cuts). It is also good practice to maintain records of test results for future documentation and analysis.

Skills

Junior (Test Executioner)

- Executes tests of software products.

- Logs results of tests.

- Documents problems and errors found in testing of software products.

- Documents results of test process.

Senior (Test Developer)

- Plans and designs tests of software products.

- Develops routines to test software products.

- Develops infrastructure to test software products including harness and logging tools.

Education

Relatively few degree programs include software testing or quality assurance courses. (The few institutions that do offer such courses tend to define their curriculum as Software Engineering rather than Computer Science.)

The scarcity of testing/QA courses is unfortunate, given the critical importance of software quality. It also means you should supplement your computer science degree with at least one testing or QA course from another source. You may find what you're looking for at the continuing education division of a college, or from a private education vendor.

Experience

You can work your way into a testing role in two ways: by starting as entry-level person whose job it is to simply execute tests, or by cross-training while working on another programming project.

It's surprising that few hiring managers or engineers realize how valuable system administration skills can be in the testing environment, especially for operating system testing. System administration provides a generalist background that helps testers identify the source of failures more efficiently, especially when developers and testers disagree. Often, developers are prepared to attribute failures to hardware or configuration problems, when a tester who has performed system administration will have the skills to isolate and reproduce the conditions of failure more consistently.

Hot Areas

In most technical job listings, roughly 10 percent of the positions available are testing-related. Since all software needs testing, these positions cover all kinds of software built with all types of languages and development tools. Most of them also build on the same set of skills. These skills include: common sense, the ability to reproduce problems on demand, in-depth product knowledge, and enough programming skill to write test routines.

Summary

In this chapter, you've taken a close look at your opportunities in software development, and the skills you'll need to take advantage of those opportunities.

Computers have always needed programming, but there's been a revolution in the relationship between computers and the creative/media communities. In the next section of *Cybercareers*, you'll take a closer look at the exciting new cyberspace opportunities for artists, writers, producers, and other media experts.

Arts and Media Skills for Your Cybercareer

- Arts and Media Overview and Content Skills

- Arts and Media Meta-Content Skills

Even though media have been produced with the help of computers for decades, the arts are a relative newcomer to cyberspace. But that's changing—fast. As computers rapidly grow more powerful, it's becoming possible to render the richness of the real world in cyberspace. Not just words: *direct sensory experiences*.

As the web grows as an advertising, education and entertainment vehicle, the contributions of arts and media people are desperately needed. However, as with all new media, the web offers new challenges and many new things to learn. On the web, art is rarely if ever simply "for art's sake": it must be functional as well. And artists are now judged on how well they reach their *target audiences*, not just their *peers*.

There's an even more profound change underway. Arts and media will need to transcend pure content.

Just as raw data has little value nowadays, raw content is also diminishing in value as so much more of it becomes available. Your keys to the cyberspace kingdom are behind-the-scenes "meta-content" or "meta-information" skills to organize content and make it manageable. Suddenly, you're not just an artist: you're bringing to bear multidisciplinary skills from psychology, information management and the cognitive sciences.

Chapter 11 presents an overview of this new environment.and looks at the content skills, many of them traditional, that you'll need to succeed in cyberspace. Finally, in Chapter 12, you'll take a closer look at tomorrow's critical meta-content skills.

11

Arts and Media Overview and Content Skills

For as long as humans have walked the planet, they've used the arts and media available to them to convey messages, evoke emotions, and motivate action. When people think about the arts and media, they typically think about the creative effort to develop an idea, and they may sometimes consider the production efforts needed to render that idea into a finished work.

In the knowledge age, creative and production work remains important, and the tools available to creators and producers are more powerful than ever. *However, creativity and production skills by themselves are no longer enough.*

It's now necessary to find strategies for managing content. These are called *meta-content* strategies. They don't deal with specific media or content. Rather, these strategies seek to unify *content, structure*, and *audience*.

Computers have transformed the arts and media: it is impossible to be creative in the new digital media without using a computer and having some degree of computer skills.

Often, general cyberspace literacy is enough. Sometimes, however, artists and media professionals fall into the trap of associating transferable skills with specific software programs (e.g., Quark Xpress or Adobe Photoshop). They're asking to become obsolete before their time.

Granted, Macintosh programs like Quark Xpress and Adobe Photoshop have remained popular for several years. But there's no guarantee they'll remain the best tools available. Moreover, it's not just software that can become obsolete nowadays: so can *media*.

As Marshall McLuhan once observed, "the medium is the message": when the medium changes, so does the messgae. As the computer world changes, and the incidence of information overload soars, fixed linear media such as this book are likely to die. Mass customization will lead from simple non-linear hypertext to custom-generated documents, with the topics you aren't interested in stripped away.

Media

Cyberspace hosts many types of media. Cyberspace media include from static images and writing much like that found in print; sound; two-dimensional animations and cartoons; 3D virtual worlds and movies; and interactive content.

Not only do new media exist in cyberspace, multiple media are often combined in new and sometimes proprietary formats. Often, a new medium has its foundation in older media.

For example, much of today's digital video (both movies and animation) simply plays many static images in a row to give the appearance of motion. The digital video professional must understand static graphics media types, how to sequence events to create the illusion, and how to record the animation using appropriate digital movie formats.

Once movies were created by people directing people and props around, and simply recording the sequence. Today's movie makers have an order of magnitude, more control at the frame level, over the placement and structure of every element. This control extends to tweaking of elements to compensate for the media format that will ultimately be presented. This is true whether the new format is a standard like MPEG, or proprietary like Macromedia's Shockwave.

Static Images

It's one of oldest cliches on Earth: *A picture is worth a thousand words*. Visual images have been a powerful element of print communication and aesthetics for thousands of years. That's unlikely to change. In fact, it was GIF and JPEG graphics that helped the World Wide Web rocket ahead of other Internet services to become the *"Killer App"* we know today.

Sound

Sound—from old speeches, to digitized special effects, to new music created in the MIDI format—is a powerful way to augment a visual message or to deliver a message that can't easily be presented otherwise.

Animation

Animation is a powerful way to communicate on the Web and in other new media. However, everyone seems to have their own way of accomplishing the same goals. There are no dominant tools now, and none in sight. This is one area where real transferable skills, not simply expertise with an individual program or media format, will be *especially* critical for anyone who expects to work past the year 2000.

3-Dimensional Environments and Movies

Jurassic Park and *Toy Story* are two powerful examples of the marriage of digital techniques with movie making. Remarkable 3-D realism sets these digital creations apart from all that's come before.

Right now, 3-D is primarily for hobbyists and those who live on the bleeding edge of technology. Today's average computer doesn't have the power or accessories to deliver a quality 3-D experience. But that's about to change, and by the year 2000, a critical mass will most likely be reached. 3-D *everything* is going to be very hot.

Today's VRML (Virtual Reality Modeling Language) is positioned to become the core technology for creating virtual environments like those described in the fiction of William Gibson and Neal Stephenson

Fixed Media

Most media is *fixed*: it is created, saved, stored, and delivered exactly the same way over and over again. This is true for print, most of television and some radio. Creating content for a fixed medium is typically less complex than developing content for a dynamic or interactive medium. Most of the skill sets learned in traditional Arts and Humanities programs focus on fixed media, and much of the following Arts and Media Content chapter will cover fixed media skills.

Dynamic or Interactive Media

Many CD-ROMs, Interactive TV, computer gaming and the Internet have created a new form of media often called *interactive*. In an interactive medium, the audience shapes the experience by their choices. This places a heavy responsibility on the shoulders of those who do the original project design, storyboarding and event sequencing.

So far, the primary way interactivity has been implemented is by changing event sequences. From the standpoint of creation and production then, most differences between interactive and fixed media are found in the early design phase. You'll learn a little more about interactive media in the Event Sequencing section of the Arts and Media Content chapter, and quite a bit more in the Arts and Media Meta-Information chapter.

Meta-Information

Meta-information strategies seek to optimize the interaction between human and media content. It includes:

- Presenting content so people receive the message efficiently. This can be tested via *Usability Testing*.

- Design interactions with content so people are comfortable with them, can easily assimilate new ones, and can figure out which interactions will accomplish their goals. This is called *Interface* or *Interactivity Design*.

- Structure the content into a coherent "knowledge space," so people can develop mental models of content, and easily navigate to the content they need (or delegate an automated proxy agent to do so for them). This is variously called *Information Design, Document Design* or *Information Abstraction.*

- Measure outcomes of human performance based upon expected goals. This is called *Human Performance* or *Performance Technology.*

Delivering Arts and Media Content in Cyberspace

In the remainder of this chapter, you'll learn about the skills you need to deliver arts and media *content* in cyberspace. Then, in Chapter 12, you'll take a closer look at the new skills you need to deliver *meta-content* specifically designed for efficient use in the knowledge age.

Visual Skills

Visual skills have traditionally fallen into two categories: *creative* and *production.* But when the medium is the computer, it's increasingly difficult to tell where creative skills leave off and production skills begin. The areas of visual skill you'll find most valuable in cyberspace are:

- Color
- Illustration or drawing
- Typography
- Iconography
- Composition and layout
- Image processing and conversion
- Lighting and perspective
- Event sequencing

It's always been difficult or impossible to objectively measure art. But when the art serves a need in cyberspace, art isn't just "for art's sake." It's there to communicate.

If communication is your goal, there are some clear, measurable metrics to determine if you've succeeded. These metrics are based upon the reaction and behavior of *your audience*—not you, the artist, nor your peers. They include:

- **Immediacy:** Was your communication immediately recognized and understood?

- **Motivation:** Did your communication set the appropriate mood or create the motivation you were seeking?

- **Consistency:** Did your visual elements avoid distracting from, or competing with, one another?

- **Communication:** Did your graphics and aesthetics serve your message, instead of detracting from it?

- **Coherency:** Did you successfully communicate your single, core message? (Of course, messages can have multiple levels of meaning—for instance, puns or double entendres. But people should always be able to quickly understand your central message.)

Experience Requires Feedback

With all visual arts and media skills, experience is best gained with the help of a mentor. Doing the work helps you learn your tools, *but* feedback from a knowledgeable source is critical for learning the essential subtleties of communication, aesthetics and technique.

Color

Color has always been a powerful tool for communicating at both the emotional and intellectual levels. Color is an important non-textual cue for managing a user's attention, and for making software easier to use. However, it needs to be used carefully.

Skill List

Color skills include:

- **The Psychological Use of Color**—Cyberspace designers need to understand the role of color in expressing emotion, managing moods, attracting and holding attention, and even in enhancing productivity. Color has long been used to affect people subconsciously. Hospital wards and schools are often painted specific colors to increase healing and learning. Color is used to warn people of important things—like ambulances and K-mart blue light specials.

- **Culturally sensitive and symbolically appropriate use of color**—Colors have cultural meanings; using them inappropriately can confuse or alienate your audience. For example, in the West, black is the color of mourning; but in many Asian cultures, *white* is.

- **Ergonomic use of color**—People become more fatigued reading a monitor than reading paper. One way to reduce fatigue is to use colors with significant luminance differences (preferably a 3:1 ratio or better)—i.e., high contrast lights and darks.

- **Color theories**—There are many theories on the use of color, and the relationships of colors with each other. Some colors are complementary; they relate harmoniously. Other color relationships can be used to highlight contrasts or even conflict.

- **Color systems**—Color has many variables and is ideally described in a 3-dimensional model which can account for all of them. However, since most training tools are two dimensional, 2-D color systems have evolved to describe colors. It is important to understand each color system, when to use each of them, how to convert among them, and which image formats are associated with each of them. The color systems you're likely to encounter include the color wheel, HSB (Hue/Saturation/Brightness, sometimes known as HLS—Hue/Lightness/Saturation), CMYK (Cyan/Magenta/Yellow/Black), RGB (Red/Green/Blue), and PANTONE™. PANTONE even offers a guide to color use on the Web, called PANTONE COLORWEB™.

Domains of Knowledge

Color isn't used in a vacuum: it's an element of a broader visual composition. Several programs can help you control color when drawing, painting, scanning or otherwise generating a composition. The most popular tool is Adobe Photoshop. DeBabelizer® from Equilibrium offers powerful capabilities for modifying color systems within files.

Color is often device specific: a color seen on a PC monitor may be different when printed, and different again when printed on another printer. Later, you'll learn more about the skills you need to reconcile these differences. But these skills all build on a general knowledge of color.

Education

Many Art departments offer courses on composition which cover color theory. A few schools offer a class devoted specifically to the use of color. Make sure the course you take covers the ergonomic use of color, a key area often ignored. (For a very different take on color use, you might investigate the oriental discipline Feng Shui.)

Illustration/Drawing

For some visual professionals, it's becoming less necessary to know how to create an image "from scratch." The use of clipart, and graphic primitives for three-dimensional worlds, offers those without strong drawing skills the ability to create at least some compositions.

Illustration or drawing is the creation of images using lines, shapes, forms and the relationships among them. In cyberspace, the ability to convert abstract mental concepts into widely meaningful images differentiates the good illustrator from the poor one.

Illustration can be done "freeform," with an eye towards visual appeal. Other times, as in engineering, illustrations must be drawn precisely. This is where CAD comes in.

CAD

CAD (Computer Assisted Design) is a technology developed to assist design people in drawing 2-D or 3-D models of objects. CAD programs like AutoCAD® from AutoDesk are now almost universally used by engineering design professionals and drafters.

One unique feature of CAD drawings is the amount of semantic knowledge embedded within the image, such as the size of threads in a screw, the type of pipe in a wall, or the notes on a drawing. Text annotations can also be added to CAD images, just as they traditionally were added to blueprints. With 3-D CAD systems, it's possible to create "wireframe" models of an object and then apply surface characteristics.

With the advent of the Web came the desire to create 3-D *worlds* and link them to the Web. This is accomplished through a platform independent language called VRML (Virtual Reality Modeling Language).

You can now use many CAD programs to create wireframes that can be converted to VRML for use on the Web. You can also create complex objects from graphics primitives or simpler objects, using other software. For example, a 3-D table can be built from cylinders (table legs) and a flat box (table top). This isn't surprising: for years, introductory drawing classes have shown students how to use circles, ovals and cylinders to draw the human body.

Skill List

• Ability to render ideas into images

Domains of Knowledge

Illustration plays a role in many different work areas, each with its own challenges. These include:

• Advertising

• Fashion

• Medical

• Technical

Illustrators can "draw upon" a wide variety of drawing and paint programs. These include Illustrator from Adobe Systems; Freehand from Macromedia, and Corel Draw from Corel Corporation. Many CAD programs are available, notably the aforementioned Autocad.

Education

Most art education programs offer drawing and illustration courses. Many schools offer computer illustration instruction on specific software programs. CAD education is often found at vocational schools, junior colleges and non-accredited education vendors. Some schools offer a single class while others offer as much as a full year's curriculum.

Typography

Typography is the use of type to communicate. Quality typography should be legible, readable, create the appropriate mood, and work together with composition and layout. These challenges are difficult in print. They're even more difficult on the Internet, where low screen resolution and low bandwidth combine with an audience that is more impatient than ever.

• Type is considered *legible* if it is easy to identify and discriminate text. Many type *faces* (also called *fonts*) now in use were developed hundreds of years ago for print, but don't work as well online. Designers need to take the limitations of cyberspace into account when choosing type. They should also know about the growing libraries of type designed specifically to be read on computer screens.

- Type is considered *readable* if its *content* can easily be assimilated. Independent of the writer's skill, the designer or typographer can make type much more readable by using the right typographic strategies. For example, choosing left-aligned text (jagged right margins) instead of justified text can make type significantly more readable.

- Typography not only can communicate a message efficiently, but can be used as a design element: a tool for emotional and psychological impact. To this end, it's important that the designer know how to make typography work in concert with other elements of a composition.

Domains of Knowledge

Font portability between hardware platforms is becoming a critical aspect of online content creation. Thus each of the common font and platform combinations is becoming domain specific. The two main domains include Adobe Postscript and Microsoft True Type.

Skill List

- Specify appropriate type face, type size and type weight for reader's ergonomic comfort and efficient reading.

- Choose type faces that harmonize with other graphical elements and create an appropriate emotional and psychological impact.

- Implement appropriate alignment, leading and kerning to create optimal spatial aspects of text.

- Define type in a style guide so others can consistently and quickly communicate basic contextual messages through the use of type.

Education

Many Art departments offer courses devoted to the use of type. As with color, it is a good idea to make sure that the course taken offers information specifically on the ergonomic use of type in the online environment, a critical area that is often ignored.

Iconography

Iconography, a subset of *semiotics,* is the use of icons to communicate in place of words.

Before literacy was common, icons were widely used—notably on shop signs, where they communicated what the store offered.

Now, in cyberspace, icons are making a return, because words are often not the best way to communicate:

- People may have language differences.

- Words may take up too much space.

- Words may take too long to read and assimilate.

- Words are difficult to render in virtual reality.

Let's take a closer look at each of these reasons for using icons:

Language differences: Over 100 countries have an Internet presence. Business is becoming global. Icons are used widely on city streets, highways, railway stations and other places where speakers of many languages converge; they're used on the Information Superhighway for the same reason.

Words aren't small: A picture is worth a thousand words. An icon is rarely worth a thousand words, but it *is* more visually compact than the few words that it does replace. In addition, icons can be uniformly sized, unlike words which have distinctly variable pixel size requirements.

Slow assimilation: In cyberspace, attention spans are short. Images can be assimilated quickly, especially by image-savvy young people conditioned by MTV, video games and new media. Icons are not only the method of choice for communicating with rushed, highly-visual people; they're also a way to add cues and hints anyone can use. On the Web, where you need to communicate abstract ideas like "where does this link lead?" icons can be invaluable.

Fish out of water: When the VRML virtual reality standard was first developed, some debated whether text should be included at all. Rendering text in a graphic environment is non-trivial: often, text must be converted to graphics before being displayed. That's one reason many games use icons such as hands for *getting* things, shoes or feet for *traveling*, a sword for *fighting*, and a starburst for the *casting* of magic.

The Swiss School was into Information Design Before the Web Was Cool According to Glenn Fleishman

The Swiss are very strong on information design as an underlying part of graphic design. There's a lot of focus there on signage, sign systems and "way finding," even when it's not high-tech. They were doing it back when metal type was strung by hand.

[Swiss design] lends itself well to information design because of its focus on regularity, consistency, and effective communication through the least number of symbols. I know many Swiss designers, and people who were trained in the Swiss school of design, who have made a very easy transition to the Web.

There's also an American school of design at Cranbrook, and some other schools teaching similar approaches, where students have also made a good transition. They're not necessarily focused on information design issues, but their aesthetics are such that web people get really excited.

—*Glenn Fleishman, formerly principal, Point of Presence Company; now, Catalog Manager, Amazon.com.*

Skill List

- Develop imagery that is recognized at a glance and is clearly and visually distinguishable from other icons.

- Create abstract, generic items that represent a class or abstract grouping.

- Create cohesive sets of icons that share formal qualities such as point of view, type of perspective, level of abstraction, consistent size, orientation, layout, color and visual weight.

Education

You may find it valuable to learn semiotics, formally defined as "the study of signs," but more broadly used to mean the study of a culture's unspoken symbols and texts to determine their true meaning. Semiotics, which includes elements of art, literature, anthropology and media studies, is more popular where multiple languages are in use. For this reason, European schools often excel in semiotics courses. It is very rare, even in Europe, to find a course devoted specifically to iconography.

Composition and Layout (Visual Design)

Layout is the arrangement of visual elements and the organization of relationships. This is sometimes called *visual design*.

Compositions are created from:

- graphics

- logos

- icons

- textual elements, including:

  —headings

  —pullquotes

  —paragraphs

  —lists

Visual design structures such as grids and layers can be used to organize the composition.

Humility is a Key Visual Design Skill According to Jakob Nielsen

One really important thing for a visual designer for user interfaces is to understand not just what *you* think is cool, but what the users can actually do. It's about humility. Many designers, especially people right out of art school, take the approach: "I know what's art. I know what's good." [User interface design] isn't art. It's functionality.

I like people to have a style and come up with suggestions. But they have to understand that when we put their work in the usability lab, we test five people, and none of them can understand it, it has to be changed—no matter how good it is.

Skill List

- Organize elements into aesthetic arrangements based upon visual design structures such as grids and layers.

- Convey information using color, specific elements, and the relationships among those elements

- Impart mood with different graphic styles, typefaces, and color

- Guide the user's attention through a composition by visually cuing the reader to the relative importance of each element or section.

Domains of Knowledge

Whether you're involved in layout for print media or for web sites, you have a wide variety of tools to choose from, and you'll need to learn at least a few of them. For print, the most popular *desktop publishing* program used by professionals is Quark XPress™ from Quark, Inc. For web work, there are no clear leaders, but popular programs include PageMill from Adobe Systems, FrontPage from Microsoft, and QuickSite from DeltaPoint. Since the leaders may well change, it's especially critical that you learn the underlying concepts of web design: the tools you choose today could quickly become obsolete.

Education

Art education programs offer a wide variety of classes devoted to the creation of visual compositions. Some courses teach specific software; others are generic. Ideally, take at least one software-specific course to give you practical skills, and one generic course to help you abstract what you've learned in your software-specific course, or in the workplace.

Image Processing and Conversion

Images come in many formats. Each format includes specific ways to identify and list the colors in an image, define the elements of an image (vector or raster), and (usually) which compression messages can be used to store the image more compactly.

Image production must confront the Web's many constraints, which often surprise designers accustomed to print. In particular, the Web forces designers to use small colormaps (sets of available colors) and small file sizes. While it's possible to "dither" the image into fewer colors, dithering can reduce image fidelity. Web designers must learn how to balance image fidelity with size requirements.

Some professionals who already understand image processing tools like Adobe Photoshop™ have encountered a steep learning curve in developing these new skills. When pressed into service as web graphic designers without help or mentoring, many have needed weeks to learn the subtleties.

Just as web designers must learn how to work within the Web's constraints, they must also understand and reconcile the differences in output hardware. Colors can vary surprisingly on PC monitors, Mac monitors, printers and scanners. Fonts can be different as well. Web designers need to know how to test for these differences, and make sure they don't interfere with the viewers' experience.

Graphics Formats

- *Vector* **images,** (also known as *object-oriented images*) are created with drawing programs. A vector file includes a list of discrete elements. Each element contains a mathematical equation describing the lines that comprise it. These elements can be manipulated individually or grouped together and manipulated. Vector graphics are resolution independent: they can be enlarged or shrunk without losing detail. Vector programs are the tool of choice when an image will be resized by the user, e.g., in Adobe Acrobat files or CAD drawings, and in images that will be used with the Virtual Reality Modeling Language (VRML).

- *Bitmapped*, **or** *raster* **graphics files** are lists of points in an image, and *color values* for each specific point. Bitmapped graphics are made with paint programs or input into the computer with a scanner. Color values may be *indexed* or *RGB*; you'll learn the difference next. GIF and JPEG, two bitmapped formats, are the standard image formats for the World Wide Web. (GIF is generally preferable for "cartoon-like" images with large blocks of solid color; JPEG for more photograph-like images.)

- *Indexed* **color, sometimes called** *mapped* color, works as follows. A *colormap* or fixed palette of colors is created. Each color is assigned an index number. The first color is 0, the second color is 1, and so on. Then, each point or pixel is listed by the index value. For example, pixel 0,0 might correspond to index color 2, pixel 0,1 to index color 8, and so on. Understanding indexing is essential to creating optimized color maps that allow for high-quality Web images of the smallest possible size; failure to index colors can lead to strange and unattractive color artifacts in many cases.

- *RGB* **color** is based on the fact that all colors can be constructed out of red, green and blue. Three values are assigned to each color: one measures the brightness of the *red* in the color, one measures the brightness of the *green*, and the last measures the brightness of the *blue*. RGB values are usually listed in hexadecimal or a decimal equivalent between 0 and 255. For example, the color white, which consists of full red, full green and full blue, can be expressed as 255,255,255. You'll need to understand these RGB numbers to create custom web colors beyond a small number of "named" colors.

Manipulating Graphics

Graphics can be manipulated in many ways:

- *Dithering* means reducing the number of colors in an indexed color image, and approximating the colors that were removed.
- *Scanning* an image means capturing it from a print source. Scanning is a complex skill in itself: for example, a designer must determine the best sampling rate, control the file size, and choose the best file format to store the image.
- Images can also have a wide variety of special effects applied to them; for example, many web images have been processed using Adobe Photoshop-compatible filters.

Skill List

You'll need the following skills to be successful with web or new media graphics:

- Adjusting gamma values and calibrating systems and programs to account for color variations among different equipment
- Manipulating colormaps, including dithering to reduce color depth and consolidating colormaps
- Sizing images
- Scanning images
- Converting graphics formats and adjusting associated color schemes
- Applying special effects to graphics

Domains of Knowledge

Many graphics processing programs are available; Adobe Photoshop is the most popular.

Education

Many vocational schools, junior colleges, art schools and non-accredited education vendors offer Photoshop training. Few teach image scanning and calibration; this is usually learned through practice.

Lighting and Perspective

3-D media producers need a sophisticated understanding of lighting and perspective to make their productions realistic. These skills have been used for many years by film professionals.

As you've learned already, 3-D graphics are created by building a "wireframe" skeleton of an object, then adding a surface with various textures and levels of reflectivity and refractivity. It's a bit like creating the structure of a pinata by blowing up balloons; then adding paper mache and decorations to the surface.

In digital compositions, perspective is as important as lighting. Perspective can be created by one or more light sources and a *virtual camera*. In the "real world," a camera records a scene and a director determines the placement of lights. When creating a digital image or movie, the placement of a "virtual" camera and the use of "cyber lights" are used to create similar perspectives. For example, you might "look from overhead on a bright day." The resulting image will be different from one you created "looking from overhead at dusk," when colors are more muted or are already fading to gray.

Computers must create these images by calculating each beam of light from each light source, calculating reflection and refraction off each element, and understanding how the lighting affects each object, e.g., where to place shadows. These *vectors* are used by virtually every *ray tracing* program available to create 3-D images. By altering the location of the virtual camera, the light sources and the attributes of the surfaces, different views can be created.

Jakob Nielsen says Designing 3-D is a Different Matter

In 2-D, navigation means scroll bars. It's so much simpler. Sensory orientation isn't a problem for anyone who's had even minimal experience using a computer. But in 3-D, it's very easy to get disoriented and not know what's happening.

—Jakob Nielsen, Distinguished Engineer, Sun Microsystems

Skill List

- Developing different perspectives by altering virtual camera placement
- Creating different effects and moods by light source placement
- Use of various textural attributes including reflectivity and refractivity

Education

Art schools teach the use of lighting and perspective. While some aspects of this are unique to the computer environment, the historical uses of light and perspective in film and painting are extremely valuable to know.

Event Sequencing

Event sequencing is the simulation of time by controlling movement through events. You can see event sequencing at work in animation, movies, and many TV shows. And it's a critical component of interactive media, including education programs and games.

The Web—A New Form of Theater, an Insight from Rosemary MacCallum

When it came to writing our web site, my background in theater helped the most. Unlike short stories or novels—but *like* writing for a web site or a catalog—theatrical productions are written in short scenes. Being trained to think in terms of small pieces that fit together to make a whole was the best training I got.

People don't read web sites and catalogs from front to back. You'll notice that many plays and films don't follow a sequence of events in linear order, either. They often jump from place to place at a fairly rapid pace. Yet they make sense.

Also, a play isn't meant to be read to oneself, but to be read aloud and performed. I constantly keep in mind how my material will be visually presented. The words will not appear to the viewer just as words on a page. They'll be accompanied by illustrations and/or photos. Even the words themselves may be turned into a graphic, with color and design.

I don't think I could've worked as well with artists, without my background in theatrical writing.

— *Rosemary MacCallum, Copywriter*

Clickstream development is a new cyberspace variant on event sequencing. A *clickstream* is a series of mouse-clicks or movements through a website. At first, companies observed how people moved through their web sites, looking for ways to improve clarity and efficiency.

Now, they're going further. They're looking for ways to customize content based on where individual users have gone before, and what they've shown interest in. These *adaptive presentations* require many of the same *storyboarding* and *path planning* skills an electronic game designer uses to plot the tasks a character can perform as a game progresses.

The most common event sequences on the Internet and many intranets now are animations. Animation is the addition of motion and time to a visual composition. Animation can be entertaining, educational or both. Animation can also include audio, making it a multi-sensory design skill.

Animations are like movies: series of pictures or frames played fast enough that we can't see the breaks. When animation was done by hand, every frame was drawn by hand, a laborious, time-consuming job that often involved large staffs. Computers can accelerate animation production. Computerized animation typically follows this process:

- An artist develops the graphic for each character and the background.

- Layering techniques similar to those used in traditional layout and composition are used to place the characters and background in the scene.

- Frames of the characters at key points, or *key-frames*, are created. These key-frames usually match the storyboard used to script the sequence.

- A computer is used to create the frames in-between each key-frame. These frames are called *tweens*.

3-D animation works much the same, except that 3-D models are used in place of the graphic characters.

A new process called *forward kinematics* can be used to make 3-D actions more lifelike. It involves capturing realistic movement by placing a real person in a body suit with lights at key points such as elbows and knees. The person's movements are recorded and fed into a computer. The key points of the recording are matched to related key points on the 3-D model. Then, the computer draws each frame by integrating the recorded action with the 3-D model.

Domains of Knowledge

Today, most web animations are either animated GIF images or Java animations. You'll most likely need to learn how to create both. You'll also have to learn when animation is appropriate, and when it isn't. Animation should be used judiciously.

Skill List

- Storyboard event sequences
- Render characters or models in key frames of the sequence
- Generate tween frames.

Education

Some art schools now educate students in computer animation; visit `http://www.gweb.org/schools-index.html` to find a current list.

Sound Skills

The more human senses you involve, the more effective and entertaining your message can be. You've learned about visual technology: sound can be just as important. For example:

- Music can establish mood and build anticipation
- Spoken messages can communicate tone and "between-the-lines" information that would get lost in text
- Sound effects can quickly communicate what's going on

Each of these audio elements can be used alone, or *mixed* together to add more impact—just as images can be layered. A sound engineer can control these multiple *tracks* to create a composition that communicates on its own, or supports visuals that appear at the same time.

Skill List

- Recording sound in digital format
- Adjusting sound parameters such as equalization and balance
- Mixing multiple tracks of sound
- Applying special effects to sounds
- Creating sound effects

Domains of Knowledge

Many sound formats are currently available, including WAV for Windows systems; AU for UNIX systems; and the proprietary RealAudio *streaming audio* format for the Internet. Streaming audio formats like RealAudio can play while they're being downloaded.

Another important format, MIDI has been used by musicians for years. It provides a very compact way of representing the sound of specific instruments. Many MIDI song libraries exist. So do many MIDI software resources; one of the leading programs is Cakewalk.

Education

Some art schools offer a few courses in sound. Often, broadcasting schools offer audio production courses. Much sound knowledge is acquired through experience.

Wordsmith Skills

Throughout this book, you've seen that communications is a core competency in cyberspace. Everyone needs to know how to communicate effectively, not just writers.

However, some writing skills go beyond the simple ability to inform. Good writers can go beyond simply informing their audiences. They can create moods, and motivate action. Sometimes this is called *persuasive* writing. Sometimes it's even more than that.

Creative Wordsmithing

Writing can be humorous, sensitive, or motivating. It can reach the heart and soul, not just the brain. It can be *art*. In cyberspace, as elsewhere, the art of writing serves commerce in at least two fields: *advertising* and *entertainment*.

Can this type of writing be learned? Recently, two theories have arisen to explain how writing can persuade in deeper more profound ways: *memetics* and *neuro-linguistic programming (NLP)*.

Memetics is the study of memes or "infectious ideas." Every time you can't get a song or slogan out of your head, you've been "infected" with it. Memetics isn't always an easy topic to understand, but Richard Brodie has brought the fire down to earth in his book, *Virus of the Mind.* Every advertising copywriter, and anyone who wants to motivate with their words, should study this book.

Like memetics, NLP studies the psychological impact of words. NLP actually goes farther, claiming that the brain is very pliable and can easily be programmed through a variety of communications methods. NLP advocates the use of certain words, phrases, and gestures to get in sync with the person you are communicating with. By communicating in the language that reaches them most potently, you can supercharge your message. By adding secondary emphasis to the right words and phrases, NLP says you can also motivate action.

NLP has primarily been used in face-to-face communications to date, because these types of communications are especially dependent on knowing what the audience is responding to. With the advent of "mass customization," a travel Web site can use what it has learned about a person to display a relaxing beach picture, a stimulating social situation, or even appeal to the sense of hearing by loading background sounds to motivate or set a mood.

Skill List

- Use communication skills to convey a message.
- Add rhyme, rhythm, and metaphor to evoke an emotional response from the audience.
- Use humor, puns, satire, and irony to add impact to a message.
- Use memetic triggers to enhance the effect of a message.
- Change modalities in communication (an NLP technique) to demonstrate greater affinity with your audience.

Education

Creative writing classes can be found in most educational institutions. A few business schools also offer copywriting courses that direct creative skills towards advertising and marketing goals. Memetics and NLP techniques aren't offered by most mainstream educational programs. Some self-help programs do cover NLP.

Experience

The best writing experience gives you immediate audience feedback. Some places to get this feedback are: live presentations, online discussion forums, and peer review forums.

There is a network of people interested in memetics; they discuss it on the Usenet Newsgroup `alt.memetics`.

Language Translation

Business is increasingly global, and the Web is *inherently* global. In such an environment, it's no surprise that the demand for capable language translators is growing. Human language remains too complex and subtle to leave translations to the computer. One classic colloquialism will make the point. "The spirit is willing but the flesh is weak" can easily be mistranslated as "The vodka is good but the meat is lousy."

It's not enough to understand the subtleties of a foreign language: you also need to understand the special vocabulary and issues surrounding the *subject matter* you're translating. If you know nothing about computers, you'll be incapable of translating a computer book no matter how well you know French.

Skill List

- Translate words accurately from one language to another
- Interpret colloquialisms into meaningful phrases
- Know subject matter vocabulary

Education

Basic foreign language skills can be acquired from many schools. Most students have the opportunity to learn more in secondary schools and still more in college. There are also schools specifically devoted to teaching foreign language skills.

Experience

Education alone cannot take the place of experience. Nothing compares with the experience of living and working in a foreign country where you can be exposed to the language as it's really used, and to the vocabulary you'll need to translate specialized subject matter.

Summary

In this chapter, you've learned the content skills you'll need to master to succeed in cyberspace creative or production tasks. Next, you'll go *beyond* traditional "content" skills. You'll learn the "meta-content" skills needed to help your audience make sense of today's deluge of information.

12

Arts and Media Meta-Information Skills

The more complex life becomes, the more valuable are *meta-information* (or *meta-content*) skills.

Meta-information means *information about information*. For example, all these are meta-information skills: the ability to create understandable structures for information; to refine data into usable knowledge; and to improve the way people interact with information.

Meta-information skills are found in many disciplines; no discipline corners the market on them. Unfortunately, people from different disciplines often have trouble recognizing others as their peers, because of the narrow orientation of classical education.

For example, some people struggle to organize information in a database, not realizing they could benefit from the knowledge librarians have developed performing similar tasks on slightly different content. Some people develop game interactions not realizing that they're using the same skills hypertext designers apply to text-based content. Since few schools have multi-disciplinary programs covering meta-information, it's likely that these disciplines won't cross-pollinate well for a long time.

It's increasingly evident that these divisions between disciplines are artificial obstacles to progress. In this chapter, we'll disregard them, seeking out important meta-content skills *wherever* they may be found.

As the brute-force production of data and content is increasingly automated, data and content are rapidly becoming commodities, of diminishing value. Meta-information will add value. This means meta-information skills will be critically important for your long-term employability.

The word data *has many definitions, depending on who's using it. In this chapter, we'll use data in the narrow computer science sense: bits and bytes of computer information. We'll use the term* content *for data structures humans can understand, like web pages.*

Human-Information Design Spectrum

Imagine a spectrum that begins with *information* and ends with *human performance*: the ability of humans to understand and act appropriately on that information. This spectrum would include a variety of design skills: interactivity design, information design, and usability testing among them. Let's take a closer look at the spectrum and the skills to be found on it:

- At the far left of the spectrum is *information*. Here, design revolves around the information, how it is processed, what forms it takes, how it is stored and retrieved. These are largely computer-based organization tactics. These types of information design involve several skillsets, including: Information Abstraction, Information Engineering, Document Design and Message Refinement.

The Technical Side isn't the Only Side as Jakob Nielsen Learned

I had two jobs at IBM. One was a short summer internship at IBM Denmark, working on what's now a completely obsolete system. My job was to create customer demo programs showing why this particular system was great.

The traditional computer science training I had taken up until then was all about learning algorithms. But doing this work, which actually led to people signing deals, helped me see that *showing* people a system's value was as useful as caring how well it was implemented.
—*Jakob Nielsen, Distinguished Engineer, Sun Microsystems*

• Take one step to the right. Interactivity Design, while certainly including the human being in the equation, still focuses on how the human can be adapted to the computer. It speaks in "computer terms" of menus, presentation and object manipulation.

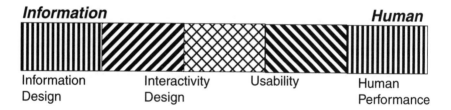

Information   **Human**

Information   Interactivity   Usability   Human
Design   Design   Performance

Figure 12–1 Design Spectrum

• Moving one step further to the right, you come to *usability*. This is the measurement of the human response to the computer environment. (Though usability can be applied to toasters as easily as computers.) The human element has come to the forefront, but still in the context of how humans relate to their computing environments.

• Finally, at the far right of the spectrum, is *human performance*. Human performance is focused entirely on the human being. It asks: how do human cognitive processes operate? Here, information technology and design is framed in cognitive and behavioral terms. By doing so, a framework can be created for measuring and improving human performance.

Information Abstraction

The first goal when creating information is to bring order to the chaos of data. This order is usually imposed through some sort of logical structure. For centuries, libraries were the only large bodies of content that required structure and organization. Librarians developed ways to impose order via category structures, often called *taxonomies*.

Once a taxonomy is defined, its individual elements (typically books and periodicals) are assigned one or more places in the structure. This process is called *cataloging*. Pertinent keywords or related ideas can be extracted from each element and referenced in an *index*.

A few high-level thinkers have gone beyond taxonomies, seeking to organize thinking in general. Formal structures of thinking are called *ontologies*. For millennia, these were the province of philosophy and metaphysics. Recently, artificial intelligence people have also ventured into this field.

Understanding how taxonomies, indexes and ontologies are created can help you design a more effective web site. Today's search indexes still overload users with thousands of listings of raw data. There's still a powerful unmet need for better ways to refine knowledge out of all that data. The best solution is likely to involve adding more meta-information to web sites so they can be more precisely indexed.

Skill List

The following skills will be valuable in cyberspace-related information abstraction:

- Classify books, periodicals and other documents into a library catalog system.

- Index materials; identify primary and subordinate terms for crossreferencing.

- Create document abstracts.

- Create a complex search using boolean operators.

- Add meta-information to pages on a web site.

Education

Many colleges offer Library Science courses and even degree programs. Classes in cataloging techniques, abstract creation, and indexing are all relevant. Some schools teach indexing in connection with technical writing or book publishing curricula.

Experience

You can gain useful experience by working on any large-scale organization project. Organizing large web sites, working at a library, and indexing a book are all good work experiences. You can also gain useful experience by participating in a usability study where test subjects sort and classify materials, and helping to document the classification systems people use in real life.

Information Engineering

Computer scientists see taxonomy development as part of a data-oriented design methodology. (See the Technical Development Skills chapter.) Most complex web sites are organized by taxonomy, i.e., they're oriented towards structuring and providing *data-oriented information*. For instance, a site may be catalogued by its contents, not the goal or process that you want to use to interact with them.

This approach has serious limitations. For one, data-oriented methods assume static content. As web use becomes more interactive, structures will be needed that are based on dynamic or interactive properties. To put this another way, the data isn't as important as what can be done with it.

Computer science has recognized both the value and limitations of the data-oriented perspective. It has supplemented them with a *process-oriented* perspective and an *object-oriented* perspective (both discussed in detail in the Technical Development Skills chapter).

A process-oriented perspective makes it possible to define both a data entity *and* its relationships with other entities. It also focuses on the processes that entities will participate in. You can build a much more goal-oriented web site using process-oriented methodology.

For example, if you're designing an electronic store, process-oriented perspectives help you account for the different approaches people take in shopping. Someone looking for the best price on a commodity item, like a hard disk drive, expects a different interface and different search techniques than someone looking for a complete value-added solution. By optimizing the shopping process, instead of simply delivering product data, site designers can better serve their users' needs.

This approach to structuring and modeling data is called *Information Engineering*. Its content-based counterpart is most often called *Information Design*.

Design of the Flow is Key According to Jakob Nielsen

You need to know *more* than the optimal way to design a screen. You also have to design the work flow. You need signing, and clear navigation through the information space you're developing. You need to nourish a rich design information structure.

Jakob Nielsen, Distinguished Engineer, Sun Microsystems

As you learned earlier in the book, an object oriented perspective defines an *entity* (object), its *attributes* or characteristics, and the processes, goals, or *methods* the object can use. These methods affect the object's attributes: they can change the object. Put another way, they create an *interactive* object that can be customized for the set of interactions it has experienced.

As mass customization sweeps the Web, this dynamic methodology will likely become dominant. Remember that object-orientation is no longer new; its methods are commonly used by software developers. Object-orientation isn't even new to multimedia. These methods are already widely used in computer games.

For example, *role playing games* often contain an object called a door. A door has certain modifiable properties or attributes: it may be locked or broken. It may have fixed attributes, such as the level of lock picking skill required to open it, or the strength required to kick it in. The door may have certain actions associated with it, including open, close, and unlock. Since an average game has many doors, this design model can be applied to many aspects of game creation. Once the designer has created the concept, or "class" of a door, specific implementations of the concept will have the same characteristics, and users will know how they can be expected to behave.

Glenn Fleishman on the Separation Between Visual Design and Information Design Skills

Information designers don't need to make things look good, or to illustrate, or draw, or even to handle type well. They do have to understand structure and presentation.

Visual designers need an aesthetic sense and an aesthetic ability. They have to be able to express themselves in whatever aspect of design they are in.

—*Glenn Fleishman, Former Principal, Point-of-Presence Company, now Catalog Manager, Amazon.com.*

Skill List

The following skills will be valuable in cyberspace-related information engineering:

- Model information in a process-oriented or object-oriented methodology.
- Define the entities and their relationships.
- Develop a dictionary of types of data elements specific to the web site.
- Create process-flow diagrams.
- Develop attribute and method definitions for objects.

Education

Information Engineering courses are offered at a few colleges and universities. Most Information Engineering courses are offered from non-accredited education vendors. Many luminaries in the field, such as Yourdon, Martin and Booch, have developed their own methodologies and teach them in partnership with certain education vendors.

Experience

At present, most Information Engineering experience comes from working specifically in software analysis and design, and especially in database development. You can gain some of the same experience if you have an Information Engineering professional mentor you through a web design project.

Document Design (SGML/HTML)

Document design is nothing new. For decades, procedural languages or typesetting "markup" instructions have been used widely. But these methods had many drawbacks.

For example, early markup languages helped a human typesetter format a document with the correct type specifications, margins, and other formatting information. But each typesetting machine had its own markup codes, so all files needed to be updated to reflect new ways of telling the typesetting system to format text or set margins. Moreover, these languages did little or nothing to capture the *structure* of the document; they simply helped with formatting.

In response to these limitations, when computers began automating typesetting, IBM developed the first *generalized markup language* (GML).

Generalized Markup Language (GML)

GMLs recognized three components of a document: the *data*, the *structure* and the *presentation format*.

- **Data,** now known as content, consists of the words, images, sounds and other media elements that convey the document's message.

- **Structure** defines the types of data elements found in a document, and the relationships between these elements. For example, a document may have a title, subheadings, paragraphs, lists, figures and tables. Structures can be nested inside of structures. For example, a *figure* can be composed of both an *image* and an associated *caption*. In GMLs, and in today's Standardized Generalized Markup Language (SGML), the structure is formally known as a *document type definition* or DTD.

- *Format* is what was previously known as markup: type specifications, margins, and other layout properties.

Generalized markup languages achieve several important goals. First, they're platform independent: documents created using these languages aren't locked into specific hardware platforms, or into specific word processing software.

Second, and potentially even more important, the structure built into these documents offers *contextual information* that can be used by automated document management systems and the humans that run them.

Formatting is segregated from content for important reasons. First, the content may stay the same, but the look of a web site may change every six months to a year. In some cases, the site may need to present a different look to different clients. With formats separate from content, these changes are easy to make.

Secondarily, today's formatting goes beyond classical fonts, white space and color control. This is because the same content may be used in several different media. In one case, it may be presented visually, as words. But what if the content is presented aurally, as a sound bite? If formatting is built into content, a human being will have to record the soundbite to accurately convey the non-verbal items that are rendered as bold or headlines in the visual version. If the formatting is *separate* from the content, what is rendered as bold on the screen can be read by a computerized text-to-speech program with a little more force or emphasis. The software simply must recognize a format called "strong"—the same instruction a word processor might render as boldface.

We already have one audience that can benefit from this: blind people. We're quickly evolving to the point where many others can benefit from it, too.

Not only that, since structural definitions now exist to describe the relative importance and relationships among content elements, you can automate the creation of new *perspectives* on a document. For example, it's easy to create an outline based solely on headings.

As the raw content of a document becomes commoditized, those who create meta-content structure definitions (DTDs) and formatting definitions (*stylesheets*) may well become equal peers to content creators.

Standard Generalized Markup Language (SGML)

IBM's GML was enhanced and formalized into an international standard (ISO 8879) in 1976: the *Standard Generalized Markup Language* (SGML). SGML covers the data and structure portions of a document. *Separate stylesheets* define the document's formatting.

SGML the Meta-Language

SGML is actually a *meta-language*: a language about *how to create* a markup language. In fact, many specialized markup languages have been created from the SGML standard, including TEI and DocBook. Each of these has its own specific structure, described in a specific DTD.

The most well-known of these SGML derivatives is HTML, the *Hypertext Markup Language*.

HyperText Markup Language (HTML)

HTML, the language of the World Wide Web, was created as a simple alternative to the complex SGML implementations used by documentation professionals. However, HTML itself has many variations, e.g., those provided by vendors who add extensions—and thus multiple DTDs. To learn higher level HTML, you still need to know how to read, modify and use DTDs in order to build universal Web pages that can be understood by any browser or device.

Stylesheets

HTML now provides a way of creating style sheets that help to organize and structure the appearance of Web pages. The HTML standard, Cascading Style Sheets (CSS), is being implemented in the latest revision of many browsers.

CSS has limitations. It describes presentation in static ways, as a desktop publishing program might. Thus different stylesheets are required for different situations.

An alternative that is far less common but has greater potential is Document Style Semantics and Specification Language (DSSSL), the style sheet standard that works with SGML. DSSSL offers the ability to generate tables of contents, outlines and other information as well as control the presentational aspects.

DSSSL (and Netscape's somewhat similar JSS) can compile tables of contents, indexes and other types of volatile layouts that may change either when content changes or when the user specifies a preference, such as "frames" or "no frames." As a result, it has the flexibility to create high-level and multilevel tables of contents. CSS, in contrast, can only create a table of contents at present by blanking out paragraph content.

Skill List

The following skills will be valuable in cyberspace-related document design:

- Create a DTD for a documentation project.
- Create a stylesheet for a documentation project.
- Develop templates and style guidelines for a documentation project.

Education

At present, there is little formal education on DTD creation. This skillset is primarily learned by reading up on SGML on the Internet and in the books that are currently available.

   Information Mapping classes offer some perspective on the theoretical aspects of creating structured documents, but these courses do not specifically cover SGML.

Experience

Many large companies with on-line documentation programs are either using SGML already, or planning ways to use it. You can get SGML experience by helping to develop the document structure for such an organization.

   Whether or not you're using SGML, you can learn about building document structures by developing style guidelines and templates for a documentation project.

Message Refinement

The goal of all meta-information skills is to refine raw data and content, thereby creating value-added knowledge. Until now, you've learned about skills for *structuring* information. Now, let's consider ways to add value by refining the information itself. Message refinement can occur in several ways:

- **Editors** modify the content of documents.

- **Interpreters** modify how words are phrased to make them equally meaningful in multiple languages.

- **Moderators** don't edit individual messages, but instead refine the discussion stream by controlling and organizing the way messages get passed on.

Editing

For hundreds of years, message refinement has been practiced. It's been known as *editing*. Editors manipulate content for a variety of specific purposes, such as:

- Making a message clearer and more concise.
- Refining a message to better meet the needs of a target audience
- Reorienting a message for a different audience
- Adding a common tone to a diverse set of messages.

Interpreting

You've already learned that translation between languages is anything but straightforward: translators need a deep understanding of the linguistic and cultural subtleties of the languages they're working with. Many multilingual professionals distinguish between pure translation and careful *interpretation* intended to maintain the impact and multiple levels of meaning contained in the original.

Moderating

The Internet is a live medium where people interact with *people*—not just computers. Discussion groups on the Web, in e-mail and newsgroups are very common and popular. Most intranets are no different, unless management limits them.

As there are all types of people, there are all types of expressions. Some messages are pertinent, insightful, and appropriately warm and respectful. These criteria are so important to civilized online discussion that a set of social conventions, called *netiquette*, have arisen to support them.

Unfortunately, other messages may be deficient in one or more of these categories. The result: recipients are subject to data overload, wasted time, or even personal abuse. These problems are occurring more and more often.

The solution: a *moderator* is assigned to wade through all the material, and refine the discussion as a whole. The moderator only passes along messages that are *on topic*, add new value instead of rehashing old points, and maintain appropriate respect for other participants.

> **Glenn Fleishman says Moderating is Different than Editing**
>
> I think it's really substantially different. Mostly because there's no requirement to what goes out. To some extent, you're trying to ensure some accuracy and that no laws are violated. But there isn't the same obligation that what goes out is A) perfectly written or B) the concepts are clear or any of that.
>
> The editorial function is certainly one level removed. It's more like planning a publication. It would be nice if we had an article like this, and if one comes in great, we'll run it, but it's not critical. If an article comes in like this we'll put that here. So it's more like doing the editorial planning, than actually editing a publication.
>
> *—Glenn Fleishman, formerly Principal, Point of Presence Company; now Catalog Manager, Amazon.com.*

Skill List

The following skills will be valuable in cyberspace-related message refinement:

- **Edit**— modify content for meaning, style, and tone.
- **Interpret**—modify content to enhance meaning when converting from one language to another.
- **Moderate**—modify the stream of content for relevance, original insight, and courtesy.

Education

It's sometimes assumed that online editors and moderators need a background in Language, especially the classical editing courses taught at many colleges and universities. Sometimes they do, sometimes not. Often, an understanding of the specific subculture holding the discussion is more valuable than generic language skills. As you might expect, nobody's teaching formal moderation skills yet.

When it comes to interpretation, there are many disciplines relating to linguistics, including courses in slang, culture and etymology—disciplines that can help you grasp the real meaning behind the words. Some anthropology classes can help you to understand the history and language of a particular group of people. Of course, no education can substitute for experience in a language.

Experience

To develop the message refinement skills you need, it's not enough to practice. By definition, the only way to find out whether you've made content clearer or more useful is to get feedback from an audience.

Interactivity Design

Designing the information itself is *one* part of the process. Next, someone must design the interaction *between* the user and the information. This is sometimes called *interface design* because it is has become familiar in connection with the design of GUI computer interfaces. However, *interactivity design* is a broader term with broader applications.

Web browsers have an interface. Web pages have their own site-specific interfaces. And interactivity design also applies to interactive multimedia educational products, virtual worlds and computer games. The components may change: graphical elements for virtual worlds; pull down menus containing text for GUIs. But the differences are shrinking (witness the trash can and recycle bin icons on many computers).

More important, the design goals are identical: to make interfaces intuitive.

Intuitiveness is in the eye of the beholder: what's intuitive to a programmer may be completely bewildering to an end-user with different background and experience to draw upon. Therefore, *audience analysis* is a core component of interactivity design. Designers need to know which words, processes and icons will really be familiar to the people who use their systems.

Even familiarity isn't enough: interactivity designers must understand how users think or move through processes. Interactivity design isn't about understanding one page or dialog box: it's about guiding users through sequences of events so they can achieve their goals.

For this reason, cognitive psychology is a key component of interactivity design theory. Often, designers diagram their intended sequence of events with flow charts, storyboards or other methods.

The third element of interactivity design has to do with learning. Often, software can do more than end users realize. Interactions must be designed to guide users through unfamiliar processes, either explicitly or by *discovery*.

Discovery learning isn't as consistent as explicit direction. It also requires more programming, because it means the program must gracefully recover from errors the user makes while learning something new. A good example are the Wizards built into many of Microsoft's leading programs. These Wizards walk users through unfamiliar processes to achieve specific goals, offering guidance and suggestions along the way. Moreover, they allow users to "go back" and change their decisions—in contrast to other programs that only allow users to "undo" the one most recent action they performed.

Interaction Design is really applied common sense. However, as Paul Massie has observed, "Common sense isn't all that common."

Interaction Skills Come From Everywhere According to Jakob Nielsen

There's no classic background for interaction design. Some people come from computer science. Some come from psychology but aren't real psychologists. Some come from architecture or advertising.

Skill List

The following skills will be valuable in cyberspace-related interactivity design:

- Analyze audiences to determine their familiarity with processes, terminology, icons, and other potential elements of an interface.

- Identify cognitive limitations of the audience and use this knowledge in critiquing designs.

- Diagram process flows and goals.

- Determine optimal interaction styles.

- Implement discovery learning and explicit guidance for less familiar activities.

Education

A few colleges and universities offer GUI design courses: often the closest thing you'll find to true interactivity design education. Some courses combine interactivity design and usability testing (discussed next).

As you've learned, however, interactivity design covers much more than GUIs; for example, it is critical to game and virtual reality design. Very few classes address game environments yet.

Experience

You can gain experience by creating a software product or a web site that uses interactivity. Again, though, feedback is critical. Unless you know what people find difficult, you can't improve.

Another less formal learning experience is hands-on training or mentoring a small audience in using a new software package. That can give you useful direct experience with the cognitive capabilities and learning patterns of others.

Usability

Usability and interaction design share the same goals. However, usability focuses on reviewing, critiquing, researching, improving and demonstrating how easy a design is to use.

Jakob Nielsen says Usability Skills Can Come from the Social Sciences

Usability professionals often have a behavioral science background. They can be psychologists or sociologists or anthropologists, or any of those "soft" human sciences.

If you think about the full set of activities in the usability engineering lifecycle, they include a lot of fieldwork, much like the work done by anthropologists. The work is commonly done by people who don't have a specialized degree but do have the right sensitivities.

—*Jakob Nielsen, Distinguished Engineer, Sun Microsystems*

Usability tests many things including:

* **Performance speed**—How fast does the computer perform its actions? How fast can a user assimilate what the computer needs, or what the user must do next?

- **Errors**—Where are users most likely to make errors? What can be done to prevent them? If errors can't be prevented, how can the software help users recover from them gracefully?

- **Learning**—Is it easy for users to learn the basic tasks involved in using the software? Can users remember what they've learned? Is it possible to learn new tasks and processes by discovery?

- **Configurability**—Can the software be modified to reflect individual tastes and learning preferences? For example, can users switch from the classic QWERTY keyboard to the Dvorak layout if they prefer it? Can they get the same tasks done using a keyboard or a mouse?

Skill List

The following skills will be valuable in cyberspace-related usability testing:

- Measure performance speeds.

- Observe work processes, and error situations.

- Monitor learning and measure learning retention and new learning effectiveness.

- Verify appropriate configurability.

Education

A few colleges and universities offer courses in usability, often at the post-graduate level or in combination with GUI design courses. You can learn much of what you need from a couple of anthropology courses, leavened with common sense and some personal reading on the topic.

Experience

You can gain relevant experience by participating in and contributing to usability studies. You can also learn by training others in using software, seeing how they learn and interact, what they understand, and what frustrates them.

Human Performance

Processes and software are subject to quality improvement: why not human beings? The study of *human performance* is intended to help people become more effective, and to find objective ways to measure competence.

- Businesses need more reliable ways to identify people who are competent in achieving specific goals.

- Businesses need to know the factors that influence competence, so they can eliminate factors in the work environment that interfere with it.

- Businesses need to identify what competencies will be required in the future, so they won't be caught without the human resources they need. (Consider the challenge companies now face in hiring or developing staff with Internet skills.)

- Businesses need ways to identify specific areas where people are not sufficiently competent, so they can provide appropriate development programs.

- Educators need ways to identify the competencies they need to teach, and they need to know the most effective ways of teaching those competencies.

- And *everyone* (employees, consultants, contractors, and managers) needs to ensure they are evaluated fairly and without prejudice, and that *all* their competencies are taken into account.

One key element of human performance in the 21st century is the learning process. It is *learning organizations* that will excel in years to come. Learning is so central that many view human performance and instructional design as synonymous.

While instructional design *is* very important, it's only a part of a mature human performance program. Human performance deals with *all* factors that affect the ability of the worker to perform, including organizational structures and obstacles, corporate processes, and management attitudes, goals and practices.

The most in-depth documentation of the human performance discipline in its entirety is the People Capability Maturity Model (P-CMM). To learn more about P-CMM, visit the Software Engineering Institute at: `http://www.sei.cmu.edu/products/prod.descriptions/p-cmm.html`

Instructional Design

Instructional design may not be everything, but it *is* critical to the learning organization. Obtaining consistent training results goes a long way towards developing high-quality personnel.

Theories of instructional design have a strong basis in cognitive psychology, behavioral psychology and the psychological theory of learning. Considerable time has been spent studying how people learn, the optimal ways to learn different types of information, the best role for instructors, and the tools most likely to facilitate various types of learning.

Education

Instructional design courses can be found at colleges and universities with degree programs in education, or more specifically adult education.

 A simplified version of these concepts can be acquired from Information Mapping core classes. Information Mapping isn't a comprehensive course in instructional design, but it does teach useful ways to organize information based upon instructional design theory.

The Software Engineering Institute offers training on P-CMM theory and applications.

Experience

As with many other meta-information skills, instructional design and human performance require not just practice but also feedback. Teaching others, developing instructional materials, and defining objective ways to describe your performance or the performance of others are all valid experiences. Education followed by experience is a good combination.

Summary

In this chapter, you've taken a look at the meta-information skills that will be critical to success in the knowledge age. In the next chapter, you'll complete your tour of *Cybercareers* with a sneak preview of the jobs you *just might* be filling in only a few years.

VI

Your Cybercareer Future

- Jobs of the Future
- Future Skills

You're just about ready to start your own Cybercareer journey.

You'll encounter work opportunities nobody's thought about yet. What will they be? Nobody can say for sure: that's why you'll have stay flexible, adaptable, and open to change. But just for the fun of it, let's travel a few years forward in time to the jobs you *just might* find yourself doing.

You can't create the future if you can't imagine it. Have your own ideas about what's ahead? We'd like to hear them. Share them with us at:w `http://www.cybercareers.com/`.

CHAPTER

13

Jobs of the Future

At first glance, tomorrow's jobs look a lot like today's. You'll dream up ideas, apply them to current problems, and create solutions. When you look closer, of course, the specific jobs are going to change dramatically-- and so are the ways you'll perform them. Here are some trends:

- **Moving from teaching to mentoring:** Teaching and learning are going to evolve dramatically, just as the rest of our lives already have. Terms like "Just-In-Time Training" will take on new meaning. Teachers will lose the hierarchical "leader" role they've held for centuries. Some instructors will specialize in helping people optimize their learning skills; others will specialize in specific subject matter. Tomorrow's teacher will be less of a drill sergeant and more of a mentor and enabler.

Jakob Nielsen on What Makes a Good Advisor

I had a lot of really good help from my thesis adviser, but more in terms of general issues—how to do research and write a good thesis. I had 5 different things I could do; choosing among them was the most important problem.

You can really tell if you've got a good advisor because they can guide you well, even if they know nothing about the topic—just because they are a good advisor.

—*Jakob Nielsen, Distinguished Engineer, Sun Microsystems*

- **Moving from mindless repetitious work to original thought:** This will be one of the biggest changes and, for many, the most unsettling. The basis of the industrial age was mindless, repetitive work; the basis of the knowledge age is the exact opposite. Unfortunately, our education system still trains people for the industrial age. We can't create a workforce of thinkers when that ability is systematically trained out of people in their formative years. We need a school system that flunks students for *failure to have an original thought*.

- **Moving from computer-centric environments to user-centric environments:** Bridging the gap between the user and the computer is the key factor in making the computer usable for everyone. "User focus" or usability will become primary.

- **Moving from atoms to bits:** Nicholas Negroponte made this point clearly in *Being Digital*. Pretty soon, all "atoms" will be commodities: added value will primarily be found in the intangible intelligence or personality we build into them.

- **Moving from gross to subtle actions:** Brute force won't stop your car from fishtailing in the snow. Nor will it stop a business from over-correcting for market conditions. But brute force isn't just going out of fashion in business decision-making. Technology will become increasingly subtle as well. For example, user interfaces may move beyond mouse-clicking, acting instead in response to your subtle movements and the direction you're looking in.

- **Moving from fixed jobs to engagements:** We must each follow our own path, develop ourselves, and set the priorities for our "company of one." Sometimes those priorities will match those of our current employers, sometimes not. More and more often, they won't. We may ultimately find some new balance that combines the autonomous nature of our farmer and hunter-gatherer forbearers, with the network-style work arrangements found in Hollywood and other contemporary media professions.

What kind of jobs might arise from these trends? Let's take a look at a few of them:

- Sensory Interface Developer
- Subject Matter Mentor
- Niche Mediators
- Reality Envisionist

Sensory Interface Developer

The Sensory Interface Developer will develop tools to bring human and computer into closer contact. He or she might develop a joystick that offers more realistic resistance, or a model of *aural iconization* (sounds that have recognizable meanings independent of language), or entirely new ways to allow a computer to recognize what the user wants and deliver more useful feedback.

Job Title: Sensory Interface Developer	
Business Skills:	• Vision
Meta-Content Skills:	• Interactivity Design • Information Design • Usability • Human Performance
Communications Skills:	• Active Listening • Tailoring the Message • Non-verbal Cue Use
Practical Reasoning:	• Logic • Problem Solving • Modeling • Perspective Changing
Change Management:	• Mentored Rollout

Subject Matter Mentor

Companies want "on-demand learning" customized to their environment. Many electronic learning systems can be designed to offer core knowledge as a first level of training. The second level of training would be the subject matter mentor. This approach resembles today's help desk strategies, where common problems are solved by front-line workers and second tier workers solve difficult or one-of-a-kind problems.

Instead of instructors teaching specific curricula, people with specific subject matter expertise will mentor students in specific applications within their fields of expertise. These mentors will possess the all-important skill of expressing knowledge in many forms to accommodate diverse learning styles.

Job Title: Subject Matter Mentor	
Business Skills:	• Awareness • Vision
Communications Skills:	• Active Listening • Empathetic Presentation • Effective Message Communication and Verification
Practical Reasoning:	• Logic • Problem Solving • Modeling • Perspective Changing
Change Management:	• Mentored Rollout

Niche Mediators

We have a long history of competitiveness. The transition to high-level cooperation is essential, but it won't always be smooth. There will be a need for mediators to resolve disputes in a non-confrontational, win-win environment -- instead of today's competitive avenues, such as price wars and industrial espionage.

Mediation has long been used as an alternative to lawsuits, as a method of resolving personal differences, and as a way of resolving labor disputes. businesses have even used it to solve business labor situations. Right now, business mediation is limited by anti-trust regulations that prevent corporations from negotiating business practices. But as the need for cooperative business practices becomes more apparent, this may well change.

Job Title: Niche Mediator	
Business Skills:	• Awareness • Vision
Communications Skills:	• Active Listening • Empathetic Presentation • Tailoring the Message • Effective Message Communication and Verification • Negotiation
Practical Reasoning:	• Logic • Problem Solving • Modeling • Perspective Changing
Change Management:	• Mentored Rollout

Reality Envisionist

We are all creatures of habit. Unfortunately, our habits and fixed opinions make it tougher to adapt to new realities, and we're usually the last ones to realize we have them. Therefore, an intelligent "mirror" is called for to point out our blind spots and make us aware.

The Reality Envisionist will be highly skilled in presenting news that is painful to hear. This requires effective communications skills, a high degree of empathy, and the principles to stand up for truth in the face of adversity. In the corporation, this person will likely be a consultant or in some other way "on the fringe." He or she may have a form of "tenure" that protects them from losing their job if they say or do the wrong thing. The Reality Envisionist will need the following skills:

Job Title: Reality Envisionist	
Business Skills:	• Awareness • Vision
Communications Skills:	• Active Listening • Empathetic Presentation • Effective Message Communication and Verification
Practical Reasoning:	• Logic • Problem Solving • Modeling • Perspective Changing
Change Management:	• Mentored Rollout • Strategic Analysis • Needs Analysis

What Do You Think?

Of course we've just scratched the surface: in your lifetime there will be hundreds of jobs not yet imagined. Visit us on the Web at `http://www.cybercareers.com/` and tell us what *you* think the jobs and skills of the future will be.

Resources

Professional Associations

American Association of Advertising Agencies
8500 Wilshire Blvd., Suite 502
Beverly Hills, CA 90211
(213) 658-5750

American Association for Artificial Intellegence
445 Burgess Dr
Menlo Park, CA 94025
(415) 328-3213

American Institute of Graphics Arts
164 Fifth Avenue
New York, NY 10010
(212) 807-1990
http://www.aiga.org/

American Marketing Association
250 S. Wacker Drive, Suite 200
Chicago, IL 60606
(312)648-0536

American Society for Information Science
8220 Georgia Ave , Suite 501
Silver Springs, MD 20910
(301) 495-0900
http://www.asis.org/

American Society for Training and Development
1640 King Street
P.O. Box 1443
Alexandria VA 22313

(703) 683-8100

American Translators Association
1735 Jefferson Davis Hwy., Suite 90
Arlington, VA 22314
(703) 683-6100
Fax (703) 683-6122

Association for Computing Machinery
1515 Broadway, 17th Floor,
New York, NY 10036-5701
(212) 626-0500
http://www.acm.org

The Association of National Advertisers
41 East 42nd St.
New York, NY 10017
(212) 697-5950

Association of Part-Time Professionals
Crescent Plaza Suite 216
7700 Leesburg Pike
Falls Church, VA 22043
(703) 734-7975

Association for Systems Management
1433 W. Bagley Rd.
P.O. Box 38370
Cleveland, OH 44138
(216) 243-6900

Association for Women in Science
1522 K St. Ste 820
Washington DC, 20005
(202) 408-0742

Association for Women in Computing
41 Sutter Street, Suite 1006
San Francisco, CA 94104
(415) 905-4663
http://www.halcyon.com/monih/awc.html

British Computer Society
1, Sanford Street
Swindon, SN1 1HJ
01793 417417

Computer Learning Foundation
P.O. Box 60007
Palo Alto, CA 94306-0007
FAX: (415) 327-3349

Computing Technology Industry Association
(708) 268-1818 ext 301

Data Processing Management Association
505 Busse Highway
Park Ridge, IL 60068
(708) 825-8124

Graphic Arts Guild
11 W 20th Street, 8th Floor
New York, NY 10011-3704
(212) 463-7730

HTML Writers Guild
`http://www.hwg.org/`

IEEE Computer Society
1730 Massachusetts Ave. NW
Washinton DC 20036
(202) 371-0101

Interactive Multimedia Association (IMA)
3 Church Circle, Suite 800,
Annapolis, MD 21401-1933
(410) 626-1380

International Interactive Communications Society (IICS)
14657 SW Teal Blvd., Suite 119,
Beavertown, OR 97007
(503) 579-4427

Internet Developers Association
http://www.association.org

The Microcomputer Industry Association, Inc
450 East 22nd Street, Suite 230
Lombard, IL 60173
(708) 240-1818

Multimedia Developers Group (MDG)
2601 Mariposa Street,
San Francisco, CA 94110
(415) 553-2300

National Association of Desktop Publishers
462 Old Boston St. Ste 62
Topsfield, MA 01983
(800) 874-4113

National Association of Personal Computer Owners
1-800-962-7261

The National Computer Graphics Association
2722 Merilee Drive,
Fairfax, VA 22031
(703) 698-9600

The National Multimedia Association of America (NMAA)
4920 Niagara Road, 3rd Floor,
College Park, MD 20740
(800) 214-9531

National Society for Performance and Instruction
1300 L Street N.W.
Suite 1250
Washington D.C. 20005
(202)408-7969

National Telecommuting and Telework Association (NTTA)
Suite 200,
1650 Tysons Blvd.
McLean VA 22102
(703) 506-3295

New Ways to Work (NWW)
785 Market St. STA 950
San Francisco, CA 94103-2016
(415) 995-9860

The Society for Technical Communication (STC)
901 N. Stuart Street, Suite 904
Arlington, VA 22203-1854
(703) 522-4114

Society of Illustrators
128 East 63rd Street
New York, NY 10021-7392
(212) 838-2560

USENIX Association
2560 Ninth Street, Suite 215
Berkeley, CA 94710
Phone: 510 528 8649
FAX: 510 548 5738
http://www.usenix.org/

Webgrrls International
http://www.webgrrls.com

Webmaster's Guild
http://www.webmaster.org

Women in Technology International (WITI)
http://www.witi.com

World Wide Web Artist Consortium
http://www.wwwac.org

Education Vendors

Council for Private Post-Secondary and Vocational Education
1027 10th Street, Fourth Floor
Sacramento, CA 95814
(916) 445-3427/327-8900

Data-Tech Institute
(201) 478-5400 (US number)
http://www.datatech.com

A list of schools that teach Computer Graphics Animation
http://www.gweb.org/schools-index.html

Learning Tree International
1-800-The-Tree
http://www.learningtree.com

Information Mapping Inc.
300 Third Avenue
Waltham MA 02154
(617) 890-7003 or 800-MAP-4544
http://www.infomap.com

Great Circle Associates, Inc.
1057 West Dana Street
Mountain View, CA 94041 USA
USA Toll Free 800-270-2562
International +1 415 962 0841
http://www.greatcircle.com

Certification Vendors

Institute for the Certification of Computer Professionals
2200 East Devon Avenue, Suite 268
Des Plaines, IL 60018
(708) 299-4227

WebPro
```
http://www.webpro.org/
```

Sylvan Prometric Banyan Systems Inc
(508) 898-1795

Suggested Readings

Here are some readings you may find especially valuable — and why you may find them valuable.

Electronic University, The; various; Peterson's Guides, Princeton NJ, 1993; ISBN 1-56079-139-X

> The book lists colleges and degree programs available *at a distance.* It's a good reference for anyone seeking non-traditional college programs. *The Internet University* is a good companion book.

Internet University, The; Dan Corrigan; Cape Software Press, Harwich MA, 1996; ISBN 0-9648112-0-0

> This book lists specific classes available from different colleges and universities via the Internet.

Capability Maturity Model, The, Guidelines for Improving the Software Process; Carnegie Mellon University Software Engineering Institute, Mark C Paulk et al.; Addison-Wesley, 1995; ISBN 0-201-54664-7

> The powerful Capability Maturity Model was designed for the Department of Defense by Carnegie Mellon University's Software Engineering Institute. It's evolved and expanded even beyond software development (e.g., to document workflow process management). The book is a classical academic text, dry and fairly heavy. However, the material is very important, and I haven't seen it covered in a *"lite"* version anywhere. *Note:* Make sure you get the version of the book that discusses CMM version 1.1.

Mythical Man-Month, The, 20th Anniversary Edition; Brooks Jr., Frederick P.; Addison-Wesley, 1995; ISBN 0-201-83595-9

> This is a wonderful remake and update of a real classic. The book was originally written as *lessons learned* in managing a large scale software project. However, it's highly relevant for any large scale knowledge project, especially today's web site development projects. If you plan to work in cyberspace, read this book!

Do What You Love, The Money Will Follow; Sinetar, Marsha; Dell Publishing, 1987; ISBN 0-440-50160-1

> This is an inspirational book. The title says it all, and the book highlights people who have succeeded in following this strategy. The book *is* realistic. The author knows that the money doesn't come immediately, and discusses compromises you can make on the road to your ideal career.

Knowledge-Value Revolution, The (or A History of the Future); Sakaiya, Taichi; Kodanasha America Inc., 1991; ISBN 4-7700-1702-2

> This book covers the social and employment implications of our first steps into the Knowledge Age. The perspective is uniquely Japanese, and very powerful. The book includes a great way to estimate the value of today's knowledge in ten or twenty years. It offers an invaluable, indepth perspective on what *value-add really means*.

End of Work, The; Rifkin, Jeremy; G.P. Putnam Sons, Ny, NY, 1995; ISBN 0-87477-824-7

> If you believe your current job — or career — will last forever, this book is a real eye-opener. It presents dramatic statistics about the demise of work for the average person. I don't agree with the math: it doesn't allow for the plateaus and growth of a real-world nonlinear system that would more closely model reality. Nonetheless, the book does paint a vivid picture of the future, and I agree that the number of jobs that will fall by the wayside will be very, very large. Read this book the summer before you start college!

Bionomics, Economy as an Ecosystem; Rothschild, Michael; Henry Holt and Company Inc., 1990; ISBN 0-8050-1979-0

> This book, along with *Crossing the Chasm*, are probably the best two books on modeling demand and understanding the economics of the knowledge industry. Knowledge, unlike material resources, doesn't have a finite limit. It just doesn't fit into 'classical' economic systems, unless you use a sledgehammer! This book compares and contrasts the punctuated equilibrium theory of evolution with modern economics. Today's business parlance is full of evolutionary metaphors: "It's a jungle out there", "Kill or be killed." Now there's a business theory that really understands evolution. If you're in business, or dreaming up a new project, this book is a must.

Emotional Intelligence; Goleman; Bantam Books, NY, NY, 1995; ISBN 0-553-09503-X

> Successful people tend to be emotionally mature, less successful people tend not to be. Sounds obvious, right? But if it's so obvious, why isn't emotional maturity more common? The Internet and most knowledge work requires more sophisticated communication and interaction skills: intangible skills that are more readily available to the emotionally mature. You shouldn't just read this book, you should *think* about it.

Empires of the Mind, Lessons to Lead and Succeed in a Knowledge-Based World; Waitley, Denis; William Morrow and Company, NY, NY, 1995; ISBN 0-688-14033-5

> The flap for this book has the presumption to declare that "standard management practices, job descriptions and career tracks are obsolete". It goes on to declare that "*individuals* at every level must reinvent themselves." The book actually shows why this is true and how to start making the difficult changes that are required.

Designing and Writing Online Documentation; Horton, William;John Wiley and Sons, NY,1994; ISBN 0-471-30635-5

> This book is routinely handed out to the students of Information Mapping seminars, and for good reason. It's an excellent primer on effective online layout and writing. It belongs in the brain and on the shelf of any cyberspace wordsmith.

Paradigms, The Business of Discovering the Future; Barker, Joel Arthur; HarperBusiness, NY, NY, 1992; ISBN 0-88730-647-0

> Understanding where radical change (i.e., paradigm shifts) will happen is the key to managing change. This is a small book that is easily read, though it will take time to absorb and apply its ideas. To really grasp the importance of these ideas, discuss this book with others who have read it.

Playing With the Future, How Kids' Culture Can Teach Us to Thrive in an Age of Chaos; Rushkoff, Douglas; Harper Collins, NY, NY, 1996; ISBN 0-06-017310-6

> This author also wrote *Media Virus*. He offers wonderful insights on how the next generation is adapting to cyberspace. What we see as negative today (decreased attention spans, and even Attention Deficit Disorder— ADD) may actually be good for the next generation, which must deal

with many order of magnitudes more data and information than we do. Rushkoff offers an entirely new perspective on the big picture.

Being Digital; Negroponte, Nickolas; Alfred A Knopf, NY, 1995; ISBN 0-679-43919-6

Negroponte outlines the critical differences between the analog world (atoms) and the digital world (bits). He previews a paradigm shift away from valuing material goods and towards the value of knowledge. This is a good easy read, recommended for all audiences.

Rise and Resurrection of the American Programmer; Yourdon, Edward; Prentice-Hall PTR, Upper Saddle River, NJ, 1996; ISBN 0-13-121831-X

A few years ago, Edward Yourdon wrote a book called the *Decline and Fall of the American Programmer* which showed how low-cost overseas job shops were taking American high-tech software jobs. Then he discovered new ways American programmers were keeping their jobs at home, and wrote a new, more optimistic book. This is an excellent look at current high-tech development trends, ideal for anyone trying to plan a technical career.

Developing Technical Training; Clark, Ruth Colvin; Buzzards Bay Press, Phoenix, Az, 1994; ISBN 0-9641045-0-4

This book was originally designed for instructional design professionals. However, it's good background for any kind of structured writing. With these skills, writers can help readers compensate for the overwhelming mass of data flooding them.

Managing Your Documentation Projects; Hackos, JoAnn T.; John Wiley and Sons, 1994; ISBN 0-471-59099-1

Modern web projects need workflow processes. "One-of-a-kind" and "sole proprietor" web development doesn't scale well. I really enjoyed this book because it tailors the Capability Maturity Model for documentation, providing an excellent set of guidelines for evolving workflow. Any manager of a media project should read this book, and it might be a good idea for all team members to read it as well.

Human Factors for Technical Communicators; Coe, Marlana; John Wiley and Sons, 1996; ISBN 0-471-03530-0

Just as the best quality assurance involves actual production people, not just measurement of finished products, good knowledge quality assurance should involve all design and production people in the workflow. This good general Human Factors textbook can help both designers and producers create more usable systems. It could use some more examples. I've tried to provide those in *Web Page Design: A Different Multimedia, a book I've co-authored with Randy Hindrichs.*

The Telecommuter's Handbook; Schepp, Debra and Brad; McGraw Hill Inc., NY, NY, 1990; ISBN 0-07-057102-3

Telecommuting isn't for everyone, but is has worked out for several million people already. This book presents a good overview of the issues, shows how to determine who is a good candidate for telecommuting, and points you to additional good reference material on telecommuting.

Awaken the Giant Within; Robbins, Anthony; Simon and Schuster, NY, 1991; ISBN 0-671-79154-0

This is a good 'psyche you up' book. It contains dozens of ways you can break away from allowing others to control your destiny. I don't think that Tony meant for this book to be used explicitly for learning to develop yourself instead of waiting for your boss or company to do it for you, but it works quite well for this purpose.

Computer Professional's Guide to Effective Communications, The; Simon, Alan R. and Simon, Jordan; McGraw-Hill; ISBN 0-07-057597-5

If you want to learn the foundations of business and technical writing, this is a good place to start. You'll learn the necessary components for many types of documents.

Art of Electronic Publishing, The; Ressler, Sandy; Prentice-Hall Professional Technical Reference; ISBN 0-13-488172-9

An exceptional book for the aspiring multimedia author. It gives a good grounding in the terms, techniques, and products currently in use for a wide range of electronic publishing media including the World Wide Web.

Hammer, Michael, et al.

- *Reengineering the Corporation*
- *The Reengineering Revolution*

Michael Hammer became famous (some would say *notorious*) with his 1993 book, *Reengineering the Corporation*. Like all other fads, companies followed his recipes with various levels of success. So he published a follow-on book, *The Reengineering Revolution,* to explain what it really takes to succeed at reengineering. Both books are intelligent and interesting.

Peters, Tom

- *The Tom Peters Seminar*
- *Liberation Management: Necessary Disorganization for the Nanosecond Nineties*
- *A Passion for Excellence*
- *The Pursuit of Wow!*
- *Thriving on Chaos*

I like Tom Peters. I like his ideas. His books offer great real world examples, and are very inspirational. There are plenty of small insights here, and Peters outlines trends very well. What you won't find here, however, are carefully outlined structures for accomplishing Peters' goals. You wouldn't, for example, write a

business plan based on Peters' books alone.

Toffler, Alvin

- *Powershift*
- *Future Shock*
- *Third Wave*

I will always think of Toffler's books fondly. *Future Shock* was my text book for a high school class that profoundly changed my perspective. There's a lot to think about in all these books.

Cook, Rick

- *The Wizardry Consulted*
- *The Wizardry Cursed*
- *The Wizardry Quested*
- *The Wizardry Compiled*
- *Wizard's Bane*

Fiction books are just as good as non-fiction for learning how to think about new things. Rick Cook's books tie fantasy and computers together. These are excellent books for anyone who wants light reading *and* some insight that can't be found elsewhere.

Neal Stephenson

- *Snow Crash*
- *The Diamond Age*

These books, while fiction, give an incredible perspective on the possible impact of the knowledge industry on the populace, and on what might follow. I highly recommend these insightful books to anyone.

Nielsen, Jakob

- *Usability Engineering*
- *Multimedia and Hypertext: The Internet and Beyond*

Jakob Nielsen, who I've quoted repeatedly in this book, has a valuable perspective on the world of usability — and is very knowledgeable in applying it to new media such as the World Wide Web.

The Mindmap Book; Buzan, Tony with Buzan, Barry; BBC Books, London, England 1995; ISBN 0-563-37101-3

Mindmapping: Your Personal Guide to Exploring Creativity and Problem-Solving; Wycoff, Joyce; Berkeley Books, NY, NY, 1991; ISBN 0-425-12780-X

This is a wonderful introduction to Mindmapping. I can't say enough about how this book helped me organize my thinking and become more creative at the same time.

Index